Human Rights, Corporate Complicity and Disinvestment

How can businesses and their shareholders avoid moral and legal complicity in human rights violations? This central and contemporary issue in the field of ethics, politics and law is of concern to intergovernmental organizations such as the UN, and to many NGOs, as well as investors and employees. In this volume legal scholars and political philosophers identify and address the intertwined issues of moral and legal complicity in human rights violations by companies and those who invest in them. By describing the legal aspects of human rights violations in the corporate sphere, addressing the complicity of companies with regard to such norms and exploring the influence of investors, the book provides a thorough introduction to corporate social responsibility. Human rights and corporate complicity will set the research agenda on socially responsible investment for years to come.

GRO NYSTUEN is Chair of the Council on Ethics for the Norwegian Government Pension Fund – Global, and is dr. juris and Associate Professor at the University of Oslo and the Defence Staff University College and senior partner in International Law and Policy Institute, Oslo.

ANDREAS FOLLESDAL is a member of the Council on Ethics for the Norwegian Government Pension Fund – Global, and is Professor and Director of Research at the Norwegian Centre for Human Rights, University of Oslo.

OLA MESTAD is Vice Chair of the Council on Ethics for the Norwegian Government Pension Fund – Global, and is Professor dr. juris at the Centre for European Law and Department of Petroleum and Energy Law, University of Oslo.

Human Rights, Corporate Complicity and Disinvestment

Edited by

Gro Nystuen, Andreas Follesdal and Ola Mestad

 CAMBRIDGE
UNIVERSITY PRESS

CAMBRIDGE UNIVERSITY PRESS
Cambridge, New York, Melbourne, Madrid, Cape Town,
Singapore, São Paulo, Delhi, Tokyo, Mexico City

Cambridge University Press
The Edinburgh Building, Cambridge CB2 8RU, UK

Published in the United States of America by Cambridge University Press,
New York

www.cambridge.org
Information on this title: www.cambridge.org/9781107012851

© Cambridge University Press 2011

First published 2011

Printed in the United Kingdom at the University Press, Cambridge

A catalogue record for this publication is available from the British Library

Library of Congress Cataloguing in Publication data
Human rights, corporate complicity and disinvestment / [edited by]
   Gro Nystuen, Andreas Follesdal, Ola Mestad.
      p.   cm.
   Includes bibliographical references and index.
   ISBN 978-1-107-01285-1 (hardback)
   1. Social responsibility of business.   2. Human rights–Economic aspects.
   3. Globalization–Social aspects.   I. Nystuen, Gro.   II. Follesdal,
   Andreas   III. Mestad, Ola.
   HD60.H85 2011
   658.4′08–dc23   2011020621

ISBN 978-1-107-01285-1 Hardback

Contents

Note on the contributors

SIMON CHESTERMAN, **Global Professor and Director, New York University School of Law Singapore Programme and Vice Dean and Professor of Law at the National University of Singapore Faculty of Law.** From 2004 to 2006 he was Executive Director of NYU's Institute for International Law and Justice. Simon's teaching experience includes periods at the Universities of Melbourne, Oxford, Southampton, Columbia and Sciences Po, as well as NYU. Previously, he was a Senior Associate at the International Peace Academy and Director of UN Relations at the International Crisis Group in New York. His books include: *Shared Secrets: Intelligence and Collective Security* (2006); *You, The People: The United Nations, Transitional Administration and State-Building* (2004); and *Just War or Just Peace? Humanitarian Intervention and International Law* (2001).

ANDREW CLAPHAM, **Professor, Graduate Institute of International and Development Studies, and Director, Geneva Academy of International Humanitarian Law and Human Rights**. He worked as Special Adviser on Corporate Responsibility to the former UN High Commissioner for Human Rights Mary Robinson and Adviser on International Humanitarian Law to Sergio Vieira de Mello, Special Representative to the UN Secretary-General in Iraq.

BRUNO DEMEYERE, **LL.M. (Harvard), a member of the Leuven Centre for Global Governance Studies**, is a PhD candidate at the Institute for International Law from Katholieke Universiteit Leuven (Belgium), where he is preparing his thesis on 'Armed Conflict-Related Trade in International Law'.

ANDREAS FOLLESDAL, **member, Council on Ethics for the Norwegian Government Pension Fund – Global, Professor and Director of Research at the Norwegian Centre for Human Rights, University of Oslo.** Andreas holds a PhD in Philosophy from Harvard University and has both studied and taught at the

University of Oslo, Harvard University and the Norwegian School of Management (BI). In 2003, he was a Fulbright 'New Century Scholar' on the topic, 'Fair Europe?' Andreas has edited books on democracy, the welfare state, consultancy and on the European constitution, and is Founding Series Editor of Themes in European Governance, Cambridge University Press.

URS GASSER, DR.IUR., LL.M. (Harvard), Executive Director, Berkman Center for Internet & Society, Harvard University. His research focuses on legal frameworks aimed at regulating information and communication processes and on the effects of structural changes in the information environment on the legal system. He has been teaching courses at St. Gallen, Harvard and Oxford. (Article written in collaboration with Silke Ernst, LL.M. and James Thurman, Esq.)

HELENE INGIERD, Director of the National Committee for Research Ethics in the Social Sciences and the Humanities, and the National Committee for Research Ethics on Human Remains in Norway. Helene holds a Cand. Polit. (MA) degree in political science from the University of Oslo and was until 2008 a Junior Researcher at the Peace Research Institute Oslo (PRIO). She has recently completed her PhD thesis 'Moral Responsibility in War: A Normative Analysis Focusing on Peacekeepers, funded by the Norwegian Ministry of Defence, which explores moral responsibility in the military setting.

CHRISTOPHER KUTZ, Professor of Law, University of California-Berkeley, Jurisprudence and Social Policy Program. Trained in philosophy and law, he specializes in moral, political and legal philosophy. His book, *Complicity: Ethics and Law for a Collective Age* (2000), concerns individual moral and legal responsibility for harms brought about through collective and corporate activity. His current work centres on democratic theory, the law of war, the metaphysics of criminal law and the nature of political legitimacy.

OLA MESTAD, Vice Chair, Council on Ethics for the Norwegian Government Pension Fund – Global, Professor dr. juris at the Centre for European Law and Department of Petroleum and Energy Law, University of Oslo. He has been a partner in the law firm BA-HR (Oslo) for many years, mainly in charge of oil and gas law. Currently, he is working with international economic law, especially trade and investment, as well as contract law and EU law. Ola has also done work on legal aspects of corruption.

GRO NYSTUEN, **Chair, Council on Ethics for the Norwegian Government Pension Fund – Global, dr. juris and Associate Professor at the University of Oslo and the Defence Staff University College**. She was Chair of the Advisory Commission on International Law for the Petroleum Fund from 2001 to 2004. Gro has been in the Foreign Service since 1991 and has been seconded to the International Conference on the Former Yugoslavia as well as the Office of the High Representative from 1995 to 1997. She was also a member of the Graver Committee which proposed the ethical guidelines for the Petroleum Fund. She is senior partner at the International Law and Policy Institute, Oslo.

HENRIK SYSE, **Senior Researcher at the Peace Research Institute Oslo (PRIO), former Head of Corporate Governance for Norges Bank Investment Management (NBIM)**. Henrik is a philosopher with an MA degree from Boston College and a PhD from the University of Oslo. He specializes in the ethics of war and international ethics. From 2005 to 2007 he was Head of Corporate Governance for Norges Bank Investment Management (NBIM). He has edited and authored several books, journals and articles. In 2007 he was named a Young Global Leader by the World Economic Forum in Davos.

Referenced case law

Acknowledgements

How, when and to what extent can corporations be held responsible, morally or legally, for human rights violations? These issues concerning corporate complicity in human rights violations have received much urgent political and academic attention lately. Among those concerned is the Council on Ethics for the Norwegian Pension Fund – Global, which has pursued several discussions regarding corporate complicity as a basis for recommending exclusion of companies from the Pension Fund.

The idea of writing and publishing this book emerged at an international conference in Oslo in 2006, initiated by the Council on Ethics, on 'Corporate Complicity in Human Rights Violations'. The conference was very productive and helpful for the Council on Ethics, and we three editors – members of the Council on Ethics – decided that the various implications of human rights abuses in relation to businesses needed to be elaborated and explored even further. That challenge was taken up by the different authors. This book has been written after the conference, by some of the participants at the conference, and about the main topic of the conference. It aspires to describe and analyse the key issues in a critical, coherent and comprehensive manner.

We would like to thank our Editorial Secretary, Kamil Zabielski, whose contributions, both substantive and administrative, to this book have been invaluable. Indeed, it would not have materialized without his very considerable efforts.

Finally, we thank all the authors who have contributed to the book, as well as fellow members of the Council on Ethics and our excellent Secretariat for support in many different ways. Anonymous referees at Cambridge University Press provided much appreciated suggestions for improvement.

1   Introduction

Gro Nystuen, Andreas Follesdal and Ola Mestad

In the twenty-first century, questions of corporate conduct in relation to human rights have come to the forefront of public attention. Globalization has brought multinational companies in closer contact with people in many countries, often countries where the state does not live up to ideals or legal obligations of protecting the human rights of their populations. The issues have reached the intergovernmental level of attention and action. It suffices here to refer to the UN Global Compact initiative launched by UN Secretary-General Kofi Annan in 2000 and the current United Nations process of establishing norms related to companies' conduct in relation to human rights led by Professor John Ruggie. Six out of ten Global Compact principles address human rights. At the same time as companies' activities have come in closer contact with people, increased use of market economy solutions through institutional investment has brought more citizens into closer contact with ownership of multinational companies. Pension funds and government funds have grown, and invest much of their stakeholders' or beneficiaries' money in listed multinational corporations. Thus people in many countries are linked with human rights violations in other countries. Such links can be seen or felt as issues of complicity in corporate wrongdoing.[1]

Several institutional investors such as pension funds, especially responsible private funds and government funds have established policies and practices to handle issues of corporate involvement which they find unethical. Basically, there are three main alternatives: (1) avoid investment in certain industries because of characteristics of the industry as such, (2) avoid investment in companies that through their conduct violate norms that the investor wants to uphold, or (3) engage directly or indirectly with specific companies with an aim to make them change their conduct or line of production. These alternatives can also

[1] The leading resource website on business and human rights is www.business-humanrights.org.

1

be combined. None of them are clearly always best, or most ethical. And they can easily conflict and create tensions between activists and investment managers.

The adoption and application of Ethical Guidelines for the Norwegian Government Pension Fund – Global, which combines all three alternatives, was the starting point for this book (see Appendices 1 and 2 below). We wanted to discuss the challenges of ethical assessments of investment and human rights on a principled as well as a practical level and invited philosophers and lawyers to take part.

1.   Three normative frameworks

The discussions of the book lie at the intersection of three important current developments relating to normative frameworks: first, the corporate social responsibility (CSR) discussion which addresses companies directly rather than the investors' perspective; second, the ethical, or responsible, investment development; and third, discussions on norms for sovereign wealth funds that are investors of a special breed. These three normative frameworks show very different approaches to human rights issues. In the Global Compact and in the work of Professor John Ruggie, human rights are at the forefront. In the principles on responsible investment, they have become included in a much wider context, as one of many considerations, and not explicitly mentioned. And in the principles for sovereign wealth funds, the impression is that it would have been better if human rights issues were avoided altogether, but indirectly, they are referred to and accepted. It is against this normative background that this book analyses the relationships between investment, companies' conduct and human rights.

With respect to corporate social responsibility, the UN Global Compact can be seen as its most 'official' expression on the global level.[2] The 'Ten Principles of the Global Compact' cover human rights, labour rights, the environment and corruption. The first two principles are that 'Business should support and respect the protection of internationally proclaimed human rights; and make sure that they are not complicit in human rights abuses.' We see here that the complicity issue is explicitly set out in this fundamental document. Also the four Global Compact principles on labour can be seen as human rights principles, especially applicable in relation to businesses. However, the broad discussions on corporate social responsibility draw mainly on theories

---

[2] See home page at www.unglobalcompact.org. The Global Compact has over 5,300 business participants as of November 2010.

from different fields of knowledge including sociology, economics, political theory and ethics. Human rights seem not to be central in the literature, but are included as only one of many ethical issues.[3] A generally agreed demarcation of CSR does not exist. But many issues covered in the discussions have repercussions on the issues of human rights and corporate complicity.

On the intergovernmental level, another initiative focuses especially on the relationship between business and human rights: the work of Professor John Ruggie, the Special Representative of the UN Secretary-General on business and human rights. This work started in 2005 and is scheduled to be finalized with a report containing guiding principles to the United Nations Human Rights Council's session in June 2011. Professor Ruggie has submitted a series of reports to the Council where he has laid out and developed the so-called 'protect, respect and remedy' policy framework. In his 2010 report, it is summarized in the following manner:

It rests on three pillars: the State duty to protect against human rights abuses by third parties, including business, through appropriate policies, regulation, and adjudication; the corporate responsibility to respect human rights, which means to act with due diligence to avoid infringing on the rights of others; and greater access by victims to effective remedy, judicial and non-judicial.[4]

This is a comprehensive take on the overall relations between business and human rights including both governments and victims while companies are at the core of the analysis and framework. Issues of company complicity arise in relation to the companies' responsibility to respect human rights.

With respect to the second development, the rise of ethical, or responsible, investment, today the most important developed initiative are the 'Principles for Responsible Investment' (PRI).[5] These principles, launched in 2006, were developed by a group of institutional investors supported by two United Nations entities: the UNEP Finance Initiative and the already mentioned UN Global Compact. The 'PRI Initiative'

---

[3] Generally, on corporate social responsibility, see Andrew Crane et al. (eds.), *The Oxford Handbook of Corporate Social Responsibility* (Oxford University Press, 2008), especially Archie B. Carrol on the history of CSR (pp. 19–46) and Domènec Melé on CSR theories (pp. 47–82). A striking feature of this handbook is that human rights appear very seldom, but see pp. 68–75 on corporate citizenship theories which relate explicitly to human rights issues.

[4] John Ruggie, 'Report of the Special Representative of the Secretary-General on the Issue of Human Rights and Transnational Corporations and Other Business Enterprises: Further Steps toward the Operationalization of the "Protect, Respect and Remedy"-Framework', UN Doc. A/HRC/14/27 (9 April 2010), para. 1.

[5] See home page at www.unpri.org.

was organized to help investors implement the principles.[6] Six short principles each list four to eight examples of possible actions. The three first principles are: (1) 'We will incorporate ESG issues into invest-ment analysis and decision-making processes', (2) 'We will be active owners and incorporate ESG issues into our ownership policies and practices' and (3) 'We will seek appropriate disclosure on ESG issues by the entities in which we invest.' The three last principles are related to cooperative initiatives within the investment industry on application of the principles and the reporting on their application.

Human rights are not explicitly mentioned in the principles. The key abbreviation ESG means 'environmental, social and corporate govern-ance issues'.[7] Neither is human rights mentioned in any of the pos-sible actions listed under each principle. Only in relation to principle 3 is there an indirect reference through the following possible action: 'Ask for information from companies regarding adoption of/adherence to relevant norms, standards, codes of conduct or international initia-tives (such as the UN Global Compact).'[8] Even if human rights are not explicitly mentioned, it seems as if it is understood to be covered by the language of 'social' issues. This is an unusual way of addressing human rights. Another important feature is that the principles do not in any way mention disinvestment, neither in the principles themselves, nor in the proposed actions. Active engagement and shareholder resolutions are suggested as well as reporting requested. Incorporation of ESG issues in analysis and decision-making processes are required. Nothing is said about the eventual effect of these analyses or the outcome of lack of reporting or non-adherence to ESG principles by the companies in which investments are made. It is possible to read the whole set of principles and actions to be without sanctions in the form of investor disinvestment no matter how a company's conduct may be.

With respect to the third current development, regarding the role of sovereign wealth funds (SWFs), the issues of human rights, companies

---

[6] As of November 2010, the initiative has 831 signatories, of which 211 are asset owners. This includes the Norwegian Government Pension Fund – Global, some other gov-ernment pension funds and many private pension funds.

[7] Jill Solomon, *Corporate Governance and Accountability*, 3rd edn (Chichester (UK): Wiley, 2010) points to the changed terminology and focus over time from ethical investment, through socially responsible investment and, from around 2003, the turn to ESG and very recently to 'extra financials', see pp. 304–7. At p. 306, she also lists eleven issues associated with ESG investment, one of which is human rights.

[8] In the annual report of the PRI Initiative 2009 it is reported that there had been a recruitment initiative undertaken by signatories writing to more than 8,400 listed companies, urging them to participate in the UN Global Compact. This demonstrates activity in relation to respect for human rights on the companies' part.

and investors have been treated differently from the ways we have already discussed. The debates on SWFs over the last few years have addressed such issues as whether they represented a threat of foreign government control over important national industries, or, during the financial crisis in 2007–8, if they could be suppliers of necessary capital to financial institutions in difficulties. These developments led to the adoption of the so-called Santiago Principles in 2008.[9] They were developed by the International Working Group of Sovereign Wealth Funds. Following completion of the principles, the working group was abolished and a new institution established to follow the functioning of the guidelines: the International Forum of Sovereign Wealth Funds (IFSWF).[10]

The twenty-four Santiago Principles and some sub-principles all address the legal framework and objectives of SWFs, their institutional framework and governance structures and frameworks for management of investment and risk. The relationship to human rights is not explicitly mentioned. An underlying idea seems to be to avoid political interference by SWFs, which also may include ethics and human rights. In the official introduction to the Principles, one of the four 'guiding objectives' is to 'invest on the basis of economic and financial risk and return-related considerations'. In the Principles themselves this is expressed in principle 19: 'The SWF's investment decisions should aim to maximize risk-adjusted financial returns in a manner consistent with its investment policy, and based on economic and financial grounds.' In the official explanation and commentary, it is stated that it 'is a core principle that SWF's overarching objective is to maximise risk-adjusted financial returns'. However, probably due to the existing practice of applying ethical considerations to investments, sub-principle 19.1 states: 'If investment decisions are subject to other than economic and financial considerations, these should be clearly set out in the investment policy and be publicly disclosed.' The explanation and commentary to this is: 'Some SWFs may exclude certain investments for various reasons, including legally binding international sanctions and social, ethical, or religious reasons (e.g., Kuwait, New Zealand, and Norway). More broadly, some SWFs may address social, environmental or other factors in their investment policy. If so, these

---

[9] Formally, the principles are named 'Sovereign Wealth Funds: Generally Accepted Principles and Practices' (abbreviated GAPP). They can be found at www.iwg-swf. org/pubs/eng/santiagoprinciples.pdf including introduction and commentaries and short presentations of the funds that participated in the preparations.

[10] See home page: www.ifswf.org. Work of the Forum is facilitated by staff from the IMF.

reasons and factors should be publicly disclosed.' The leading analyst of SWFs, Edwin M. Truman, concludes with respect to sub-principle 19.1 that 'the US authorities did not get their way in the GAPP on the principle that SWF investment decisions should be based solely on economic grounds rather than political or foreign policy considerations'.[11] The official commentary, however, at least tries to make the exceptions as narrow as possible. The exercise of shareholder ownership rights is also addressed in the Principles. It should be done 'in a manner that is consistent with its investment policy and protects the financial value of its investments' (principle 21). The fund's 'general approach to voting securities of listed entities, including the key factors guiding its exercise of ownership rights' should be publicly disclosed. In the commentary, the rationale behind the principle is explained to be to 'dispel concerns about potential noneconomic or nonfinancial objectives'. Any informal engagement with the management of listed companies, in which the fund holds shares, is not covered by the Principles.

2.   The Ethical Guidelines for the Norwegian Government Pension Fund – Global

This book discusses in general terms questions of principles and of practical application of ethical norms. No systematic mapping of different types of ethical guidelines will be given. In this section, however, we will briefly present the ethical guidelines of the Norwegian Government Pension Fund – Global. They are important in their own right since the Fund is by far the world's largest investor applying ethical assessments. Further, they give an insight into the different issues that have to be addressed when developing such guidelines and issues surrounding the Guidelines and some of the recommendations are explicitly discussed in several of the chapters that follow.

The Norwegian Government Pension Fund – Global is the world's second largest sovereign wealth fund, with a value of assets of approximately US$432 billion (NOK 2,792 billion) as of 30 June 2010.[12] The Fund receives all net government petroleum sector income and

---

[11] Edwin M. Truman, *Sovereign Wealth Funds: Threat or Salvation?* (Washington, DC: Peterson Institute for International Economics, 2010), pp. 136–7.

[12] For a ranking of the world's sovereign wealth funds as well as government pension funds, see ibid., pp. 12–15. Truman's table has Abu Dhabi Investment Authority as the largest SWF (US$620 billion), but Japan's Government Pension Investment Fund, which is not a SWF, is twice that size again, although it invests mostly domestically. In spite of its name, the Norwegian Government Pension Fund is no pension fund in the sense that citizens have an entitlement to any part of the Fund.

transfers yearly to the state budget approximately four per cent of the Fund. Currently, approximately sixty per cent of the Fund is invested in equities (shares) and forty per cent in interest-earning securities (bonds). The Fund is in a process of diversifying into real estate as well. All investments are outside Norway. Investment of equities is spread out in international markets. The Fund holds approximately one per cent of the total value of the world's listed shares.[13] The Fund can hold up to ten per cent of the shares in one company.[14] Normally, the holding is much lower as the Fund is what is sometimes called a universal owner which follows the markets more generally.[15] Performance of the Fund is measured against a benchmark portfolio set by the Ministry of Finance. Basically, the benchmark portfolio also guides the distribution of the investments.

Following a public debate on the ethics of the (increasingly) sizeable Norwegian government fund generated by income from offshore oil and gas, Ethical Guidelines for the Norwegian Petroleum Fund (later renamed the Government Pension Fund – Global) were adopted in 2004 and amended in 2010.[16] A Council on Ethics, with a mandate to make recommendations to the Ministry of Finance on exclusion of certain companies, based on the criteria in the Guidelines, was also established. And the central bank of Norway, Norges Bank, which manages the fund, was entrusted with the task of shareholder engagement.[17]

Two sets of ethical considerations constituted the foundation for the Guidelines. First, the Fund should benefit future generations and thus secure 'a sound return in the long term, which is contingent on a sustainable development in the economic, environmental and social sense'. Second, while securing returns, the Fund should not contribute to serious unethical conduct.[18] Two main mechanisms were established in order to achieve these goals. First, the exercise of ownership rights,

---

[13] See Chart 1–4 of Government Pension Fund – Global report for second quarter of 2010, at www.nbim.no/Global/Reports/2010/Q2_2010%20eng.pdf.

[14] Section 6 of Regulations on the Management of the Government Pension Fund – Global dated 22 December 2005, No. 1725 (as amended).

[15] On universal owners, see Lloyd Kurtz, 'Socially Responsible Investment and Shareholder Activism', in Crane et al. (eds.), *The Oxford Handbook of Corporate Social Responsibility*, pp. 259–61.

[16] The original and the current guidelines are included as appendices to this book. On the development of the guidelines, see Norwegian Government White Paper, NOU 2003:22, on the Ethical Guidelines of the Government Pension Fund (Report from the Graver Committee).

[17] The part of the bank that manages the fund is Norges Bank Investment Management (NBIM).

[18] Norwegian Government Pension Fund – Global: Ethical Guidelines 2004 ('Ethical Guidelines'), para. 1 (see Appendix 2 below).

including engaging with companies, which is the responsibility of Norges Bank. Engagement with companies in the portfolio and shareholder activism shall be based on the UN Global Compact, the OECD Guidelines on Corporate Governance and the OECD Guidelines for Multinational Enterprises.[19] Second, recommending *exclusion of companies* from the Fund's portfolio; this is the responsibility of the Council on Ethics which is an independent council appointed by the Ministry of Finance.[20] The exclusion mechanism is divided in two sub-categories; exclusion on the basis of certain *products* and exclusion of companies on the basis of company *conduct*. The chapters of this book that relate to the Ethical Guidelines of the Norwegian Pension Fund deal mainly with this second mechanism, but investor engagement with companies is also discussed.

Exclusion of companies related to specific *products* entails screening of all companies in the portfolio with a view to identifying companies involved in the following: production of weapons that through normal use may violate fundamental humanitarian principles, production of tobacco, and sale of weapons or military material to Burma. The humanitarian principles related to weapons are known as the principle of distinction (between civilians and military targets) and of proportion (avoidance of unnecessary suffering or superfluous injury). The predetermined list of such weapons includes weapons of mass destruction as well as anti-personnel mines, cluster munitions and certain other weapons deemed to violate humanitarian principles. All companies involved in the production of such weapons will be excluded from the Fund. This mechanism is therefore sometimes referred to as 'negative screening'. The term 'screening' indicates that the aim is to exclude *all* companies in the investment universe involved in the production of these weapons.

Exclusion of companies because of the company's *conduct* is a mechanism that requires more reasoned judgment in its application. A company can be excluded from the Fund if there is 'an unacceptable risk that the company contributes to or is responsible for:'

- serious or systematic human rights violations, such as murder, torture, deprivation of liberty, forced labour, the worst forms of child labour and other forms of child exploitation,

---

[19] Guidelines for Norges Bank's work on responsible management and active ownership of the Government Pension Fund – Global (1 March 2010), Section 2(2) (see Appendix 3 below).
[20] Norwegian Government Pension Fund – Global: Ethical Guidelines 2010, Section 4 (see Appendix 1 below).

- serious violations of the rights of individuals in situations of war or conflict,
- severe environmental damage,
- gross corruption,
- other particularly serious violations of fundamental ethical norms.[21]

We see here that human rights violations are listed as the first category on the list. While the *product*-related screening aims for the exclusion of all companies within the Fund involved in specific weapons production, the *conduct*-related exclusion mechanism does not aim for an actual investigation of all companies in the portfolio with regard to every incident of human rights violations, environmental damage, corruption, etc. The aim is to target worst case companies within the different categories.

The formulation of the standards and requirements in the Ethical Guidelines for the Pension Fund do not necessarily reflect general rules or standards for company conduct. The threshold for determining complicity in human rights abuses within the scope of the Ethical Guidelines must also be seen in the context of the political compromise that constituted the Norwegian parliamentary consensus at the time of adoption of the Guidelines.

2.1   Processing of cases under the Ethical Guidelines

The Council on Ethics comprises five persons, appointed by the Ministry of Finance. They are selected because of their expertise in various areas covered by the guidelines. The Council makes written recommendations to the Ministry of Finance, mostly on the exclusion of specific companies. The Ministry decides on whether to follow the recommendations, but all recommendations by the Council must eventually be made public.

The Council meets on average once a month, and has a Secretariat with eight full-time staff members who cover different fields of expertise relevant to the Council's mandate. The Secretariat collects information and prepares cases for the Council. The approximately 8,300 companies in the Fund are screened electronically on a daily basis against specific search criteria and databases. The Secretariat moreover collects specific information about companies from the public domain – news articles, websites, NGO reports and company reports – and solicits new information by commissioned consultants. In some cases Secretariat

---

[21] Ibid., Section 2(3).

members conduct field-level visits to verify the quality of commissioned work and to obtain first-hand knowledge on specific company cases. Issues pertaining to child labour and labour conditions have been the theme of some previous fact-finding visits to developing countries, as has the issue of environmental damage caused by mining operations.

Because the recommendations on exclusion and the reasoning behind them are publicly available, the cases must be well documented. The Secretariat often works for many months with fact-finding and collecting documentation regarding one single company. The Council assesses the facts against the wording of the relevant part of the Guidelines, in addition to considering the Guidelines' preparatory work and previous recommendations.

If the Council finds that a company should be investigated more closely, the Council will normally contact the company to get information on the facts and on the company's intentions and plans. When a draft recommendation is completed, it is also always sent to the relevant company for comments, corrections, etc.[22] The company will normally be given several weeks to respond, and will also be granted extensions of the deadline if requested. In some cases, the response from the company has led to a case being dropped. In other cases, responses have led to amendments of the recommendation with no change of the conclusion. In yet other cases, the company in question has not responded at all.

Based on the investigations and possible input from the company, the Council issues a final recommendation to the Ministry of Finance. The recommendation is then subject to political processing among relevant ministries depending on the subject matter. This process can take several months. If the Ministry decides to exclude a company, the Central Bank is directed to sell its holdings, usually within two months. After this point the Ministry will publicize the recommendation in its entirety, also if exclusion has not been decided. Until publication, the Council on Ethics is not at liberty to comment on that specific case, or even to confirm that a certain case is under consideration. It follows from this that recommendations may have been submitted a fairly long time before they become public.

2.2   *Recommendations related to human rights issues*

Four recommendations on exclusion due to complicity in human rights violations have been made public as at October 2010.[23] These are the

---

[22] Ibid., Section 5(3).
[23] All publicized recommendations can be found in English at www.etikkradet.no.

recommendations with respect to Total in Burma and Wal-Mart regarding mainly supply-chain issues, both from 2005. Further, there is the recommendation on Vedanta from 2007, which was excluded based on violation of the environmental damage criterion as well as human rights with respect to indigenous peoples' rights in India. These three will be discussed in Chapter 2.

The fourth publicized recommendation on human rights is on Monsanto from 2006, regarding the worst forms of child labour. The Ministry of Finance decided not to follow the recommendation. Instead, the Ministry found that engagement with the company and other participants in the same line of production was a better alternative, as the Bank had recently decided to make child labour a priority in its engagement.[24] This development illustrates the interplay between different types of mechanisms under the guidelines.

3.   Contents of the book

Concepts of complicity in human rights violations are at the core of this book. They are discussed from several philosophical as well as several legal perspectives. The underlying discussion is how to establish norms for assessing corporate conduct and investors' relationships to such conduct, and how to apply them?

In Chapter 2, *Disinvestment on the basis of corporate contribution to human rights violations: the case of the Norwegian Government Pension Fund*, Gro Nystuen discusses the understanding of corporate complicity in human rights violations and how the Ethical Guidelines for the Norwegian Government Pension Fund – Global have been analysed and applied by the Council on Ethics. The discussion is situated in a wider context before she goes on to deal with three specific cases relating to Total, Wal-Mart and Vedanta and explains the forward-looking approach of the analysis due to the Guidelines' requirement of the risk of future complicity as a basis for exclusion from the investment universe of the Fund. She also emphasizes the Council's restrictive approach to the relationship between companies and human rights violations: protecting human rights is basically an obligation of the state, but companies can be involved in – complicit to – such violations. And she explains the human rights concept of the Guidelines as including labour rights.

---

[24] For the recommendation, see Council on Ethics, Annual Report 2008, pp. 16–35 and 36–42, as well as an explanation of the process at p. 5. This work has resulted in the Central Bank's expectation document on children's rights, see www.e-pages.dk/ nbim/7/.

In Chapter 3, *Laws, standards or voluntary guidelines?*, Simon Chesterman critically scrutinizes some of the reasoning by the Council on Ethics as well as situates the Guidelines and the recommendations within a framework of other legal and voluntary instruments. Special emphasis is put on the analysis of the notion of complicity in the Guidelines and the recommendations. Possible future alternatives are also sketched: will the development lead to legal norms or will ethical guidelines be substitutes for generating legal norms?

In Chapter 4, *Responsibility beyond the law?*, Christopher Kutz lifts the discussion to a more principled and conceptual level. As his starting point, he takes the separation of ownership and management in corporate capitalism and the ethical implications of this for the investors who do not take a direct part in the activities of a corporation. He sees corporate conduct as a situation of what he calls collective agency with its expanded power and ensuing complicated ethical issues. The main part of the analysis concentrates on the differing interpretations of legal and ethical complicity in this context, and the analysis is extended to the special case of collective agency when the investor is a government entity – owned by its citizens – with an analysis of the relevance of politics in the management of collective ethical concerns.

In Chapter 5, *Attribution of responsibility to listed companies*, Ola Mestad dives into analysis of some of the complex corporate structures under which companies are acting in real life. In nearly all cases, unethical conduct takes place organizationally and often geographically far away from the large listed parent companies in which the investor holds shares. Typically this will be in sub-subsidiaries, in activities through joint ventures or in companies outside the corporate structure but inside the supply chain. A sphere of control criterion is developed to serve as a basis for attributing responsibility. The analysis is based on facts from cases from the Council on Ethics and on cases decided under the US Alien Tort Claims Act. Attribution of ethical responsibility from an investor perspective is compared with attribution of responsibility seen from the perspective of victims of corporate wrongdoing.

In Chapter 6, *Responsibility for human rights violations, acts or omissions, within the 'sphere of influence' of companies*, problems related to the discussions in Chapter 5 are taken further. Urs Gasser, in collaboration with Silke Ernst and James Thurman, takes seriously the concept of *sphere of influence* which has taken a central position in discussions and guidelines on corporate responsibility. An account of the historical development of the concept is given with a focal point in the Global Compact Principles from 2000. Further, legislation and case law are examined to find whether the concept has entered legal rules or discourse. The

conclusion is that the concept has not yet become a practical legal concept and the reasons for this are analysed through discussion of actual
cases (Yahoo, Microsoft and Google in China). This leads to further
theoretical discussion, first of the top-down approach to the 'sphere of
influence' concept, and, second, to an analysis of the use of the concept
in actual corporate documents on human rights issues as a bottom-up
approach. Interestingly, this research reveals that a substantial amount
of corporate policies apply the concept. The chapter concludes that
the concept has become a driver in the paradigm shift away from the
state-oriented human rights approach to a broader and more holistic
approach, but that the direction of further development is still open.

In Chapter 7, *Human rights investment filters: a defence*, Andreas
Follesdal first points to the old seventeenth-century discussions among
Quakers on ownership of shares in slave-trade companies like the Dutch
East India Company and shows the long roots of today's discussions on
ethical investment. The discussion is on whether it is ethically right to
avoid investment in some companies, leading to a social contract theory
analysis of obligations on businesses regarding human rights based on
analysis of the complex social institutions of today's globalized economy. His main argument is that the normative aim must be both to
avoid moral complicity in the worst consequences of the present global basic structure and to promote its longer-term improvement. This
leads to a norm of respect for vital human interests. His analysis also
discusses some important objections like 'If I don't invest, someone
else will' and the question of whether disinvestment will draw attention
away from an ethical principle to prevent harm.

Specification of ethical norms for investors is also part of the task
of Chapter 8, *The moral responsibilities of shareholders: a conceptual map*.
Helene Ingierd and Henrik Syse start out by discussing different types
of responsibility which may be argued or applied in relation to the
'socially responsible investment' requirements of a large institutional
investor. The investigation draws, *inter alia*, on Christopher Kutz' work
but it is directly related to the complex relationships that are involved
in managing a large institutional investor entity. Two main types of
responsibility are analysed: causal responsibility, especially in the form
of complicity and role responsibility, especially in the form of what they
term 'attitude responsibility'. The discussion also addresses the important and practical issue of priorities between several moral obligations,
leading up to identification of an obligation for investors to use their
ownership rights to influence companies in which they are invested.
The authors further try to identify which issues to address. Also attitude responsibility is identified as an obligation for large institutional

investors. This implies taking the lead on issues where other investors, or states, have not necessarily shouldered their own responsibilities.

The two last chapters draw on more direct, but different legal perspectives. In Chapter 9, *Sovereign wealth funds and (un)ethical investment: using 'due diligence' to avoid contributing to human rights violations committed by companies in the investment portfolio*, Bruno Demeyere takes a legal and especially an international law approach to questions of responsibility for human rights violations. He does this with a starting point in the sovereign wealth funds, not institutional investors in general. This leads to an examination of state responsibility due to sovereign wealth funds' closeness to states. State responsibility through holding shares in corporations complicit in human rights violations is rejected as a matter of public international law. But Demeyere also discusses some special treaties which may form a basis for state responsibility under those treaties. Further, he brings in an international law concept of 'due diligence', somewhat different from the 'due diligence' concept applied in the financial sector, and discusses how sovereign wealth funds could apply 'due diligence' procedures in their investment activities as a policy matter.

In Chapter 10, *Corporations and criminal complicity*, which concludes the book, Andrew Clapham also addresses issues of legal responsibility under international law but he focuses on a criminal law perspective: corporate criminal liability through complicity in war crimes and genocide. This perspective has been one of the central dimensions in the evolution of ethical discussion of corporate conduct. Clapham lays out the importance of the corporate complicity discussion in human rights organisations' interest in reporting on the behaviour of multinational corporations in the end of the 1990s and in the Global Compact framework as well as the emerging Alien Tort Claims Act cases relating to companies. He then focuses the discussion on today's issues through addressing the complicity rules of the statute of the International Criminal Court (ICC). He assumes that, even if not all human rights violations represent international crimes, the rules will nevertheless inform the future discussion of complicity in relation to ethical guidelines, even if the ICC statute does not cover corporations.

The book brings together lawyers and philosophers to investigate this emerging field. They come from different traditions of thinking, but concepts of complicity are central in the different traditions. Discussion on such concepts often needs concreteness. One main feature of the book is that the published recommendations of the Council on Ethics of the Norwegian Government Pension Fund give the discussions more specific content than most analysis of the issues of companies and human rights, both with respect to facts and with respect to specific assessments. Through investigations leading to recommendations on exclusion of corporations from the Fund, the Council has gained practical experience and also met theoretical challenges. At the same time, the recommendations gave others a basis for reflections and critical as well as welcoming comments. This spurred the Council on Ethics for the Fund to organize a workshop in 2006 on corporate complicity in human rights violations. From this workshop and later discussions the chapters of this book have been developed.

The book focuses on the human rights issues which have partly been sidelined in the current discussions on responsible investment. Human rights and business raise challenging factual and analytical matters. In addition to complicity issues that are discussed in all of the chapters, five further themes run through the book. First, the clarification of the legal concept of human rights as a matter between states and citizens, and the resulting complicated relationship between companies and human rights (See especially Nystuen in Chapter 2). Second, the structure of international capitalism today, as a structure with emphasis on an international market economy as well as national market economies, but at the same time with government and other institutional investors playing increasingly important roles (See Kutz in Chapter 4, Follesdal in Chapter 7, Ingierd and Syse in Chapter 8 and Demeyere in Chapter 9). Third, the increasing spheres of influence resulting from the enormous expansion of multinational (transnational) companies (See Gasser et al. in Chapter 6 and Mestad in Chapter 5). Fourth, the complex structures of multinational company groups with their subsidiaries in many countries and activities structured through joint ventures and other vehicles (See Mestad in Chapter 5). And fifth, types of actions by investors that the reasoning on complicity leads to (See Follesdal in Chapter 7, Ingierd and Syse in Chapter 8 and Demeyere in Chapter 9). All of these themes are important to grasp the actual implications of human rights for investors.

2 Disinvestment on the basis of corporate contribution to human rights violations: the case of the Norwegian Government Pension Fund

Gro Nystuen

1. Introduction

To what extent can *companies* be morally, or even legally, responsible for human rights abuses that take place in connection with their conduct of business? Moreover, to what extent can *investors* be responsible for unethical conduct by companies within their portfolio?

Such questions have been discussed for many years and in many different settings; within religious groups, in financial institutions and, not least, in civil society. There has been extensive debate over the past years in many international fora, including the UN, about the concept of corporate responsibility for human rights abuses. The launching of the UN Global Compact in 1999, as well as the 'Draft Norms on the Responsibilities of Transnational Corporations and Other Business Enterprises with Regard to Human Rights' (the Draft Norms), which were discussed but not adopted by the UN Commission on Human Rights in 2004, reflect such debates. The Secretary-General's Special Representative on business and human rights, John Ruggie, has contributed to these discussions, as have a number of other intergovernmental organizations, non-governmental organizations, academics, companies and governments.

The international debate(s) on corporate responsibility for human rights abuses generate two main categories of questions. The *first* category pertains to the formal, structural and legal questions that entail the controversial issue of whether entities other than states can violate human rights. This is linked to the question of whether individuals or companies or investors can be bound directly by international law. Already the heading of this chapter reveals a position on this issue; the term *contribution* has been chosen in order to indicate that corporations are not considered to be directly responsible under international human rights law. The *second* category of questions pertains to the actual assessment of what acts or omissions on behalf of a company or an investor could generate responsibility, be it legally or morally. What kind of linkage is required between a company and human rights abuses? Must a main perpetrator be identified in order to assert responsibility for an accomplice? Is it a requirement that the company in question benefits from the human rights abuses? What exactly is a company's 'sphere of influence'?

As a point of departure, there are no general rules or principles that determine to what extent companies can be held 'responsible' for human rights abuses. First of all, it would depend on whether the term 'responsible' entailed *criminal liability* for a company, whether it entailed liability for *compensation* or *tort*, or whether it entailed other forms of consequences, such as exclusion from fund portfolios. Secondly, the requirements for establishing corporate responsibility vary from jurisdiction to jurisdiction and from one corporate responsibility regime to another. There is no common standard for determining in what situations a corporation may be held accountable or responsible for human rights violations.

This chapter will discuss these topics, both from a general point of view as well as from the more narrow perspective of the Ethical Guidelines for the Norwegian Government Pension Fund – Global (the 'Ethical Guidelines'). It will focus on some of the main questions pertaining to the issue of corporations and human rights violations, using the implementation and interpretation of the Ethical Guidelines as an illustration. The recommendations generated through this system represent one of the few publicly available examples of concrete assessments of company conduct against a set of rules pertaining to, *inter alia*, human rights. Other examples of such assessments would be jurisprudence from national courts (mainly US courts under the Alien Tort Claims Act).

The Council on Ethics has, in three of its publicized recommendations, discussed concrete cases where companies have been accused of being involved in human rights abuses. A short outline of the three cases will be presented below. Subsequently, the questions pertaining to the application of the Ethical Guidelines on the three cases will be discussed. Issues such as the extent to which companies' presence in oppressive states can constitute contribution to human rights violations, whether the violations must be ongoing or be likely to happen in the future and the question of to what extent companies can be held accountable for human rights abuses in connection with their business activities will be at the centre of the discussions.

1.1   *Three recommendations regarding human rights abuses*

One of the first cases that was brought to the attention of the Council
on Ethics was the case of the French oil company *Total* and its operations in Burma. This case had been subject to massive media focus.
The Ministry of Finance sent a letter to the Council on Ethics soon
after the Council had been established, asking for an assessment of
whether or not Total should be excluded from the Fund because of
alleged contribution to human rights abuses in Burma. It was in particular the human rights abuses that took place in connection with the
construction of the Yadana gas pipeline between 1995 and 1998 that
were the focus of the allegations against Total. Burmese military troops
were used as security forces to ensure the building of the pipeline, and
they were responsible for numerous human rights violations such as
violence, threats, deportations and, not least, forced labour in connection with the ongoing pipeline construction. The Council considered
it likely that Total had been aware of the severe human rights abuses
that took place in connection with the construction of the gas pipeline. Based on the wording of the Guidelines, however, the Council
found that companies could only be subject to exclusion if there were
a future risk of the company contributing to human rights violations.
The Council found that in the case of Total and its activities in Burma,
this was not the case. The Council on Ethics issued its recommendation to the Ministry on 14 November 2005, advising the Ministry to not
exclude Total from the Fund.[1]

Wal-Mart was another company that came to the Council's attention
quite early. Being the world's largest retailer, they buy goods from suppliers in around seventy countries around the world. The allegations
against Wal-Mart pertain to business conduct of a manner that contra-
dicts internationally recognized human rights and labour standards,
both at its suppliers in a number of countries in Asia, Africa and Latin
America, and at its own operations in North America. Such allegations
include employment of minors in contravention of international rules,
dangerous and health-hazardous working conditions in supply-chain
operations, forced overtime work without compensation, gender discrimination and a systematic policy to suppress attempts to establish
trade unions. In the case of Wal-Mart, the Council on Ethics did find
links between the company's conduct and the human rights violations,

---

[1] Council on Ethics, 'Recommendation of 14 November 2005, Concerning Whether
Investments in Total, Due to the Company's Operations in Burma, are Contrary to
the Petroleum Fund's Ethical Guidelines' (Total Recommendation).

and an unacceptable risk that the unethical conduct would continue in the future. It issued its recommendation to exclude Wal-Mart to the Ministry of Finance on 15 November 2005, and the recommendation was publicized on 6 June 2006, when the exclusion of the company had been implemented.[2]

The third case that was (partly) human rights related was the exclusion of the British mining company *Vedanta*. This company was excluded mainly because of its systematic and serious contribution to environmental damage. The Council did, however, also consider claims that the company contributed to displacement and deportation of tribal people in some of the areas of its operations, and found that there was an unacceptable risk that these were ongoing human rights violations which the company did contribute to.[3]

It should be noted that the first of these three cases is not a typical recommendation; the Council on Ethics rarely makes public statements with regard to companies that are *not* recommended for exclusion. The reason for this in the Total case was that the Ministry of Finance specifically asked the Council to assess Total and its operations in Burma in relation to the Guidelines. The Council's mandate pertains to making recommendations on *exclusion* of companies, and it will normally not make statements on non-exclusion unless asked about specific companies or situations by the Ministry. This has happened in a few cases, and the exchange of letters between the Ministry and the Council in each case is publicly available.[4] For example, because of the situation in Burma in the fall of 2007, the Ministry asked the Council to give out information on what cases the Council was assessing in Burma. The Council's answer to this letter was publicized in October 2007, and will be subject to discussion below.[5]

2.   Framing the issues

As mentioned above, the issues at hand pertain both to the structural discourse regarding *which* entities can be responsible under human rights law, as well as to the actual determination of whether human

---

[2] Council on Ethics, 'Recommendation of 15 November 2005 on the exclusion of Wal-Mart Stores Inc.' (Wal-Mart Stores Inc. Recommendation).

[3] Council on Ethics, 'Recommendation of 15 May 2007 on exclusion of Vedanta Resources Plc', Section 5.3.1: 'Forced eviction of tribal peoples', pp. 20–1, Section 5.4.6: 'Involvement in human rights violations', pp. 27–32 and Section 7.2: 'The Council's Assessment: Human rights violations', pp. 36–8.

[4] See 'Other documents', on the Council on Ethics website; www.etikkradet.no.

[5] Council on Ethics, 'Letter dated 11 October 2007, on the Council's Assessment of Companies with Operations in Burma.'

rights abuses have taken place and if so, the extent to which companies or corporations can be seen to have legal or ethical co-responsibility for that. The first issue is linked to a debate on the content of public international law, and is discussed below under the heading '*Non-state entities and human rights violations*'. The second set of issues pertains to the interpretation and application of one (of many) set of rules regarding company conduct and human rights, namely the Ethical Guidelines for the Pension Fund, discussed under the heading '*The human rights criterion in the Ethical Guidelines*'.

The Council on Ethics has dealt with both of these main categories of questions, albeit relatively briefly with respect to the first. In the Total case, the Council stated that: 'Only states can violate human rights directly. Companies can ... contribute to human rights violations committed by states. The Fund may in its turn contribute to companies' complicity through its ownership. It is such complicity in a state's human rights violations which is to be assessed under this provision.'[6] The main focus of the Council has thus been to establish a credible link between unethical acts (which may constitute human rights abuses for the affected individuals) and a company (which is owned by the Pension Fund).

This does not mean that the doctrinal question of whether entities other than states can violate human rights is unimportant. The reason why the Council did not go any further in discussing the conceptual difficulties and legal controversies that surround the issue of non-state entities and potential human rights responsibility was that it was not considered necessary. The wording of the Ethical Guidelines refers to contribution or complicity to human rights abuses, and it is not contested that companies can contribute to such abuses.

3.   Non-state entities and human rights violations

The doctrinal debate on how business corporations can have responsibility with regard to human rights, takes place in many different settings. The adoption of the UN Global Compact, the proposed Draft Norms on Transnational Corporations by the UN Sub-Commission on Human Rights, and the establishment of a Special Representative for human rights and business, all represent developments that have generated much debate amongst governments, non-governmental organizations, academics, corporations and other stakeholders.

---

[6] Total Recommendation, Section 3.1: 'Further details on para. 4.4, second sentence, first alternative: Human rights.'

One of the divides in this debate has evolved around the issue of whether companies have human rights obligations under international law. This question is decisive for how one defines the responsibility of companies and corporations; do they have a moral or ethical obligation to ensure human rights, do they have a legal obligation and if they do, is the legal basis for this obligation international law or national law?

There have been several strong proponents from both sides of this divide. Representatives from civil society have for example often leaned towards assuming that corporations do have human rights responsibilities. An aspect of this debate is that the distinction between *lex lata* and *lex ferenda* sometimes tends to get blurred. This entails that differences over whether or not non-state entities have human rights obligations are not always as deep as they may seem. The UN Special Representative on business and human rights suggests that while much can be done for increased corporate responsibility for human rights around the world, the attempts to tie such a responsibility to international legal obligations for companies may serve to distract and obscure the focus of the process.[7] Several non-governmental organizations have opposed the Special Representative's views on this.[8] Academics have also contributed substantially to the debate.[9] It thus seems appropriate to shed some light on why the Council on Ethics has placed itself among those who find that corporations, under the current regime of international human rights law, are not bound by human rights instruments.

The above mentioned quotation from the Total case[10] expresses the basic view of the Council that under international human rights treaty law, it is only the parties to a treaty that are bound by its provisions.[11] The *lex lata* point of departure is that human rights treaties are inter-state agreements regarding how each state shall secure human rights to the

---

[7] John Ruggie, 'Interim Report of the Special Representative of the Secretary-General on the issue of Human Rights and Transnational Corporations and other Business Enterprises' (Interim Report 2006), UN Human Rights Council, UN Doc. E/CN. 4/2006/97 (22 February 2006), para. 60.

[8] See for example Position Paper by *Federation Internationale des ligues des droits de l'Homme (FIDH)*; www.fidh.org/IMG/pdf/business442a.pdf.

[9] See in particular Andrew Clapham, *Human Rights Obligations of Non-State Actors* (Oxford University Press, 2006).

[10] 'Only states can violate human rights directly. Companies can, as indicated in paragraph 4.4, contribute to human rights violations committed by states.'

[11] Also international organizations can be party to certain treaties, and it has been established that international organizations in certain cases can have rights and obligations under international law. See, for example, 'Advisory Opinion of the International Court of Justice, ICJ Reports on Reparation For Injuries Suffered in the Service of the United Nations', 11 April 1949.

individuals (and persons[12]) in its territory and/or under its jurisdiction.[13] Also the monitoring mechanisms of the human rights treaties imply that only states can be subject to the various proceedings established for complaints of violations of various human rights.[14]

The UN Universal Declaration on Human Rights states that 'everyone is entitled to all the rights and freedoms set forth in this Declaration ...', without specifying who the duty holders are. This may be attributed to the fact that this is a declaration, which at the time was not legally binding on states.[15] Normally, however, if someone has a right, then somebody else has an obligation to fulfil that right. It may be argued that everyone should be entitled to all human rights, but for those human rights that still do not constitute customary law, an individual must be within the jurisdiction of a state which has undertaken to secure a specific obligation in order to claim this as a human right under an international human rights treaty.

The point of departure for treaty interpretation is the wording of the relevant (binding) text.[16] The ordinary meaning of the terms of the treaty shall also be interpreted in light of the treaty's 'object and purpose'. Many human rights bodies, including the European Court of Human Rights, have interpreted human rights treaty texts in a more dynamic or expansive manner than other international courts have interpreted international law in general.[17] This has often implicitly or explicitly been linked to the requirement that treaties shall be interpreted 'in light of its object and purpose'. The 'object and purpose' of human rights conventions is undoubtedly to secure human rights to everyone, irrespective of where they live and who they are. In this context, human rights protection includes protection by state authorities against violations committed by private actors, including non-state entities. This cannot, however, reasonably make others than the parties to a treaty legally bound by it.

One reason behind some of the uncertainty as to whether or not non-state entities can be legally responsible for human rights violations

---

[12] Under the European Convention on Human Rights (ECHR) legal persons also have protection under the Convention, see Article 1 of the ECHR.

[13] For example Article 2 of the International Covenant on Civil and Political Rights (ICCPR) and the International Covenant on Economic, Social and Cultural Rights (ICESCR).

[14] Including the Treaty Bodies under the UN system, as well as the European Court of Human Rights.

[15] Most of the substantive rights contained in the Universal Declaration on Human Rights from 1948 are assumed to have the character of international customary law now.

[16] Vienna Convention on the Law of Treaties, Article 31.

[17] See for example *Wemhoff* v. *Germany*, Judgment of June 1968, ECHR, Series A 7, para. 8 (under 'As to the law').

is that human rights law often gets mixed up with international humanitarian law (and international criminal law). One difference between international human rights law, on the one hand, and international humanitarian law/criminal law on the other, is the issue of *who* are right-holders and duty-bearers under the different regimes. Under international humanitarian law, both individuals and states can be prosecuted for violations. In some states, legal persons can also be prosecuted for such violations. A government can be held responsible for war crimes committed by its armed forces, and the individuals who committed the war crimes or ordered them can be held individually responsible both under national legal systems and, to a certain extent, under international legal systems.[18] Companies that are responsible for international crimes can, under some states' jurisdictions, be held responsible for compensation to victims,[19] and under a few jurisdictions, even be criminally liable.[20] Under international criminal law only natural persons can be prosecuted and punished for such crimes.[21]

It is important to distinguish between international human rights law and international humanitarian law, also because similar terms within the two regimes sometimes cover dissimilar acts. All acts or omissions that may generate human rights responsibility or criminal liability (under international humanitarian law) must be assessed within a context. Even to cause someone's death can be justified, for example if the killer were a privileged combatant, or if the requirements for necessity were fulfilled. The very same physical acts can thus be regarded differently under different legal regimes, depending on the context. Illustrative of this are the legal rules pertaining to *torture*. Under a human rights regime, torture has to be administered 'by or at the instigation of or with the consent or acquiescence of a public official or other person acting in an official capacity'.[22] Under the regime for war crimes (international humanitarian law and international criminal law), there is no requirement that the torturer

---

[18] After the two tribunals established in the aftermath of the Second World War (Nuremberg and Tokyo), examples of such international systems are the two ad hoc criminal tribunals for the Former Yugoslavia and for Rwanda, as well as the Permanent International Criminal Court (ICC) which was established in 1998.

[19] For example companies which fall within the jurisdiction of the Alien Tort Claims Act in the United States.

[20] This is the case in, for example, Norway. FAFO, 'Project on Business and International Crimes: Assessing the Liability of Business Entities for Grave Violations of International Law, Nation survey on Norway' (2004), and 'Assessing the Liability of Business Entities for Grave Violations of International Law'; www.fafo.no/liabilities/index.htm.

[21] See Article 25 of the International Criminal Court (ICC) Statute.

[22] Article 1 of the Convention Against Torture and Other Cruel, Inhuman or Degrading Treatment or Punishment.

must have acted on behalf of a government.[23] In a decision from 2001, the International Criminal Tribunal for the former Yugoslavia (ICTY) held that:

> ... the definition of torture under international humanitarian law does not comprise the same elements as the definition of torture generally applied under human rights law. In particular, The Trial Chamber is of the view that the presence of a state official or any other authority-wielding person in the torture process is not necessary for the offence to be regarded as torture under international humanitarian law.[24]

The fact that non-state entities can have responsibilities, and can even be prosecuted for violations of international humanitarian law, does not mean that they have human rights obligations under the international human rights system. The value of analogy between the two regimes is in some respects limited. The main focus of human rights law is to regulate state conduct vis-à-vis its individuals and to protect individuals against abuse, discrimination, etc. also by non-state actors. The main focus of international humanitarian law, in addition to regulating reciprocal state conduct in situations of armed conflict, is to protect individuals through regulation of conduct of individual soldiers and other participants in hostilities.

It has been pointed out that the lack of an enforcement system or a mechanism for prosecution for non-state entities does not necessarily exclude the existence of obligations for such entities with regard to human rights.[25] Obligations can exist even when there is no enforcement mechanism. While this is clearly true, the main question remains: under what legal basis can non-state entities be considered to have human rights obligations?

One might well argue that certain non-state entities *ought* to have human rights obligations. There are a number of good arguments for why large companies and multinational corporations should have responsibilities for human rights.[26] Many developing countries host companies whose returns are more substantial than the host states' annual budgets. Clearly, there is a need to involve companies and corporations in human rights issues – particularly in areas where they can make a difference. The proposal of the UN Draft Norms on the

---

[23] See, for example, the ICC Statute Article 8(2)(a)(ii), which is applicable in international armed conflicts and 8(2)(c)(i) and (ii) which is applicable in non-international armed conflicts.

[24] ICTY Judgment, *The Prosecutor v. Kunarac et al.* (IT 96–23 & 23/1, 22 February 2001), paras. 483–96.

[25] See for example Clapham, *Human Rights Obligations*, p. 74.

[26] Ibid., chapter 6: 'Corporations and Human Rights'.

Responsibilities of Transnational Corporations and Other Business Enterprises with Regard to Human Rights (the 'Draft Norms') was an attempt to present a set of rules that would set some standards for company conduct with regard to *inter alia* human rights.[27] The Draft Norms were, however, never adopted by the Commission (now Council) on Human Rights, mainly because of their declaratory treaty-like language and pretence of being binding on corporations. As the UN Special Representative on business and human rights, John Ruggie, pointed out in his interim report in 2006: 'What the Norms have done, in fact, is to take existing State-based human rights instruments and simply assert that many of their provisions are binding on corporations as well. But that assertion itself has little authoritative basis in international law – hard, soft or otherwise.'[28] Present work in the UN is thus focused on examining *states' obligations* in relation to regulating actions of business enterprises with regard to the core human rights treaties.[29]

Notwithstanding the situation as it is today, inter-state agreements with regard to human rights responsibilities for corporations are clearly a conceptual possibility; states could agree on human rights standards that companies must adhere to, in host states or the home states of companies or both. John Ruggie makes this point in his interim report, and then goes on to specify that '... these are not propositions about established law; they are normative commitments and policy preferences about what the law should become and that require State action for them to take effect'.[30]

Thus, it may well be the case that international agreements regulating company conduct with regard to human rights will be negotiated in the future. There are several examples of international agreements on national legislative regulation of corporate conduct in areas such as, for example, combat of international terrorism, trafficking and corruption. Andrew Clapham points out that it would be possible to develop 'a new treaty to set out what States must do to ensure that "their" corporations abide by international human rights law. Such a treaty could be modelled on the corruption treaties, now widely understood and accepted.'[31] Such a treaty would, however, be directly binding only on entities with

---

[27] Sub-Commission on the Promotion and Protection of Human Rights, Resolution 2003/16 of 13 August 2003.
[28] Ruggie, Interim Report 2006, para. 60.
[29] See John Ruggie, 'State Responsibilities to Regulate and Adjudicate Corporate Activities under the United Nations' Core Human Rights Treaties', Report No. 4 (2007).
[30] Ruggie, Interim Report 2006, para. 65.
[31] Clapham, *Human Rights Obligations*, p. 268.

international legal personality (in other words entities that can become party to the relevant treaty), and such entities (states) would have to take national measures to make its content binding on companies or investors.

4.   The human rights criterion in the Ethical Guidelines

When trying to determine whether a concrete company in the Fund's portfolio should be excluded, the wording of the Ethical Guidelines is of course the first and most important legal source against which to assess the relevant company. One might say that the implementation of the Guidelines requires two basic elements: (1) documentation about individual companies and their conduct and (2) assessing this documentation against the relevant rule. The documentation element will not itself be dealt with in this chapter – all of the sources that have been used in the individual recommendations are indicated in the text of the recommendations themselves and in the relevant footnotes. The topic for this chapter is the content of the legal assessments made by the Council with regard to the human rights criterion.

The human rights criterion in the Ethical Guidelines is formulated as follows:

The ministry of Finance may, on the advice of the Council on Ethics, exclude companies from the investment universe of the Fund if there is an unacceptable risk that the company contributes to or is responsible for:

a) serious or systematic human rights violations, such as murder, torture, deprivation of liberty, forced labour, the worst forms of child labour and other child exploitation;
b) serious violations of the rights of individuals in situations of war or conflict;
c) etc.[32]

A number of different questions can be asked with regard to this rule: What exactly are 'human rights violations', and where is the threshold for such abuses being 'serious or systematic'? How does one define the term 'contributing to'? What kind of link between human rights abuses and company conduct is required? What is an 'unacceptable risk'? And how does this specific approach to disinvestment from companies because of human rights abuses compare to the general thinking around corporate responsibility in connection with human rights violations?

---

[32] Norwegian Government Pension Fund – Global: Ethical Guidelines 2010, Section 2(3) (see Appendix 1 below).

4.1   The wording of the criterion – interpretation

The actual wording of the Guidelines lists several specific examples of human rights abuses: 'Serious or systematic human rights violations, such as murder, torture, deprivation of liberty, forced labour, the worst forms of child labour and other child exploitation'. It is clear, however, from the term 'such as' before the list of examples, that this is not intended to be an exhaustive list. Moreover, the examples make it clear that the term 'human rights' also includes labour rights. This was emphasized by the Council in the Total recommendation, where, in referring to the preparatory work of the Guidelines, the Council took 'as its point of departure that the reference to human rights pertains to internationally recognized human rights and labour rights'.[33] The Council moreover stated that the qualification 'serious or systematic' must be assessed in each individual case, but that 'a limited number of violations could suffice if they were very serious, while the character of a violation need not be equally serious if it were perpetrated in a systematic manner'.[34]

In the three above-mentioned cases pertaining to human rights, the violations have been both serious and systematic. In the Total case the reported incidents entailed forced labour, violence, including murder and rape, perpetrated by government security forces, and a number of other abuses of fundamental human rights. In the Wal-Mart case, the human rights topics extended to labour rights including allegations of forced labour, of compulsory unpaid overtime, of child labour and unacceptable working environments. In the Vedanta case, the main focus was on the environmental aspects of the company's activity, but the Council did find that violations of fundamental rights of tribal people had also taken place in connection with the company's conduct of business.

The Ethical Guidelines require that there must be an 'unacceptable risk' that unethical corporate conduct takes place in connection with the potential exclusions of companies. This wording reflects the mandate of the Council on Ethics, which is to avoid *contributing* to unethical acts through investment. The Guidelines thus have no penal or retrospective objective; the aim is to avoid present and future complicity, not to punish companies for what they may have done in the past. The Council made the following interpretation of the Guidelines and their preparatory work in the Total Recommendation:

The term *risk* is associated with the degree of probability that unethical actions will take place in the future. The NOU states that 'the objective is to decide

---

[33] Total Recommendation, Section 3.1, p. 8.   [34] Ibid., pp. 8–9.

whether the company in the future will represent an unacceptable ethical risk for the Petroleum Fund.'[35] The wording of Point 4.4[36] makes it clear that what is to be assessed is the likelihood of contributing to 'present and future' acts or omissions. The Council accordingly assumes that actions or omissions that took place in the past will not, in themselves, provide a basis for exclusion of companies under this provision. However, earlier patterns of conduct might give some indications as to what will happen ahead. It is hence also relevant to examine companies' previous practice when future risk of complicity in violations is to be assessed.[37]

The Council furthermore assumed that the reference to an 'unacceptable risk' allowed the Council to recommend exclusion of a company without necessarily providing the kind of evidence that would be required in a court case: 'The acts or omissions must constitute an unacceptable risk of complicity on the part of the Fund. This means that it is not necessary to prove that such complicity will take place – the presence of an unacceptable risk suffices.'[38] These two elements of the concept of 'unacceptable risk' are closely linked. The word 'risk' indicates that the unacceptable conduct that should be avoided (through disinvestment) is in the future (or present). It is impossible to *verify* that something might happen in the future, and it is often very difficult to prove on-going seriously unethical conduct. Moreover, when discovered and exposed, it will often subside.

The Council on Ethics has used the term 'contribution to' as synonymous with 'complicit' in. This is due to the fact that the original Norwegian word used in the Guidelines ('medvirker') has both of these meanings. As such, it is not a determination that generates any legal consequences; the term has no specific implications beyond describing what the Council finds it reasonable to hold a company responsible for. Use of the term 'complicity' in the Council's Recommendations thus does not indicate an assessment of criminal liability or any other specific form of legal responsibility – it is simply used to indicate that an act or omission can be attributed to a company.[39] As stated in the Total case; 'The term complicity is used in many different contexts, *inter alia*, both as legal and ethical categorisation of acts.'

When trying to define *complicity* in the context of the Guidelines, the Council had to base its assessments on the preparatory work of the Guidelines, a Government White Paper, drafted by a commission

---

[35] Norwegian Government White Paper, NOU 2003:22, p. 35.
[36] Now Section 2(4) of the Ethical Guidelines 2010.
[37] Total Recommendation, p. 9.   [38] Ibid.
[39] The Ethical Guidelines could of course not infer any kind of liability or responsibility of a legal nature on any entity; they simply guide the investment policy of a pension fund.

whose mandate had been to propose ethical guidelines for the Fund.[40] This White Paper, which did contain the proposed guidelines and detailed reasoning for them, was discussed in the Government, as well as in the Parliament (*Stortinget*), and the guidelines were accepted as proposed, without any significant amendments. The Guidelines are not statutory law, and have not been subject to formal adoption as such by the Parliament. Nevertheless, since the Parliament and Government agreed with what was proposed, the assumption is that these bodies agree with the argumentation contained in the White Paper. The preparatory work (the White Paper) is thus an important factor when interpreting the wording of the Guidelines.

A number of other factors which might assist in the interpretation of the complicity concept include national and international compensation law and criminal law, relevant national and international practice and jurisprudence, principles regarding complicity in the documents pertaining to the UN Global Compact, the assessments reflected in the reports of the UN Special Representative on business and human rights, and various codes of conduct for corporations, to mention some. It was thus specified in the Total Recommendation that: 'The Council considers that the term complicity in paragraph 4.4 of the guidelines must be interpreted on the basis of the preparatory work and in light of perceptions of national and international law and practice.'[41]

4.2   The concept of 'contribution' or 'complicity' under the Guidelines

As mentioned above, the term 'complicity' has been used synonymously with 'contributing to' in the English versions of the recommendations. The Ethical Guidelines specifically refer to this concept when describing the criteria for exclusion of companies because of human rights violations. This seems to be a relatively common approach. As Clapham points out: 'Complicity is the concept which helps lawyers and human rights organisations to fuse the state/non-state actor divide and apply international human rights law to non-state actor corporations.'[42] The term 'complicity', however, is not self-explanatory. It is often used to describe moral or legal responsibility for wrongdoings when someone is not necessarily the only, or the main, perpetrator. It can be used to describe intentional complicity as well as unintended or passive or indifferent conduct.

---

[40] Known as the 'Graver Commission', see Norwegian Government White Paper, NOU 2003:22.

[41] Total Recommendation, p. 10.   [42] Clapham, *Human Rights Obligations*, p. 563.

Under national penal legal systems, it is often not necessary to establish that there has been a 'main perpetrator' in order to convict someone of complicity. There can be cases where there are several perpetrators and it is impossible to know or prove who actually performed the decisive act. In such cases, all of the involved can be convicted of 'complicity' even if no one is convicted of the main offence.[43] When it comes to corporate complicity in human rights violations, it may not be necessary to establish that a specific state has violated human rights in order to be able to hold a company responsible for complicity/contribution to human rights violations. In many cases the alleged human rights violation in question will consist of weak or lacking national legislation, or lack of implementation or enforcement of such legislation, and will thus lead to non-fulfilment of human rights obligations under international treaties. When trying to establish blameworthy conduct for a corporation, it seems unnecessary to engage in discussions about the scope of each state's human rights obligations and how this translates to requirements for and enforcement of national legislation.[44]

In the Wal-Mart Recommendation, the Council on Ethics thus noted that: 'The Council presumes that it was hardly the intention that the Council, as a precondition for establishing companies' complicity in human rights violations, should be required to determine whether states violate such rights.'[45] As their basis for this assertion, the Council referred to the following sequence of the preparatory work of the Ethical Guidelines: 'Since international law expresses a balancing of interests between states, it is difficult to derive norms of action for market actors from sources of international law. On the other hand, international conventions give concrete form to the content of an international consensus on minimum requirements which should be imposed regarding respect for basic rights worldwide.'[46]

The Council then summed up its position:

In other words, international standards and norms can be indicative of which acts or omissions are deemed unacceptable, without asserting that companies are legally responsible for violations of international conventions. The Council

---

[43] This was the case in 'Orderud-saken', *Eidsivating lagmannsrett*, 5 April 2002 (High Court of Eidsivating, Norway).

[44] This is what all the Treaty Bodies, as well as the international human rights courts, are mandated to adjudicate in individual complaints cases, or in their assessment of periodical State Reports.

[45] Wal-Mart Stores Inc. Recommendation, Section 3.2: 'Complicity in human rights violations with regard to the relationship between states and companies', p. 5.

[46] Norwegian Government White Paper, NOU 2003:22, p. 96.

accordingly assumes that the wording of Point 4.4[47] of the Ethical Guidelines does not require the Council to consider whether individual states violate human rights or labour rights standards each time it assesses a company's conduct in relation to this provision. It is sufficient to establish the presence of an unacceptable risk of companies acting in such a way as to entail serious or systematic breaches of internationally recognised minimum standards for the rights of individuals.[48]

Use of the term 'complicity' in connection with company conduct and violations of human rights standards therefore does not require that a main perpetrator must be identified. Rather, the use of this term in such cases points to the conceptual and doctrinal difficulties in trying to make corporations legal subjects under human rights treaty law.

4.3   Investor 'contribution'

The wording of the Guidelines assume that the Pension Fund may contribute to unethical actions through owning shares in companies that are responsible for unethical conduct. The preparatory work thus deals with the issue of investor complicity:

In order (for an investor) to be complicit in an action, the action must be possible to anticipate for the investor. There must be some form of systematic or causal relationship between the company's operations and the actions in which the investor does not wish to be complicit. Investments in the company cannot be regarded as complicity in actions which one could not possibly expect or be aware of or circumstances over which the company has no significant control.[49]

This passage implies that circumstances beyond the company's control cannot entail complicity for the investor. This must also mean that the company itself cannot be considered to be complicit in ethical norm breaches that are beyond the company's control or which the company could not possibly expect or be aware of.

4.4   Application of the 'complicity' standard

The White Paper addresses more specifically the issue of complicity in states where human rights violations take place:

Particular problems arise in connection with companies operating in states where severe human rights violations occur. Such violations can also occur

---

[47] Now Section 2(3) of the Ethical Guidelines 2010.
[48] Wal-Mart Stores Inc. Recommendation, p. 5.
[49] Norwegian Government White Paper, NOU 2003:22, pp. 164–5.

in connection with the companies' operations, for example through the use of security forces that commit abuses to protect the company's property and installations, deportation of people and environmental damage to facilitate the company's projects, or arrest and persecution of workers seeking to promote trade union rights. A company may be regarded as complicit to such actions only when those actions are taken in order to protect the company's property or investment and the company has not taken reasonable measures to prevent the abuses.[50]

The Council has, in its recommendations, interpreted the above quotations from the White Paper as follows:

… it is only when the unethical actions are carried out in order to protect or to facilitate a company's activities, and the company has failed to 'take reasonable measures to prevent the abuses', that the company, and thus also the Fund, can be held liable for complicity under the guidelines. If the company (and the Fund) is aware of unethical actions carried out in the company's interest but choose to remain passive, this may be regarded as complicity. NOU 2003:22 thus appears to imply that companies cannot justify plain passivity if they could have taken steps to prevent unethical conduct. The requirement of taking 'reasonable measures' is assumed to refer to circumstances over which the company has control. The question is whether the responsibility is limited to this. It would be natural to interpret 'reasonable measures' as also applying to circumstances where the company has a genuine possibility to exert influence, even though it does not necessarily have control.[51]

The Council has noted in its recommendations that under Norwegian penal law, the main rule is that passive complicity is not a criminal offence. The thresholds, however, for criminal liability and, for example, invoking responsibility for compensation, are not necessarily the same. The harsher the sanctions are, the higher the thresholds. One might suggest that for disinvestment, which in itself can hardly be seen as a sanction at all, the threshold need not be very high.

There are not many examples of legal assessments of company complicity in human rights violations, neither from the sphere of criminal law, nor from tort or compensation cases. There are hardly any examples of criminal liability for companies under international law. During the Nuremberg trials, individual company representatives, such as Alfred Krupp, were prosecuted for complicity in crimes against humanity, but the company itself was outside the jurisdiction of the tribunal.[52] In the Statute for the Permanent International Criminal Court (ICC),

---

[50] Ibid., Section 5.3.2.3: 'Contribution and delimitation of corporate responsibility'.
[51] Total Recommendation, p. 11 and Wal-Mart Stores Inc. Recommendation, p. 5.
[52] See Knut Dörmann, *Elements of War Crimes under the Rome Statute of the International Criminal Court* (Cambridge University Press, 2003), pp. 35–7. (The Zyklon B Case, UNWCC, LRTWC; Vol. I, pp. 93–103, 13 AD 250.)

Article 25 specifies that only natural persons can be subject to the jurisdiction of the Court. Some states, however, have domestic legislation that prescribes criminal liability for legal persons.[53]

There is more relevant jurisprudence to be found with regard to corporate responsibility for *tort* or *compensation*. In particular the newly invigorated US Alien Tort Claims Act (ATCA) from 1789 has been subject to international attention as several large multinational corporations have found themselves in lawsuits where large compensation sums have been at stake. The act refers to violations of 'the law of nations', which by US courts have been specified to include genocide, slave trade, forced labour, war crimes, rape, torture and summary executions.[54]

One case under this act was especially relevant to the Council on Ethics while assessing the Total case; the Unocal case. This case was settled following a ruling that allowed judicial consideration of Unocal's alleged complicity in the Burmese authorities' human rights abuses in connection with the construction of a gas pipeline.[55] The case was of direct significance for Total, which collaborated closely with Unocal in Burma in the period in question.

The first instance court (the US District Court) did not find it likely that Unocal had been complicit in human rights abuses, because the company's actions/omissions did not constitute what the court defined as 'active participation' in breaches of international norms. This view, however, was not shared by the Court of Appeals whose conclusion was that there existed sufficient evidence of complicity on the part of Unocal to warrant judicial consideration of the merits of the case. One key factor was that Unocal had knowledge of the abuses perpetrated by the military. Although the case was of a procedural nature, the judges came very close to presuming Unocal's guilt regarding its complicity in human rights violations in connection with the construction of the pipeline. This was based, *inter alia*, on presumptions that the company had paid for the use of Burmese military forces to attend to pipeline security and construction of infrastructure along the pipeline route, and that they undoubtedly knew that these forces resorted to forced labour and were guilty of violence, rape and so forth.[56] The decision was partly based on testimony of witnesses and reports that persons in the company's management, on several occasions,

---

[53] FAFO, 'Project on Business and International Crimes: Assessing the Liability of Business Entities for Grave Violations of International Law.'

[54] Clapham, *Human Rights Obligations*, p. 253 (*Wiwa* v. *Shell*, *Kadic* v. *Karadic*).

[55] *Doe I* v. *Unocal Corp.* (United States Court of Appeals for the Ninth Circuit, Nos. 00–56603, 00–57197, D.C. No. CV–96–06959–RSWL).

[56] See for example *Doe I* v. *Unocal Corp.*, para. 14.

had acknowledged that they knew of abuses in connection with the construction project.

The Council on Ethics drew heavily on the Unocal case when discussing the Total case:

> According to the grounds for the finding in the above-mentioned Unocal case, Total is presumed to have had the same knowledge of, and responsibility for, the human rights violations in connection with the pipeline construction as Unocal. The Council accepts this as a fact. There were procedural reasons why the complaint, which originally referred to Total, Unocal and MOGE alike, only was raised against Unocal.[57] Actions for damages have been brought against Total in Belgium and France in connection with their activities in Burma. No such action has been subject to final judgment.[58]

Thus, the Council did find that Total's actions in Burma during this time period were equally blameworthy as those attributed to Unocal. Nevertheless, the Council did not find that Total should be excluded from the Fund. The different objectives and functions of a Court on the one hand and the Council on Ethics on the other explain this; courts have a retrospective and penal focus. The Council on Ethics has a forward-looking perspective; the aim of exclusion is to avoid contributing to unethical conduct. There must exist an unacceptable risk of breaches taking place in the future.

Based on discussions of the Total case, the Council on Ethics summarized its criteria for establishing complicity for human rights violations for companies in the following four points:

- There must exist some kind of linkage between the company's operations and the existing breaches of the guidelines, which must be visible to the Fund.
- The breaches must have been carried out with a view to serving the company's interests or to facilitate conditions for the company.
- The company must either have contributed actively to the breaches, or had knowledge of the breaches, but without seeking to prevent them.
- The norm breaches must either be ongoing, or there must exist an unacceptable risk that norm breaches will occur in the future. Earlier norm breaches might indicate future patterns of conduct.[59]

---

[57] *Doe I* v. *Unocal Corp.*, D, 14205, states: 'The District Court later denied the Doe-plaintiffs' motion for class certification and dismissed their claims against Total for lack of personal jurisdiction.'

[58] One action brought against Total was recently denied in Belgium on procedural grounds. See Total Recommendation, Section 3.2: 'More about the term complicity', p. 10.

[59] Ibid., p. 12.

The Council referred to the guidelines' preparatory work as the main source for these criteria and indicated that they were not necessarily required to be cumulatively fulfilled, but that they constituted 'decisive elements in an overall assessment of whether there exists an unacceptable risk of the Fund contributing to human rights violations'.[60]

4.5   Links between company conduct and human rights violations

One of the reasons for not recommending exclusion of Total was the lack of a linkage between the ongoing human rights abuses in Burma and the company's operations. The Council did not question the gravity or extent of human rights abuses in Burma. On the contrary, it acknowledged the very high likelihood of them continuing in the foreseeable future:[61]

The Council expects the human rights violations in Burma to continue, cf. the UN Commission on Human Rights' resolution from 2005 expressing deep concern over: 'the ongoing and systematic violation of human rights, including civil, political, economic, social and cultural rights of the people of Myanmar, in particular discrimination and violations suffered by persons belonging to ethnic minorities, women and children, ... harassment of members of the National League for Democracy ..., forced relocation, ... forced labour, including child labour, ... denial of freedom of assembly, association, expression and movement, ... wide disrespect for the rule of law and lack of independence of the judiciary.'[62]

The Council, nevertheless, found that:

There is no obvious direct linkage between these serious violations of human rights and Total's operations today. There appears to be general agreement, also within NGO circles, that human rights violations are not a significant feature in the pipeline area today. The Council is unable to see any direct linkage between Total's present operations and the human rights violations taking place elsewhere in Burma. Nor is the Council able to see that the human rights violations in Burma, which are largely perpetrated by the military and security forces, are designed to protect the company's interests or to facilitate the company's projects.[63]

The Council thus did not find a strong enough connection between the company's operations and the regime's human rights abuses.

---

[60] Ibid.   [61] Ibid., pp. 21–2.

[62] UN Commission on Human Rights, 'Situation of Human Rights in Myanmar: Report of the Special Rapporteur, Paulo Sérgio Pinheiro', UN Doc. E/CN.4/2005/36 (2 December 2004).

[63] Ibid., p. 22.

In the Wal-Mart case, the Council did find such a connection:

There is no doubt that working conditions at textile factories in Asia, Africa and Latin America can be abysmal, and that Wal-Mart purchases a number of products that are manufactured under unacceptable conditions. There are numerous reports of child labour, serious violations of working hour regulations, wages below the local minimum, health-hazardous working conditions, unreasonable punishment, prohibition of unionisation and extensive use of a production system that fosters working conditions bordering on forced labour, and of employees being locked into production premises etc. in Wal-Mart's supply chain.[64]

The Council also found that there were substantiated allegations against Wal-Mart in North America, particularly with regard to a practice of gender discrimination, as well as with regard to freedom of organization, association and assembly. The company seems to have an effective policy of preventing any attempt by employees to form trade unions. The Council found that the above examples showed that there had been violations of internationally recognized standards for labour rights and human rights.[65]

The Council found several links between the human rights violations in question and the conduct of the company. In its recommendation, the Council stated that:

The violations of standards discussed above have taken place either in connection with the company's operations and activity in North America, or in connection with the manufacturing of goods for sale in Wal-Mart's stores. While it may be difficult to prove that Wal-Mart is directly responsible for violations of labour rights at its suppliers in the developing world, the Council considers there is an unacceptable risk that such a linkage exists. Where the violations of standards in the company's own business are concerned, the linkage between this business and the violations is relatively clear-cut. The linkage in this case is highly visible due to the keen public interest in Wal-Mart shown by the press and by a number of NGO's.[66]

The Council also found that the violations had been carried out with a view to serving the company's interests, or to facilitate conditions for the company:

---

[64] Wal-Mart Stores Inc. Recommendation, Section 6.1: 'Violations of standards in the supplier chain', p. 17.
[65] See Article 8, ICESCR which establishes the right to form trade unions, and Article 21 and 22, ICCPR, which also establishes the right to form trade unions in addition to the right of assembly and organization in general, as well as the Convention on the Rights of the Child (1980) and ILO Convention no. 182, 'Worst Forms of Child Labour' (1999), Article 8(3) ICCPR, ILO Convention no. 29, 'Forced Labour' (1930 and 1957), ILO Convention no. 87, 'Freedom of Association' (1948).
[66] Wal-Mart Stores Inc. Recommendation, Section 6.3: 'The company's responsibility', p. 21.

In the view of the Council, the type of violation focused on in this recommendation in Wal-Mart's business operations has been undertaken with the intention
of increasing the company's profits. The Council considers that even though
all companies aim at maximising their profits, it is ethically unacceptable to do
so by committing, or tacitly accepting, serious and systematic violations of ethical norms. The Council finds that the violations have been undertaken with a
view to facilitate or serving the company's interests.[67]

One element (included in the third bullet point) pertained to whether
the company had contributed actively to the violations, or had knowledge of the violations without seeking to prevent them. In light of the
fact that the Council deemed Wal-Mart to be directly responsible for
the reported violations in their own operations in North America, this
requirement was clearly met. With regard to reported patterns of violations in the supply chain in third world countries, the Council assumed
that Wal-Mart was largely aware of them and largely refrained from
seeking to prevent them. The Council also recognized that Wal-Mart
had considerable influence with regard to working environment, wages
etc., particularly in relation to the manufacturers that the company
itself describes as 'direct suppliers'. This influence is due to the company's size and widespread presence in many countries, and thus also
due to its engagement with a large number of supply-chain entities.

When the Council summarized its complicity standard in the four
bullet points set forth in the Total recommendation, those elements
were seen to constitute *decisive factors in an overall assessment*, and it
was thus not necessary that all four criteria were met in order for a
company to be considered complicit in human rights violations. With
regard to the Wal-Mart case, however, the Council found that all of the
four requirements were met.

The Council made it clear that isolated labour standard violations or
human rights violations, even if serious, would not suffice to exclude
a company because they would not constitute sufficient grounds for
establishing a risk of violation in the future. Moreover, the Council
explicitly stated that the violations of working environment standards,
prevention of unionization and gender-based discrimination, would not
in themselves suffice to recommend exclusion, even in cases where they
must be regarded as systematic. The Council recommended exclusion
of Wal-Mart because of

... the total sum of violations of standards, both in the company's own business
operations and in the supply chain. It appears to be a systematic and planned
practice on the part of the company to operate on, or below, the threshold of

[67] Ibid.

what are accepted standards for the work environment. Many of the violations are serious, most appear to be systematic, and altogether they form a picture of a company whose overall activity displays a lack of willingness to countervail violations of standards in its business operations.[68]

The Wal-Mart exclusion was thus a result of an overall assessment of the entire operation of the largest, and clearly one of the most influential, retail companies in the world.

4.6   Future complicity

The last of the above four bullet points, '*The norm breaches must either be ongoing, or there must exist an unacceptable risk that norm breaches will occur in the future. Earlier norm breaches might indicate future patterns of conduct*',[69] reflects the actual wording of the Guidelines themselves; it refers to the requirement that there must exist an 'unacceptable risk' of complicity taking place. As indicated above, this requirement is a direct result of the fact that the entire reason for the exclusion mechanism within the Ethical Guidelines is to avoid complicity in unethical acts through ownership.

It was in particular the last bullet point which prevented the Council from recommending that Total should be excluded from the Fund in 2005. The Council did not find it likely that Total would continue to contribute to the human rights violations that had been associated with the company in the past. First of all, the actual construction work with the pipeline had been completed. Moreover, it seemed that the company had improved its work and public profile with regard to human rights and social responsibility. One might question whether this human rights focus was credible, as the actual construction work had been completed. However, the Council presumed that in future construction projects Total was not likely to put itself in a situation in which it could be associated with the use of forced labour. The Council assumed that 'any financial gain accruing to Total thanks to forced labour is assumed to be far outweighed by the negative light in which the accusations have placed the company'.[70] The Council thus found it unlikely that Total would start future projects without taking steps to avoid human rights violations in connection with its operations. This assessment was built on available facts about the situation concerning Total's operation in Burma in 2005. Needless to say, the situation can change, and companies operating in Burma, including Total, are being monitored closely by the Council on Ethics.

[68] Ibid., p. 22.   [69] Total Recommendation, p. 12.   [70] Ibid., p. 18.

With regard to the Wal-Mart case, however, the Council assumed that an unacceptable risk of future violations, linked to the company's operations, existed. To the Council's knowledge, there were no indications that the company had plans to revise its approach in terms of seeking to prevent violations of labour rights taking place in its supply chain, or with regard to violations of standards for labour rights, including gender discrimination and prevention of unionization, within its own business operations in North America. In this regard it is worth noting that the Council had not received a reply to its enquiry to the company, which was sent before the recommendation on exclusion was finalized.

The term 'unacceptable risk' gives the Council a discretionary mandate. The final assessment of what constitutes an unacceptable risk is a subjective one. In the case of Burma, however, the Council did make it relatively clear that it would be difficult to imagine any large infrastructure construction work, such as clearing areas for and building gas pipelines, without massive human rights violations taking place in connection with this. As mentioned above, Total was largely identified with Unocal, and the Council did not doubt that both Total and Unocal had been complicit in the human rights violations that took place in Burma during the pipeline construction. The building of such large infrastructure projects in Burma can therefore be seen to be almost an objective criterion – if a company is involved in such projects, then there is an unacceptable risk that it will be complicit in the seemingly unavoidable forthcoming human rights violations generated by the project.

In October 2007, following the military regime's violent attacks on Buddhist monks, students and others, the Ministry of Finance asked the Council on Ethics in a letter to give an update on the Council's work with regard to investments in companies that had operations in Burma. The Council, in its response, reiterated that the risk of grave human rights violations in connection with construction of infrastructure in Burma is extensive. The Council stated:

Grave human rights violations such as forced displacement of people and extensive use of forced labour can be expected. This is particularly so in the first stages of large construction projects, when preparations are made for constructions, areas are cleared and roads are built. Even though it is the Burmese authorities and not the companies who principally commit the violations, it is likely to be a connection between the violations and the companies' operations, in the sense that the violations take place to facilitate for companies' future operations.[71]

---

[71] Council on Ethics, 'Letter dated 11 October 2007, on the Council's assessment of companies with operations in Burma', p. 2.

The Council went on to state that several companies, to the Council's knowledge, had 'engaged in negotiations regarding the construction of oil and gas pipelines from Burma to India, China and Thailand. A number of alternative projects have been discussed between the Burmese authorities and different groups of companies. Since the Council on Ethics is particularly aware of the risk of violations of human rights in connection with large construction projects in Burma, it has especially surveyed the possible role of companies in the Fund in similar, new projects.'[72]

Among the companies looked into by the Council were, according to the letter, the South Korean company Daewoo International Corp. and the Chinese company Petrochina Co. Ltd. The Council found indications that there were political agreements on sale of gas to China, and that it thus was to be expected that construction of gas pipelines between the two countries would take place. The Council, however, had at the time of the writing of the letter, not been able to establish that any contracts or formal agreements were entered into. Nevertheless, the Council stated that: 'If companies in the Fund's portfolio were to enter into contract agreements regarding the construction of such pipelines, the Council may recommend the exclusion of these companies *already from the time of entering into the agreements*. Because such undertakings would most likely involve an unacceptable risk of contributing to human rights violations, it is not considered necessary to wait until the violations actually take place.'[73] The Council thus considers it to be practically impossible to be party to a project that requires large infrastructure construction work, such as gas pipelines, without being complicit in the massive human rights violations that would be generated by such projects under the current military regime in Burma.

4.7   Presence in states with oppressive regimes

Many organizations, journalists, politicians and other individuals have made the point that being present in states with oppressive regimes and generating income for such regimes, can be seen as complicity to human rights violations in itself. Not least with regard to Burma, this has been a view supported by many. It stands to reason that generating income, for example through taxes, for a regime will enable that regime to carry out its oppressive policies.

Depending on the interpretation of the term 'complicity', financial activities that facilitate the activities of an offender could easily fall into

[72] Ibid.   [73] Ibid, p. 3.

this category, both from a political or moral point of view, but also from a legal point of view. One recent example of how extensively the term 'complicity' can be interpreted is international regulations on transfer of money to groups or institutions labelled as terrorist organizations. National as well as international legislative rules[74] have treated all forms of transfer of money to such organizations as support to and complicity in the activities of such groups, irrespective of the aim of the individual transfer. Even to finance travel expenses in order to facilitate participation in peace talks could violate the prohibition on transfer, directly or indirectly, of financial goods to such persons.

Whether or not an act or omission is considered to constitute 'complicity', in the sense that it generates some kind of sanction, depends entirely on the applicable legal regime. Based on the Ethical Guidelines, the Council on Ethics thus has made it clear that generating revenues for an oppressive state is not in itself sufficient grounds for a company to be excluded from the Fund. The wording of the Guidelines themselves does not deal specifically with this issue. Interpreted in isolation, the Council may well have determined that 'unacceptable risk of contributing to … human rights violations' included financial activities that clearly benefited oppressive regimes. The preparatory work of the Guidelines, however, indicates that it was not the intention of the government to let the Ethical Guidelines cover this kind of activity. As has been explained above, there are clear indications that there must be a concrete link between a company's conduct and the relevant human rights abuses. Human rights abuses that have no causal link to the activities of a company seem to fall short of the requirement.

The Council on Ethics has also indicated that it falls outside its mandate to assess whether companies should be excluded because of presence in very oppressive states, because this would in fact require that the Council make assessments of states and not companies. In the Total case, the Council therefore briefly dismissed undertaking a general assessment of Burma because this 'would moreover raise questions about whether the human rights situation of *other* regimes is sufficiently bad to warrant the same considerations. This entails an assessment of *states*, which the guidelines do not require the Council to embark on.'[75] It is not difficult to understand the reason for this limitation on the Council's mandate or to foresee what kind of discussions the Council on Ethics would generate in trying to apply the criteria even handedly with regard to states. There are at least a dozen states that would easily

---

[74] See for example Security Council Resolution 1373, 28 September 2001.
[75] Total Recommendation, Section 4.2.2: 'The Council's assessment', p. 19.

qualify as extremely bad from a human rights point of view, not least states in which Norwegian petroleum companies are present and generating income for the regimes in question.

In the Guidelines' preparatory work, it has been underlined that the guidelines are not meant to deal with foreign policy concerns. If the government wants to pursue foreign policy issues, it has a wide range of more effective instruments and tools than the investment policy of the Fund.[76] The Council stated, both in the Total recommendation in 2005 and in its letter to the Ministry of Finance in 2007 that: 'The Ethical Guidelines' preparatory work states that the objective to be achieved by excluding companies is to avoid the Fund's contribution to grave unethical actions. It is beyond the Council's mandate to assess whether the exclusion of companies could have effects, such as improvement of the political situation in a state, beyond this.'

The political limitations in the case of the Ethical Guidelines must be seen in connection with the fact that this is a governmental Fund, owned and administered by the state, and that the Council on Ethics' mandate is to advise the relevant state organs. Private investors, or investors with a specific profile, will perhaps be more willing to apply political considerations pertaining also to states in their investment policies.

5.   Summing up

The exclusion mechanism in the Ethical Guidelines for the Norwegian Government Pension Fund represents one of the very few existing systems which entail disinvestment based on a set of fixed criteria. Clearly, disinvestment as an instrument for achieving ethical aims is relatively rare within the sphere of corporate social responsibility. Engagement with companies through dialogue and exercise of ownership rights, with the aim of improving company conduct, is a far more common approach to ethical challenges. Once a company is excluded from a portfolio, the means of influencing that company is considerably weakened. One might thus argue that exclusion of companies on ethical grounds does not in itself contribute to improve the state of the world.

The Ethical Guidelines, however, also contain a mechanism that entails engagement and dialogue with companies.[77] It seems reasonable to assume that efforts to engage companies in dialogue on ethical

[76] Norwegian Government White Paper, NOU 2003:22, p. 22.
[77] Guidelines for Norges Bank's Work on Responsible Management and Active Ownership of the Government Pension Fund – Global (1 March 2010) (see Appendix 3 below).

issues get more attention from the companies in question when they are aware of the possibility of being excluded. The engagement mandate (exercised by the Central Bank) and the exclusion mandate (exercised by the Council on Ethics) must be seen as integral parts of the overall ethical management of the Fund.

The exclusion mechanism is, as mentioned above, based on the aspiration to *avoid complicity* in unethical conduct, and does not seek to influence company conduct or policies. This is the reason why the ethical criteria are applied with a view to ongoing and future unethical conduct, but not retrospectively. One might, from this point of view, suggest that the exclusion of companies from the Fund has a 100 per cent effect; when a company is excluded, the Fund no longer has a part in what the company does.

One might ask to what extent exclusions under this regime have effects beyond mere avoidance of complicity. While it can be assumed that the exclusion mechanism in some instances is conducive to achieving meaningful dialogues with companies, it probably has no such effect in other cases. Attempting to estimate effects of publicly announced exclusion decisions based on ethical criteria is hardly an accurate science. However, the fact that the Fund is so large, and the fact that the exclusion decisions are detailed and are being made publicly available, increases the possibility of them having some influence with regard to other investors and funds, as well as on companies.

One final question, which is perhaps more interesting in the context of the topic for this chapter, is to what extent the exclusion mechanism can contribute to ongoing discussions on corporate responsibility, *lex lata* as well as *lex ferenda*, for violations of human rights in connection with company conduct. The hope of this author would be that the recommendations produced by the Council on Ethics will play a part in future discussions on ways of enhancing company accountability and responsibility for the consequences of their activities which might have a negative human rights impact.

3   Laws, standards or voluntary guidelines?

Simon Chesterman

1.   Introduction

The question of how to influence the human rights behaviour of multi-national corporations has long been a concern of non-governmental organizations, scholars and governments. Their efforts at mobilization, analysis and regulation have achieved mixed results. More recently, pension funds and other institutional investors have assumed an important role in channelling such influence into a form that may exert greater leverage on the decision-making process of a multinational: through its shareholders. Companies with operations in Myanmar (Burma) and Sudan have been punished for their ties to governments engaged in human rights abuses; a far larger number have signed onto voluntary principles and codes of conduct embracing best practice in the field of human rights. These various efforts to shape behaviour through inducements and public pressure are an admission that traditional regulation through coercion for violations of specific rights is not working. Praise for 'corporate social responsibility' generally assumes that traditional regulation *cannot* work; criticism often asserts that the illusion of accountability undermines the prospects of establishing an effective mechanism with teeth and is worse than nothing at all.

Leaving aside that larger question of whether formal regulation – such as through treaty or legislation – is desirable or possible, should the ad hoc efforts of investors to shape the human rights behaviour of the companies in which they own shares themselves be regulated? That is, by what standard, if any, should the activist shareholder be judged? This chapter will consider this question in the context of the Council on Ethics of the Norwegian Government Pension Fund – Global.

I am grateful to Franco Ferrari, Benedict Kingsbury, Christopher L. Kutz, Ola Mestad, John Ruggie and Wee Meng Seng for comments on an earlier draft of this paper. An earlier version was published as 'The Turn to Ethics: Disinvestment from Multinational Corporations for Human Rights Violations – The Case of Norways's Sovereign Wealth Fund', *American University International Law Review* 23 (2008), pp. 577–615.

Section 2 briefly introduces the Pension Fund and the Council on Ethics, surveying the recommendations the Council has made since its creation in November 2004. Section 3 then situates the Council's work in the context of other legal and voluntary frameworks. Section 4 considers an issue that has posed a key challenge to the Council's work: the meaning of 'complicity'. Section 5 then returns to the question of whether the Council's work is best seen as legal or purely 'ethical.'

2. The Norwegian Government Pension Fund and the Council on Ethics

The Norwegian Government Pension Fund – Global (*Statens pensjonsfond – Utland*) invests surplus wealth produced by Norway's petroleum sector, principally revenue from taxes and licensing agreements. Known until January 2006 as the Petroleum Fund of Norway, it is the second largest pension fund in the world with assets in excess of US$400 billion.

The Fund was created in 1990 by an act of the Norwegian Parliament (*Stortinget*). Since its mandate was to receive money when there was a budget surplus, however, the first transfer was made only in 1996 for fiscal year 1995. Subsequent years were more bountiful and the fund has now grown well beyond Norway's annual gross domestic product (GDP) – US$369 billion in 2007 – and is projected to reach a level of around 250 per cent of GDP by 2030. As oil revenues diminish, it is then expected gradually to decline. (Crude oil production is believed to have peaked; natural gas production will peak around 2013.)[1]

The purpose of the fund was, first, to avoid the wide fluctuations of economic activity caused by the petroleum sector. By limiting the impact of variable oil revenues on government spending and investing a substantial portion of those revenues abroad, the fund reduces these fluctuations and stabilizes the exchange rate. Second, the fund provides a savings vehicle for future generations of Norwegians – an aim reflected in its re-branding in 2006 as a 'Government Pension' Fund.[2]

2.1 The turn to ethics

In addition to these domestic considerations of economic stability and intergenerational equity, the government of Norway later adopted two mechanisms addressing the impact of its international investments. In 2001 an 'Environmental Fund' was established within the larger fund.

---

[1] Tore Eriksen, 'The Norwegian Petroleum Sector and the Government Pension Fund – Global' (Oslo: Norwegian Ministry of Finance, June 2006).
[2] Ibid.

This new instrument invested exclusively in developed markets and was restricted to acquiring equity in companies assumed to have limited negative influence on the environment, and which met specific environmental reporting and certification requirements based on analysis from the British consulting firm Ethical Investment Research Services (EIRiS).[3]

In the same year, the Ministry of Finance appointed an Advisory Commission on International Law for the fund. The Commission responded to requests from the Ministry as to whether specific investments were in conflict with Norway's commitments under international law. In March 2002, the Commission responded to such a request concerning Singapore Technologies Engineering. It concluded that, as there was 'a large degree of probability' that the company through a subsidiary produced anti-personnel mines, even modest investments in the company could constitute a violation of Norway's obligations under the Ottawa Convention on Anti-Personnel Mines. Such an investment could imply a violation of the Ottawa Convention prohibition on 'assist[ing]' the production of anti-personnel mines. A month later the government formally excluded Singapore Technologies Engineering from the fund's investment universe.[4]

In Autumn 2002, the government appointed a committee to develop more general ethical guidelines for the fund's investments. The committee, which was chaired by Professor Hans Petter Graver, reported on 25 June 2003. In recognition of the pluralism of Norwegian society and the fact that beneficiaries of the fund included future generations, the foundation of the ethical guidelines was made broad and relatively vague. The Graver Report sought to identify an overlapping consensus of ethical values that were consistent over time, relying largely on internationally accepted principles rather than seeking to develop a separate basis founded on Norwegian national culture or policy. The Report specifically cited principles on protection of the environment, human rights, labour standards and corporate governance embodied in the UN Global Compact and adopted by the International Labour Organization (ILO), the Organisation for Economic Co-operation and Development (OECD) and the UN Sub-Commission on the Promotion and Protection of Human Rights.[5]

Such a pragmatic formulation of substantive obligations was also an attempt to avoid problems of theory. The Report explicitly sought

[3] Council on Ethics, 'Annual Report 2005' (Oslo: Government Pension Fund – Global, January 2006).
[4] Norwegian Petroleum Fund Advisory Commission on International Law, 'Memorandum to the Ministry of Finance: Question of whether Investments in Singapore Technologies Engineering Can Imply a Violation of Norway's International Obligations' (Oslo, 22 March 2002).
[5] Norwegian Government White Paper, NOU 2003:22.

to embrace both teleological and deontological schools of ethics: teleological ethics, such as utilitarianism, emphasize the importance of consequences; deontological ethics, such as Kant's categorical imperative, hold that one should do the right thing not in order to achieve a goal but simply because it is right. The two schools are also known as consequentialism and non-consequentialism respectively. Though the division is not quite so neat, these two approaches to ethics are broadly reflected in the two instruments ultimately adopted to implement the general standards to which the Norwegian fund would be held.

The first, reflecting the teleological conception of ethics, was the exercise of active ownership rights to promote long-term financial returns – explicitly understood as including protection of human rights and sustainability of the environment. When the Ministry of Finance adopted ethical guidelines that included environmental considerations, the Environmental Fund as a separate entity was discontinued. Those general guidelines now provide that the overall objective remains safeguarding the fund's financial interests, but that the exercise of ownership rights 'shall primarily be based on the UN's Global Compact and the OECD Guidelines for Corporate Governance and for Multinational Enterprises'.[6] Norges Bank, which administers the fund, is required to report on how it has acted as owner representative, 'including a description of the work to promote special interests relating to the long-term horizon and diversification of investments in accordance with' the guidelines on ownership.[7]

The second instrument is the exclusion from the investment universe, either through negative screening or disinvestment, of companies where there is an unacceptable risk as an owner of complicity in gross or systematic breaches of ethical norms within the areas of human rights and the environment. Though exclusion may in some circumstances influence the behaviour of companies, the Graver Report focused on the importance of exclusion as a means of avoiding one's own complicity in ethically suspect activity, rather than as a means of influencing the activity itself.[8] This was seen as an extension of the work of the Advisory Commission on International Law, which was replaced in December 2004 by a five-member Council on Ethics. Reflecting the deontological conception of ethics, the focus of the Council's work is on avoiding the risk of doing the wrong thing rather than ensuring a

---

[6] Norwegian Government Pension Fund – Global: Ethical Guidelines 2004, para. 3.1 (see Appendix 2 below).
[7] Ibid., para. 3.2.
[8] Norwegian Government White Paper, NOU 2003:22, para. 5.1.

desirable course of action is followed. Moreover, the Council's examination is focused – at least technically – on the potential for Norwegian complicity rather than the actual conduct of the company in question. As the Graver Report observed, 'the Council does not have to prove that a company is guilty of unethical practices'.[9] As we shall see, for some companies this is a distinction without a difference.

Formally, the Council submits recommendations to the Ministry of Finance, which makes final decisions on negative screening and exclusion of companies from the investment universe.[10] These recommendations and decisions are to be made public, though there is provision for a delay in publication in order to 'ensure a financially sound implementation of the exclusion of the company concerned'.[11] This recognizes the likelihood that knowledge of an imminent, concentrated sale may have a negative impact on the share price of the company in question; keeping notice of the sale closely held enables the Fund to sell at what would presumably be a higher share price.

The Council is given a broad power to make recommendations on its own initiative. The first basis for exclusion of a company is for 'production of weapons that through their normal use may violate fundamental humanitarian principles'. In addition, the Council may issue a recommendation because of acts or omissions that constitute an unacceptable risk of the Fund contributing to:

- Serious or systematic human rights violations, such as murder, torture, deprivation of liberty, forced labour, the worst forms of child labour and other forms of child exploitation
- Grave breaches of individual rights in situations of war or conflict
- Severe environmental damages
- Gross corruption
- Other particularly serious violations of fundamental ethical norms.[12]

This allows, clearly, wide discretion on the part of the Council, which is not constituted as a court but nevertheless required to 'gather all necessary information at its own discretion and … ensure that the matter is documented as fully as possible'. When the Council is considering recommending exclusion, 'the company in question shall receive the draft recommendation and the reasons for it, for comment'.[13] As might be expected, questions of burden of proof and natural justice swiftly arose.

---

[9] Ibid., para. 5.4.   [10] Ethical Guidelines 2004, para. 4.1.
[11] Ibid.   [12] Ibid., para. 4.4.   [13] Ibid., para. 4.5.

The Council is also tasked with reviewing 'on a regular basis' whether the grounds for exclusion of a particular company continue to apply; on the basis of new information it may recommend to the Ministry of Finance the revocation of a decision to exclude.[14]

2.2   The Council's recommendations

By the end of 2009, the Council had recommended the exclusion of forty-eight companies. In the product exclusion category this included eight companies linked to cluster weapons, ten to nuclear weapons, one to anti-personnel landmines and seventeen to tobacco. One company was excluded due to its supply of military equipment to Burma. A further eight were excluded for environmental damage, two for human rights concerns, and one for 'other particularly serious violations of fundamental ethical norms' (surveillance systems sold to Israel for use in the West Bank). The Norwegian Ministry of Finance has followed most of all published recommendations. The Fund's portfolio presently includes about 8,000 companies.

In addition to predictable unhappiness on the part of companies publicly excluded from investment by the fund, there has been some measure of criticism within Norway of the Council's activity. The Chair of the Council, Gro Nystuen, responded to some of these criticisms in an article published in the newspaper *Dagens Næringsliv*, including claims that the Council did not allow companies the opportunity to rebut accusations of improper activity, and that companies that did answer accusations were nevertheless excluded anyway. Nystuen explained that allegations are substantiated with 'concrete references to sources' and that companies being assessed for exclusion are sent a letter and invited to 'comment on the allegations':

I would assume that this process represents a more or less universal method for processing allegations and accusations. Whether one wants to complain about an administrative decision, respond to a complaint from the neighbour or challenge a criminal indictment, it is a basic requirement that the claims which are presented are concrete and that they are well substantiated and documented. It is much more difficult to respond to, or counter, vague allegations or rumours.[15]

The response was suggestive of the unusual nature of the Council on Ethics. Technically it is not a legal tribunal bound by rules of due process; technically it focuses on the risk of complicity on the part of

---

[14] Ibid., para. 4.6.
[15] Gro Nystuen, 'Response to Criticism Concerning the Exclusion of Companies from the Norwegian Government Pension Fund', *Dagens Næringsliv* (11 September 2006).

the fund rather than proof of allegations against a given company. In practice, however, it has justified its decisions on quasi-legal grounds, establishing precedent and following or distinguishing prior decisions; building on the provisions of the Ethical Guidelines it has also adopted a quasi-adversarial procedure, allowing companies the opportunity to know allegations and respond to them, though without the full trappings of legal process. This begs the question of whether the Council is properly seen as an ethical or legal body, a point to which we will return in section 5.

3.   Legal and non-legal approaches to regulating multinational corporations

Regulating the activities of corporations that operate across national borders poses a challenge to the international legal order, which is premised on the centrality of states.[16] The largest multinationals dwarf the economies of many countries; frequently they are also able to mobilize greater political influence. As the Council on Ethics noted in its exclusion of Wal-Mart recommendation, Wal-Mart's annual turnover is larger than the GDP of 161 of the world's states.[17]

Nevertheless, efforts to analyse and delimit the international legal status of natural persons have had far more success than comparable efforts with respect to their juridical counterparts. This is due in part to the longer history of prosecuting individuals. The Nuremberg trials are the iconic example of this, but these built upon a tradition of individual responsibility under international law, most consistently with respect to pirates. In addition, however, war criminals and *génocidaires* have fewer defenders in the governments of wealthy countries that frequently drive transformations in the law.

Evidence of this different treatment is found in the debates over whether to include corporations within the jurisdiction of the International Criminal Court. At the negotiations in Rome in 1998, the delegation of France pushed for inclusion of the criminal liability of 'legal persons' or 'juridical persons' on the basis that this would make it easier for victims of crimes to sue for restitution and compensation. Differences in the forms of accountability of corporate entities across jurisdictions – where they existed at all – meant that

---

[16] Some passages in this section first appeared in Simon Chesterman, 'Oil and Water: Regulating the Behavior of Multinational Corporations Through Law', *New York University Journal of International Law and Politics*, 36 (2004), p. 307.

[17] Wal-Mart Stores Inc. Recommendation (14 November 2005), Section 4.1.2.

consensus was impossible and the language was ultimately dropped.[18] The International Criminal Court was ultimately created, but there is no comparable regulatory framework for corporations. Instead, six months after the Rome Statute was adopted, United Nations Secretary-General Kofi Annan proposed a 'Global Compact', challenging business leaders to abide by principles on human rights, labour and the environment that are essentially voluntary.

In theory, of course, legal controls on the activities of a multinational corporation do exist. This section will briefly review the possibility of holding a corporation to account before considering the impact of non-legal mechanisms on corporate behaviour.

3.1   Regulation in the local jurisdiction

First, it is appropriate to regulate the activities of a corporation in the jurisdiction within which it is actually operating. Wrongs committed by multinational actors will generally occur within a given jurisdiction; primary responsibility for pursuing a remedy lies with the state in which the wrong occurs. This is supported by a general principle in human rights and other conventions that states parties undertake 'to respect and to ensure' certain rights.

This will not always be effective, however. A state may be unable or unwilling to regulate the activities of an entity with far greater economic and political power than the institutions of government. In some cases, the government itself may be perpetrating abuses in which a corporation is complicit. In those situations it may be more appropriate or more effective to seek redress in other jurisdictions. The most obvious is to go to the jurisdiction in which the corporation has its base – and, as importantly, its assets.

3.2   Regulation in the home jurisdiction of a multinational corporation

Secondly, therefore, legal remedies may in some circumstances be pursued in the home jurisdiction of a multinational corporation – particularly when that jurisdiction is the United States. When it can be established that a corporation or its officers have violated the laws of

---

[18] Albin Eser, 'Individual Criminal Responsibility', in Antonio Cassese (ed.), *The Rome Statute of the International Criminal Court: A Commentary* (Oxford University Press, 2002), p. 779, and Per Saland, 'International Criminal Law Principles', in Roy S. K. Lee (ed.), *The International Criminal Court: The Making of the Rome Statute* (The Hague: Kluwer, 1999), p. 199.

the country in which it is incorporated or in which it maintains its registered offices, for example by engaging in practices that are proscribed even if they take place extraterritorially, bringing an action against the corporation in that home jurisdiction might be an attractive avenue. This section will briefly consider one important barrier to such proceedings – the doctrine of *forum non conveniens* – and the most important means of avoiding it in the most important jurisdiction: the US Alien Tort Claims Act.

Forum non conveniens is a principle in the conflict of laws whereby a forum – in other words, a court – technically entitled to exercise jurisdiction over a matter may forgo its jurisdiction in favour of another forum that could entertain the case more conveniently. In the *Bhopal* case, for example, a pesticide plant in India run by the subsidiary of the US company Union Carbide malfunctioned. Clouds of toxic gas were released, killing thousands and crippling many more. India filed a civil suit in the US federal courts against the parent company, alleging that it functioned in all material respects as the same enterprise as the Indian subsidiary and that relevant conduct occurred in the United States. The trial judge accepted the defendant's argument of *forum non conveniens*. Soon after the US proceedings were dismissed, a US$500 million settlement was brokered under the auspices of the Indian Supreme Court – a large amount by Indian standards but far less than what a US civil jury might have awarded.[19]

This approach was followed in subsequent cases in the United States until the late 1990s, including a large number of cases against the extractive industry. Wrongs alleged range from harm to the environment and harm to human health, to corporate complicity in physical brutality (including forced labour, torture and slavery). More recently, however, there is evidence of moves by courts to reduce the use of this doctrine in bad faith, such as making its invocation subject to an agreement actually to submit the claim to a court in the other jurisdiction.[20]

One way of avoiding these procedural hurdles in the United States is through recourse to the Alien Tort Claims Act, which has become central to the recent history of such proceedings against multinational corporations. The act was originally intended to bring pirates to justice and was enacted in the first session of the US Congress in 1789.

---

[19] Craig Scott, 'Multinational Enterprises and Emergent Jurisprudence on Violations of Economic, Social and Cultural Rights', in Asbjørn Eide, Catarina Krause and Allan Rosas (eds.), *Economic, Social and Cultural Rights: A Textbook* (The Hague: Nijhoff, 2001), p. 588.

[20] Chesterman, 'Oil and Water', pp. 317–18.

It authorizes civil lawsuits in US courts by aliens for torts committed 'in violation of the law of nations or a treaty of the United States'. Rediscovered almost two centuries later in a case brought in the United States by Paraguayan citizens against a former Inspector General of Police in Paraguay, the procedure is unique to the United States.

Alien Tort actions were largely thought of as symbolic as no judgment has yet been enforced, but in 2005 Unocal settled an action that had been brought against it alleging that it used forced labour in Myanmar. Ironically, this sole example of the Alien Tort Claims Act leading to money changing hands corresponds to the factual situation in which the Council on Ethics issued its only recommendation for *non*-exclusion of a specific company, in the case of Total's operations in Myanmar.[21]

3.3 International law

International law may, in some circumstances, provide a third arena in which legal remedies may be pursued, particularly through the emerging discourse of international criminal law. Some international crimes may be committed by individuals: for example, piracy (including aircraft hijacking), enslavement (including forced labour), genocide, war crimes and crimes against humanity. Other crimes may be committed only by states.[22] It has been accepted at least since the war crimes trials after the Second World War that individuals may be held accountable for acts undertaken through corporations. A more controversial possibility is that corporations themselves may be held liable.

In general, international criminal prosecution has tended to pursue the individual. As the Nuremberg Tribunal observed, 'Crimes against international law are committed by men, not by abstract entities, and only by punishing individuals who commit such crimes can the provisions of international law be enforced.' The court was referring to the danger of allowing individuals to hide behind the veil of the state, but the principle might be seen as applying equally to the corporate veil. Nevertheless, establishing the liability of a corporation itself may be appropriate, especially if the organizational structure made it difficult to establish the criminal responsibility of a particular individual. In practice, however, this area of international law remains of academic rather than practical interest.

---

[21] Total Recommendation (14 November 2005).
[22] Ian Brownlie, *Principles of Public International Law*, 5th edn (Oxford: Clarendon Press, 1998), p. 511.

3.4   *Voluntary codes*

A few days after the Rome Statute of the International Criminal Court was adopted in July 1998, the *Financial Times* published an article warning that the accomplice liability provisions in the treaty 'could create international criminal liability for employees, officers and directors of corporations'.[23] This was technically true, but the failure to include the liability of juridical persons within the Court's jurisdiction and the likely difficulties of establishing individual guilt on the part of corporate officers mean that the breathless tone was somewhat exaggerated.

Six months later, at the 1999 World Economic Forum in Davos, UN Secretary-General Kofi Annan proposed the Global Compact. The Compact is not a regulatory instrument – it does not 'police', enforce or measure the behaviour or actions of companies. Instead, it relies on 'public accountability, transparency and the enlightened self-interest of companies, labour and civil society to initiate and share substantive action in pursuing the principles upon which the Global Compact is based'.[24]

The emergence of this and other codes of conduct that are essentially voluntary is an acknowledgement of the inadequacy of efforts to protect the environment, human rights and labour standards through traditional governmental and intergovernmental regulation. It also reflects the preference of many governments, particularly those in the industrialized world, for minimal regulation generally. In such an economic environment, many governments opt for voluntary undertakings on the part of companies themselves, perhaps supplemented through market mechanisms, over legislation to compel companies to comply with particular standards – and perhaps putting them at a competitive disadvantage with respect to their global competitors.[25]

Such codes are, therefore, essentially marketing tools, but this is hardly unusual. The Alien Tort Claims Act has been influential despite the practical impossibility of enforcing judgments. It played an important role, for example, in encouraging companies to contribute to the 'voluntary' slave labour fund in Germany.[26] Actions against Unocal for

---

[23] Maurice Nyberg, 'At Risk from Complicity with Crime', *Financial Times* (27 July 1998), p. 15.

[24] The Ten Principles of the Global Compact 2004; www.unglobalcompact.org.

[25] Chris Jochnick, 'Confronting the Impunity of Non-State Actors: New Fields for the Promotion of Human Rights', *Human Rights Quarterly*, 21 (1999), pp. 67–8.

[26] Michael J. Bazyler, 'Litigating the Holocaust', *University of Richmond Law Review*, 33 (2000), pp. 613–17.

its activities in Myanmar were also intended to put pressure on the military government; there is some evidence that the lawsuits also influenced US policy towards that military government.[27] In the absence of a global enforcement regime, such tactical litigation is most effective when combined with broader norm-generating activities. In its application to multinational corporations, this is presently an early state of development. A voluntarist regime may not seem to be the most efficient means of advancing this cause, but an analogy may be drawn with the development of international law, which is itself not far removed from voluntarism.[28]

An optimistic analogy might also be drawn with the emergence of human rights in Eastern Europe. In 1975 the Conference on Security and Cooperation in Europe's Final Act of the Helsinki Conference included human rights provisions that were, at the time, derided as laughably unenforceable.[29] Despite the scorn of western international relations scholars, dissidents were later able to co-opt the language of such documents to call for union rights in Poland, glasnost in Russia and, after 1989, multi-party elections.[30] These weak norms provided a language for the articulation of rights that later transformed societies. It would be overly optimistic to suggest that corporate social responsibility is laying similar foundations for regulation of multinational corporations, but it is possible that regimes such as the Global Compact, 'enforced' through mechanisms such as the Council on Ethics, are at least changing the language.

4.   Ethics, complicity and responsibility

Though the Council on Ethics is not a court and its recommendations do not have the force of law, it swiftly assumed a legal character. Through careful interpretation of its mandate, evaluation of evidence and justification of decisions, the recommendations resemble judgments of a rudimentary court of first instance – rudimentary not because of the quality of the reasoning but because of the limited resources available to make independent findings of fact, and the absence of discipline imposed by

---

[27] Jim Lobe, 'U.S. –Burma: Sanctions Campaign Keeps Rolling', *IPS-Inter Press Service* (15 May 1997).

[28] Michael Byers, *Custom, Power and the Power of Rules: International Relations and Customary International Law* (Cambridge University Press, 1999).

[29] Daniel C. Thomas, *The Helsinki Effect: International Norms, Human Rights, and the Demise of Communism* (Princeton University Press, 2001), pp. 244–55.

[30] Michael Ignatieff, 'Human Rights, Power, and the State', in Simon Chesterman, Michael Ignatieff and Ramesh Thakur (eds.), *Making States Work: State Failure and the Crisis of Governance* (Tokyo: United Nations University Press, 2005), p. 62.

the possibility of formal appeal. The decisions are ultimately administrative recommendations, yet the nature of the ethical judgments being made and the dispositions of the individuals making them has led to a kind of jurisprudence of ethics.

Though the Ethical Guidelines do not mention the word,[31] the touchstone of this jurisprudence has been the notion of 'complicity'. The term was used in the Graver Report to explain the reasons why investment in a company may itself raise human rights concerns:

> Even though the issue of complicity raises difficult questions, the Committee considers, in principle, that owning shares or bonds in a company that can be expected to commit grossly unethical actions may be regarded as complicity in these actions. The reason for this is that such investments are directly intended to achieve returns from the company, that a permanent connection is thus established between the Petroleum Fund and the company and that the question of whether or not to invest in a company is a matter of free choice.[32]

This and other fairly broad references to complicity were not elaborated. By its fifth and sixth recommendations, however, the Council on Ethics was using complicity to define the human rights obligations relevant to its decisions. In the *Recommendation on Total*, quoted again in the *Exclusion of Wal-Mart*, the idea of complicity is introduced. Whereas complicity had previously been understood in terms of explaining Norway's ancillary responsibility for wrongs through investment of its resources, complicity was now invoked to justify the reference to human rights treaties that apply in a formal sense only to states:

> Only states can violate human rights directly. Companies can, as indicated in paragraph 4.4 [of the Ethical Guidelines], contribute to human rights violations committed by states. The Fund may in its turn contribute to companies' complicity through its ownership. It is such complicity in a state's human rights violations which is to be assessed under this provision.[33]

This is, of course, partly correct but conflates the ethical and legal conceptions of complicity: a company may indeed contribute to a violation, but this is quite separate from the legal notion of complicity as a form of ancillary responsibility.[34] The reason only states can violate human rights in the sense of rights protected by treaty is that the parties to those treaties are *states*. Individuals (arguably including juridical as well as natural persons) can violate international criminal law, either directly

---

[31] This may be in part due to problems of translation, discussed below.
[32] Norwegian Government White Paper, NOU 2003:22, para. 2.2.
[33] Total Recommendation, Section 3.1.
[34] Christopher Kutz, *Complicity: Ethics and Law for a Collective Age* (New York: Cambridge University Press, 2000).

or through ancillary offences, but the insertion of complicity in these two ways – both explaining the company's and Norway's relationship to the alleged violation – seems confusing, unnecessary and unhelpful.

Confusion arises from the multiple ways in which complicity is simultaneously invoked – as ethical and legal principle – as applicable to a company and to the fund itself (and thereby to Norway). Its use derives in part from principle 2 of the Global Compact, which provides that 'Businesses should make sure they are not complicit in human rights abuses.' The Global Compact itself acknowledges the difficulty of defining complicity, outlining three distinct meanings relevant to businesses:

Direct Complicity

Occurs when a company knowingly assists a state in violating human rights. An example of this is in the case where a company assists in the forced relocation of peoples in circumstances related to business activity.

Beneficial Complicity

Suggests that a company benefits directly from human rights abuses committed by someone else. For example, violations committed by security forces, such as the suppression of a peaceful protest against business activities or the use of repressive measures while guarding company facilities, are often cited in this context.

Silent complicity

Describes the way human rights advocates see the failure by a company to raise the question of systematic or continuous human rights violations in its interactions with the appropriate authorities. For example, inaction or acceptance by companies of systematic discrimination in employment law against particular groups on the grounds of ethnicity or gender could bring accusations of silent complicity.[35]

Direct and beneficial complicity are clearly intended to be covered by the Ethical Guidelines, but the notion of 'silent complicity' would appear to go well beyond those Guidelines, which requires some form of contribution to a wrongful act. This was partly acknowledged by the Council when it distinguished purely 'passive complicity' as it is understood in Norwegian criminal law from situations where a defendant knows that such passivity assists the main perpetrator's commission of the criminal act. Again, however, the importing of criminal law concepts to delimit ethical responsibility blurs the nature of the enquiry – among other things undermining assertions by the Council that it does not need to prove the existence of a human rights violation or other wrong to recommend exclusion of a company.

[35] The Ten Principles of the Global Compact 2004.

Reference to complicity is unnecessary in any case. As indicated earlier, the Ethical Guidelines do not mention complicity. And, indeed, in formulating criteria for the exclusion of a company, the Council on Ethics itself included the term only in passing:

Based on the preparatory work to the guidelines the Council accepts as a fact that the Fund, through its ownership interests in companies, can be said to contribute to companies' complicity in states' human rights violations. The guidelines are principally concerned with *existing* and *future* breaches of the ethical guidelines, although earlier breaches might give an indication of future conduct. The point is that there must exist an unacceptable risk of breaches taking place in the future. Complicity includes actions carried out to protect or to facilitate the company's activities, and refers to circumstances which are under the company's control or circumstances which the company could have been in a position to countervail or to prevent. Based on the guidelines' preparatory work, the Council lists the following criteria which constitute decisive elements in an overall assessment of whether there exists an unacceptable risk of the Fund contributing to human rights violations:

- There must exist some kind of linkage between the company's operations and the existing breaches of the guidelines, which must be visible to the Fund.
- The breaches must have been carried out with a view to serving the company's interests or to facilitate conditions for the company.
- The company must either have contributed actively to the breaches, or had knowledge of the breaches, but without seeking to prevent them.
- The norm breaches must either be ongoing, or there must exist an unacceptable risk that norm breaches will occur in the future. Earlier norm breaches might indicate future patterns of conduct.[36]

These four criteria make clear the pragmatic approach that is to be adopted, focusing on the risk of *contributing to* a potential violation rather than being *complicit in* a wrong. The distinction is comparable to that between a risk assessment for the purpose of insurance estimation or intelligence analysis, and evidence produced in a criminal trial. In the first case, no formal judgment is made about the propriety of the conduct being examined and the focus is on the significance of that risk analysis – for present purposes its significance for the fund.

For this reason, reference to complicity also appears to be unhelpful because it imports a quasi-legal standard that runs the risk of setting too high a threshold for exclusion, or else implicitly asserting that a wrong has been perpetrated without the obligation to prove that it has. This is an understandable response to the problem of holding multinationals to account, described in section 3. But the Council does not

---

[36] Total Recommendation, Section 3.3.

provide an adequate alternative forum to supplement such legal forms of accountability; if it pursued the complicity line to its natural conclusion, the Council would not merely depart from its position that the recommendations are not judgments of the company in question – it would also be making a judgment about every other investor in that company.

Part of the problem may be basic questions of translation from Norwegian to English, and from civil law conceptions to common law assumptions. As Ola Mestad points out in his chapter in this book, the Norwegian original for the key phrase 'unacceptable risk of the Fund *contributing to*' uses the term *medvirker til*, which is closer in meaning to the civil law concept of complicity. Mestad offers a thoughtful study of the ways in which complicity operates and suggests a test of 'sphere of control' for determining the key question of determining the ethical responsibility of a company.

Such a reconceptualization of complicity may help, but the foundational problem appears to be the theoretical sleight of hand that made creation of the Council possible in the first place. In contrast to the active ownership rights that are to be exercised by Norges Bank, reflecting the teleological ethical framework that seeks to bring about good outcomes, the Council embodies the deontological school of ethics that seeks to do that which is right, or to avoid doing that which is wrong. In practice, however, deontology has imported law to justify determinations of right and wrong, with the result that the Council has focused on the unacceptable risk of contributing to a *legal* wrong. This substantially narrows its ability to protect Norway from complicity in conduct that is not *ethical*, but demonstrates the difficulty of keeping law, ethics and politics distinct.

5.   Law, ethics and politics

The virtue of law as a means of regulating behaviour is clarity; the virtue of politics is flexibility. The principled use of disinvestment stems from an ethical commitment on the part of Norway to avoid participation in a wrong, but exercise of that discretion has demonstrated a discomfort with doing so on what might be seen as an arbitrary basis. One mechanism through which the Council has sought to avoid arbitrariness is through reference to 'complicity'. A second manifestation of arbitrariness is less obvious and yet may be, in the end, even desirable.

Quite apart from the uncertain use of complicity as a touchstone of exclusion, discussed earlier, a second set of concerns relate to the link between the '*unacceptable risk* that the Fund contributes to ... violations' and an implication of a need to prove actual or potential causation:

The acts or omissions must constitute 'an unacceptable risk of (the Fund) contributing to ...'. This means that it is not necessary to prove that such contribution will take place – the presence of an unacceptable risk suffices. The term unacceptable risk is not specifically defined in the preparatory work. NOU (Norwegian Official Report) 2003:22 states that 'Criteria should therefore be established for determining the existence of unacceptable ethical risk. These criteria can be based on the international instruments that also apply to the Fund's exercise of ownership interests. Only the most serious forms of violations of these standards should provide a basis for exclusion.' In other words, the fact that a risk is deemed unacceptable is linked to the seriousness of the act.

The term risk is associated with the degree of probability that unethical actions will take place in the future. The NOU states that 'the objective is to decide whether the company in the future will represent an unacceptable ethical risk for the Petroleum Fund.' The wording of paragraph 4.4 makes it clear that what is to be assessed is the likelihood of contributing to 'present and future' actions or omissions. The Council accordingly assumes that actions or omissions that took place in the past will not, in themselves, provide a basis for exclusion of companies under this provision. However, earlier patterns of conduct might give some indications as to what will happen ahead. Hence it is also relevant to examine companies' previous practice when future risk of complicity in violations is to be assessed.[37]

The Council thereby also avoided defining unacceptable risk, but qualified its examination by finding that acceptability is linked to the gravity of the harm – thus a one per cent chance of arbitrary killing might be less acceptable than, say, a thirty per cent chance of arbitrary detention.

In addition to the components of probability and gravity, however, there is a third implicit variable: unacceptable *to whom*? This is distinct from the general question of what ethical framework is adopted as it relates not merely to the determination of wrongs but to the tolerance for risk. The answer would appear to be linked to Norwegian sensibilities as well as to market constraints. To be absolutely certain of avoiding complicity in any wrong Norway could disinvest from *all* companies. This would clearly be unsatisfactory – and would undermine key economic functions that the fund is intended to play. It would also be self-defeating if that line were drawn at the other extreme of precluding investment only where actual proof of a legal wrong could be established.

It is, nevertheless, important to draw a line somewhere and it is possible to do so in a non-arbitrary way. As the Council demonstrated in

---

[37] Ibid., Section 3.1.

Freeport, certain harms can be ranked and the unacceptable probability determined accordingly.[38] The problem lies in how that line is justified to the company in question, and to third parties who may be adversely affected by the decision to disinvest. If one abandons complicity as a tool for justifying disinvestment on the basis that the company and all other investors must also be said to be complicit in the wrong, how is that line to be justified?

This became a particular issue in the case of the fund's disinvestment from Wal-Mart.[39] The decision drew a sharp protest from the US ambassador, Benson K. Whitney, who accused Norway of a sloppy screening process and unfairly singling out US companies.[40] In a subsequent speech to the Norwegian Institute of International Affairs, he outlined a more nuanced critique:

I respectfully ask the Norwegian government and people to fully recognize the seriousness of what Norway is doing with divestment decisions like these. Norway is not just selling stock – it is publicly alleging profoundly bad ethical behaviour by real people. These companies are not lifeless corporate shells. They represent millions of hard working employees, thousands of shareholders, managers and Directors, all now accused by Norway of actively participating in and supporting a highly unethical operation. The stain of an official accusation of bad ethics harms reputations and can have serious economic implications, not just to the company and big mutual funds, but to the pocketbooks of workers and small investors.[41]

These accusations are not without merit. Indeed, the practice of disinvesting prior to making decisions public implicitly acknowledges the harm that disinvestment might cause. One solution would be to avoid public justification altogether. If the purpose of the Council on Ethics is genuinely and solely to reduce the risk of Norwegian complicity in unethical activities, it could make disinvestment recommendations secretly, implemented with discretion by the Norges Bank as part of the regular trading undertaken by its investment arm. There might be speculation as to why the fund is moving assets, but as the fund is limited to owning at most ten per cent of the voting rights in any one company this is unlikely to have major consequences. If the Council on Ethics eschews disinvestment either as a tool to change behaviour or as

---

[38] Recommendation on Exclusion of Freeport McMoRan Copper & Gold Inc. (15 February 2006), Section 2.2.

[39] Wal-Mart Stores Inc. Recommendation (15 November 2005).

[40] Mark Landler, 'Norway Keeps Nest Egg From Some U.S. Companies', *New York Times* (4 May 2007).

[41] Benson K. Whitney, 'Pension Fund Divestment: Meeting Norwegian Fairness Standards?' (Oslo: Norwegian Institute of International Affairs (NUPI), 1 September 2006).

a form of punishment, the need for public scrutiny of such decisions is not justified as an element of natural justice: if a company is not being penalized or accused directly of wrongdoing, it has no right to hear charges against it or be given an opportunity to rebut them.

Secrecy is proposed here only hypothetically – apart from anything else, public scrutiny of how Norwegian public funds are invested is appropriate – but is intended to highlight that the Council on Ethics should not be seen as a substitute for a legal regime that *is* intended to change the behaviour of multinational corporations. Indeed, there is a danger that Norway, a good global citizen, may feel that by adopting these guidelines it is doing 'its bit' to promote good corporate behaviour. It may well be doing more than most countries, but the structure of the disinvestment regime is clearly intended to be more of a political framework than a legal regime, and with domestic rather than international consequences.

An alternative, also proposed hypothetically, would be to use this political framework explicitly to change behaviour of multinationals. If one takes seriously the international impact of Council recommendations, the real influence lies not in the nominal punishment of disinvestment, but the *threat* of disinvestment and the possibility of further investment. In other words, whereas the law typically operates as a stick, Norway's oil wealth may be more appropriately used as a carrot. At its most extreme, one could conceive of an effort to link the Council's work with the active ownership rights exercised by the Norges Bank: when confronted with a company operating unethically, one way of changing its behaviour would be not to sell but to *buy*.

There has been some movement on this front. A review process begun in 2008 culminated in a report to the *Stortinget* that the main purpose of the Guidelines was to contribute to change. Revisions to the Ethical Guidelines now allow the Council to establish direct contact with companies at an early stage of investigation; the Ministry of Finance has also established a watch-list for companies where there is uncertainty as to whether the conditions for exclusion have been met. Such reforms may increase the scope for more nuanced interactions than exclusion, though it is too early to tell how effective such interactions will be.[42]

6.   Conclusion

The appearance of regulation may, in some circumstances, be worse than no regulation at all. The turn to ethics as a means of improving

[42] Disclosure: the author was a consultant to the Norwegian government in the early stages of the review process.

behaviour of multinational corporations offers an opportunity but also an opportunity cost: ethics can be a means of generating legal norms, through changing the reference points of the market and providing a language for the articulation of rights; yet they can also be a substitute for generating those norms.

The Norwegian Council on Ethics demonstrates both tendencies. The tendency to conceive its work in quasi-legal terms, justifying disinvestment decisions by reference to complicity in wrongs, suggests where its work may lead – even as those terms perhaps overstate how much has already been achieved. At the same time, however, the artifice of a trial in which a company's conduct is examined and judged without serious consequences may create the illusion of accountability and thus reduce the demand for actual change.[43]

These tensions will, eventually, need to be resolved. How they are resolved will depend on whether the ethical precepts on which the Council bases its recommendations are dismissed as Scandinavian self-righteousness, in which case their publicity and wider significance are suspect, or as the precursor to a wider adoption of normative constraints on corporate entities operating in jurisdictions without the capacity to control their behaviour. In the latter case, the Council's work may serve as this new regime's foundational jurisprudence.

---

[43] Thomas Nagel, 'The Problem of Global Justice', *Philosophy & Public Affairs*, 33 (2005), p. 113.

4   Responsibility beyond the law?

Christopher Kutz

1.   Ownership and responsibility

The central project of corporate capitalism is separation of the function of ownership from management. Financial capital can purchase human capital, but beyond that there is no reason the twain should meet, except through periodic meetings of the corporate board. As a way to raise the large amounts of capital necessary for complex industrial operations, the separation strategy is functionally ideal. The ownership of industrial enterprise, whether direct or mediated through an investment fund, can be conceived as a discrete activity whose sole aim is to send money to its site of most efficient deployment, as measured by financial return. The managers and workers of the enterprise can, for their part, concentrate on doing what they do best: maximizing the efficient production of their product or services.

The separation of ownership and management has also enabled another separation: between investment and ethics. Once owners of enterprises are spared the operational duties of industry, and moreover are generally restricted in their capacities to set constraints on those operations, their companies' activities no longer figure in their own sense of ethical agency. What their companies do is not something they have done, for which they are responsible. Ownership is not participation (through investment) in strip-mining, munitions manufacturing, strike-breaking, greenhouse-gas emitting; but simply a reason to enter a figure on a portfolio spreadsheet, and perhaps to expect a dividend check from time to time. Further, in the case of publicly traded companies, even significant stakes in ownership are dwarfed by the fraction of equity owned by others. And given that selling one's own shares would simply lead to their repurchase on the secondary market by others, one can easily tell oneself that ownership makes no difference to the financing of the company as well.

Of course, it does not follow that the separation of capital from management entails the absence of owner responsibility. But insofar as our sense of moral agency is sustained and affirmed by the experience of doing things, making things happen, this separation works beautifully to sustain the illusion of moral indifference to the doings of one's investments. More perversely yet, since managers see themselves as under a fiduciary duty to maximize owners' financial return, they easily come to see ethical principles not embodied in hard positive law as improper distractions from the business at hand. The entire burden of constraint on corporate activities will come to rest on law – and in the case of multinational industry, or corporate activities in largely ungoverned territories, that burden will fail to be met.

The problem I have just sketched, of the illusion of morally costless investment and ungoverned multinational enterprise, has been the basis of the movement of socially conscious investment.[1] But while socially conscious investment is a robust and growing phenomenon, it is still a relatively small part of the international capital pool. Thus Norway's decision to submit its national oil wealth to ambitious ethical principles represents a major advance towards ethical capitalism. The sheer size of the Pension Fund, coupled with its natural salience as the investment vehicle of a nation-state, means that decisions about investment, and divestment, will attract attention as few other funds can.[2]

What does it mean for a nation to decide that its wealth should be invested ethically? In particular, what are the moral costs of failing to apply ethical principles to national investment? The Graver Commission, which laid out the basic principles of Norway's investment system, has put the matter in terms of a concern with complicity in its investment objects' activities. But the concept of complicity is under so many layers that the concept demands some excavation. Take, for example, the Council on Ethics' recent deliberations on investment in Caterpillar, Inc., a company whose bulldozers are purchased by the Israeli government and used by its army to flatten Palestinian homes, potentially in violation of the inhabitants' human rights.[3] The question before the Council was whether Caterpillar's sale of equipment rendered the company complicit in Israel's human rights violations; and, in turn, whether Caterpillar's complicity might expose the Fund to an unacceptable risk

---

[1] This problem is also one I have pursued at length in my *Complicity: Ethics and Law for a Collective Age* (New York: Cambridge University Press, 2000).

[2] Notwithstanding the fact that the Fund can own only up to ten per cent of a given company's equity (previously five per cent).

[3] I will assume the human rights violation for the purpose of discussion, as does the Council of Ethics. See its 'Letter to the Ministry of Finance', 15 May 2006, reprinted in the Council's 'Annual Report 2006', p. 69. Like the Council, I think in fact that the question of rights violation is clear, but will not discuss it here.

that they themselves are contributing to these violations.[4] Under the Council's interpretation of its charter, the risk of 'contributing' to an investment object's complicity is itself a matter of the Fund becoming complicit in those acts.[5]

Thus, the question of complicity is buried at least three layers deep. What matters ultimately is not the ethical standing of the Fund itself (which is simply money), but the standing of its owners and beneficiaries, the people of Norway: will the people of Norway be complicit, through the Fund's complicity, in Caterpillar's complicity in Israel's violation of Palestinian rights? Indeed, we can add yet further layers, for Israel's violation of those rights is itself a function of the acts of particular soldiers, operating under orders; and the question of state ethical responsibility is itself a question of citizen responsibility for state acts done through its agents. How can a Norwegian citizen assess her complicity (let alone the risk of complicity) in an act done thousands of miles away by someone driving a bulldozer, with so many intermediaries involved? The question is indeed difficult. Layer onto that yet further the question of how these ethical matters might be resolved in a way that can generate firm decision principles regarding exclusion, and the complexity of the task before the Council is clear.

My charge in this chapter is to illuminate some of these concepts: to discuss the transition from issues of legal complicity to issues of ethical complicity; and second, to fill out the discussion of ethical complicity in the particular context of investment. I will add a third point as well: to show that giving ethical complicity its full, warranted scope would go far beyond the screening criteria of the Pension Fund. In particular, ethical complicity can include responsibility for acts we could not have known about in advance, or we could not have controlled. Our complicity might be, in a relevant sense, entirely non-voluntary, and entirely a matter of post hoc discovery. There may well be practical reasons to limit the scope of divestment decisions to complicity in acts that the investment target could have known about or avoided, but those reasons have to do with the feasibility of managing an investment fund by reference to indeterminate ethical criteria, and not because determinate ethical criteria establish those more restrictive guidelines. Thus, I hope and expect that the lessons of the Norwegian experiment will sound beyond its borders, into the general matter of citizen and investor responsibility.

---

[4] Norwegian Government Pension Fund – Global: Ethical Guidelines (2004), para. 4.4 (see Appendix 2 below).
[5] Total Recommendation, reprinted in 'Annual Report 2005', p. 46.

2. Complicity as an ethical versus a legal concept

Let me first clarify the general notion of ethics. By that term, I do not mean some special set of professional rules governing professional behaviour. I mean, rather, ethics in something like the classical sense, as a set of concerns about how we ought to live our lives with others, and how we ought to think and feel about the terms in which we do so. Ethical conduct is, thus, a much broader conception than legal conduct, or even than morally permissible conduct. Living ethically means aspiring to live in a way such that one can regard one's life as good and well lived, and that includes, but means more than, just playing by the rules. I can violate no one's rights, yet live a life that is less than admirable, simply because it is largely self-enclosed. Ethics goes both beyond law, and in this sense, beyond morality.[6]

More specifically, what I will discuss is the ethics of indirect action: how we should think about our involvement in acts and projects that also reflect the efforts of other people. There is much to say about our involvement in good projects, and the field of socially conscious investment concerns both investments in positive social projects, as well as avoiding involvement in negative projects. Here, however, I will accentuate the negative, and focus on investments that contribute to suffering. What I will do is to offer some truisms about our responsibilities for harms caused by others – truisms that, notwithstanding their truth, are often denied, sometimes by philosophers. These truisms have to do, first, with how our ethical responsibilities for harm increase rather than decrease as we expand the scope of our powers through working with others; and, second, with the relation between politics and ethics that is a consequence of our expanded powers of collective agency.

The central ethical concept for present purposes is **complicity**. Being complicit in another's act is a complicated relationship to that person and their act, and to the system that subjects one to accountability. Indeed, strictly speaking, claims of complicity involve five different elements: the **subject** accomplice (you), the **principal** (the party who directly brought about the wrong or harm in question), the **object** of complicity (the harm or wrong itself), the **basis** of complicity (your relation to the principal) and the **response** owed (what you ought to do in virtue of your complicity).

---

[6] This distinction between the broader concept of ethics and morality has become a commonplace, but was initiated by Bernard Williams, e.g., in his *Ethics and the Limits of Philosophy* (Cambridge, MA: Harvard University Press, 1986).

In legal contexts, these relations are well defined. For instance, usually in criminal law one person is an accomplice in another person's crime when, and only when, the putative accomplice (**subject**) has aided or encouraged (**basis**) another party (**the principal**) who himself or herself has committed a criminal act with the requisite intent (**object**), perhaps causing some further set of concrete harms.[7] The result will be a jail term (**response**), usually equivalent to that of the principal party. The basis of accomplice criminal liability might be further specified in terms of parity of moral deserts, or incentives not to contribute to wrongdoing, etc. At root, however, will be a relatively robust relationship, in both thought and deed, between the accomplice and the principal, whereby the accomplice affirmatively seeks to produce the required result.

In civil law, the terminology differs – sometimes it is termed 'vicarious' or 'joint' liability – but the concept is structurally similar. A secondary party, for example an employer (**subject**), is liable for the monetary damages (**response**) caused by an employee's (**principal**) accident (**object**) in virtue of the employment relation (**basis**). Again, the basis might be further specified in terms of corrective justice, or of a fair allocation of the risks of an enterprise, among victims, direct actors or those profiting from the principal's activities; or in terms of the efficiency of certain actors as risk-bearers, etc. But fundamentally, indirect civil liability will be grounded in some way in which the accomplice (secondary party) contributed to, facilitated or enabled the principal to cause the harm, albeit frequently without criminal law's requirement of intent or purpose.

This basic structure of complicity is fairly well established in the law, despite underlying variations in the particular items related. This is not to say there cannot be hard cases, for instance under what conditions enterprises can be viewed as accomplices to their managers' delicts, or whether whispering encouragement to someone hard of hearing can suffice for criminal liability, or whether routinely employed independent

---

[7] Generally speaking, Anglo-American criminal law permits liability for mere encouragement, while European criminal law requires the accomplice to promise, threaten, or order the principal to commit the crime. Compare, e.g., the US Model Penal Code Sec. 2.06 (93)(a)(i) and Sec. 5.02(1), establishing that solicitation is a basis for accomplice liability, and is established by 'command[ing], encourage[ing], or request[ing]' another to commit a crime; with the French *Code Penal* Art. 121–7: 'Est complicé ... la personne qui par don, promesse, menace, ordre, abus d'autorité ou de pouvoir aura provoqué a une infraction ou donnée des instructions pour la commettre.' Thus, mere advice would suffice in Anglo-American but not French law. Germany, similarly, requires inducement (*Anstiftung*) as a basis for non-aid-based accomplice liability, thus going beyond mere advice.

contractors who cause accidents can generate liability for their employers. More difficult still are situations wherein the accomplice knows
that his conduct will facilitate the principal's wrongful act, but does
not himself intend that the wrongful act be performed, as when a gun
merchant sells guns to someone obviously intent on robbery. But even
here the nature of the question at issue is clear: given the accomplice's
positive, contributory role in the principal's act, should liability be
forthcoming?

Not so in the ethical domain. Many of the questions closed off by law,
by its restrictive band of relations, are laid open. This is partly a function of the quite different scope of response. Once the power of the state
to imprison or extract a fine is off the table, a new range of responses
and corresponding sentiments is in place. Put another way, once blame
and guilt become mere options among alternatives, the full scope of
complicity reveals itself, with all the complications of our actual social
thought and practice. We can be answerable for things in lots of ways
that don't involve blame. If my dog digs up your garden, or I hit a wet
patch while riding my bike and hit your car, I can be answerable for
the damage done, even though I may not be in any way to blame for
it – it might just have been a pure accident. And my liability, apart from
blame, might not even be financial – maybe, even if I should offer to pay
for your tulip bulbs, or to fix your dent, you should decline my offer.
What I really owe you is a kind of apology, an acknowledgement of your
loss and my role in it. That broad sense of liability, as a consequence of
ethical complicity, is what is under discussion, so that we can be complicit in, but not necessarily to blame, for others' actions.

I shall try to make this clearer through an example, to which I shall
recur later as well: Imagine that you are a member of a family of significant wealth, not given to living ostentatiously, but nonetheless enjoying
a level of comfort and security from fear that many would covet. You
were raised in the belief that your family acquired its wealth through
the hard work of your grandfather, who owned a textile mill. But you
now discover that the initial stock of wealth (re-invested) owed much to
your grandfather's business during the war, when much of the labour
for the mill was supplied by captive soldiers. Imagine also that while the
prisoners who worked in the mill are dead, there are clear legacies of
their labour, in the form of lower levels of wealth and education among
their descendants.

This discovery would surely be disorienting to you, not just to your
ideal of your grandfather, but to your sense of your family's ethical
standing, and your sense of entitlement to your financial security. Put
crisply, you would probably feel tainted by your grandfather's actions,

and as a result, specially connected to the victims of his enterprise, with duties of acknowledgement and perhaps repair to them. Living on and through wealth acquired through wrongdoing would render the decent life you try to live essentially hypocritical: moral on the surface, but corrupt in its foundations. Perhaps this seems priggish, and maybe the skeletons can be locked into the closet, a psychological manœuvre easily rationalized by the (true) observation that many families harbour similar secrets. But the point I want to make here is that the concerns raised by inherited wealth built on crimes are real concerns for one concerned with living ethically. They demand reflection and perhaps response. And they have nothing to do with choice, control or knowledge.

The Graver Commission, and subsequent decisions by the Council on Ethics, seem to have opted for a legal standard of liability, rather than the broader ethical conception of answerability, mooted above:

In order (for an investor) to be complicit in an action, the action must be possible to anticipate for the investor. There must be some sort of systematic or causal relationship between the company's operations and the actions in which the investor does not wish to be complicit. Investments in the company cannot be regarded as complicity in actions which one could not possibly expect or be aware of or circumstances over which the company has no significant control.[8]

I say that this conception is legalistic, in that it requires some degree of *mens rea*, or culpability, on the part of the investor: actual, imputed or potential knowledge by the investor of the risk of wrongdoing. Within Anglo-American law, this is actually an intermediate standard of culpability, between criminal law, which largely requires purpose, and civil liability, which is frequently strict (independent of fault or culpability). It thus roughly tracks the ethical category of blameworthiness.

There is, however, one crucial way in which the Graver Commission departs from the liability model: it is exclusively forward-looking, while liability (criminal or civil) is, by definition, a retrospective matter either of punishment or responsibility for rectifying wrongs. Under Point 4.4 and in the Commission's Report, the charge of the Council is to evaluate the risk of **present or future** complicity in serious wrongdoing.[9] Strictly speaking, there is still a retrospective element, in that the risk is that the Fund will have been complicit in wrongdoing, through the company's acts. But, combining the requirements of control or knowledge with prospectivity, the result is that examples of ethical taint

---

[8] Norwegian Government White Paper, NOU 2003:22 (quoted in Total Recommendation, p. 46).
[9] Ibid.

simply do not apply. Thus, while Total S.A. may have been complicit in systematic human rights abuses in Burma in the past, evidence of its reform and the new incentive structure it faces, with harsh scrutiny of potential future abuses, was sufficient to retain it within the Fund's investment universe.

3.   Corporate complicity versus individual complicity

What I now want to show is that while the Graver Commission's principles are legitimate interpretations of the complicity of the Fund itself, considered on an essentially legal model, they fail to describe the potential complicity ultimately at issue: individual, personal complicity on the part of the Fund's beneficiaries.

Because corporations enjoy a legal personality, it is tempting to think that they enjoy a moral personality as well.[10] We talk about corporations paying taxes, influencing elections, making contracts, hiring and firing workers. It is easy to forget that all of these things happen because individual people – accountants, managers, executives, workers – act in complexly coordinated ways. Many years ago, in a US debate on corporate taxation, President Ronald Reagan said, 'You know, corporations don't pay taxes. People pay taxes.' He meant this as part of an argument that ultimately all corporate taxes are paid by consumers in the form of higher prices, and he was not necessarily correct about that. But the broader point is true: ultimately, the incidence of corporate taxation lies with individual people – shareholders, employees, bondholders, consumers. The corporate form is just a legal technology, a profoundly useful system for mobilizing capital and distributing risk. At the end of the day, corporations are just people, usually many people, joined together by various forms of contracts. There is no inherent nature of the corporation such that it ought to be taxed – which is not to say that a separate level of corporate taxation might not be good policy.

There is an analogy between corporate taxation and corporate morality. People – philosophers, political activists – sometimes talk about corporate morality, and about the moral responsibility of corporations. It certainly can make sense to talk about what a given corporation should or should not do – whether, for example, Exxon ought to partner with a given state, or DynCorp ought not to send its employees to participate in a given conflict. These are claims about what the entity ought to do, and they cannot be expressed in any other form, except derivatively – it

[10] An entertaining recent example of moral personification is Joel Bakan's *The Corporation: The Pathological Pursuit of Profit and Power* (New York: Free Press, 2005).

is because Exxon shouldn't engage in the partnership that its managers ought to decline the deal. But these questions about what corporations ought to do are distinct from questions about moral responsibility, about who is answerable, ethically speaking, when corporations do harm. Legal personality is not the same thing as moral personality, and talk about the moral or social responsibility of corporations obscures the fact that what is really at issue is our responsibility, as individuals, for the bad things our corporate instruments do.

Moral responsibility, on my view, is a system through which we humans attempt to regulate our behaviour towards each other and the world, to minimize the amount of suffering we cause and perhaps even make some improvements here and there. This system of social control works through our individual psychologies, our motivations to avoid criticism and to receive praise – to feel that our lives have been well lived. Given such a conception of moral responsibility, it is rather beside the point to talk in terms of corporate or collective entities – the system of moral responsibility functions, when it functions at all, through our individual consciences.

Focusing attention at the corporate or collective level can lead to dangerous psychological and ethical mistakes. These mistakes have to do with thinking of corporations, or governments for that matter, as remote agents of a sort, with us as principals. We have a disturbing tendency to think of principal–agent relations as having distinct ethical effects. In particular, there's a tendency for people to think that their agents can do things that they themselves are not permitted to do – that, for example, one can keep one's hands clean by paying someone else to perform some ugly act – oust poor squatters from corporate property, or pay exploitative wages, or the like. And on the other side of things, there is a tendency for individuals to regard themselves as morally free to do things on behalf of their clients that they regard personally as wrong – this is an especially pernicious tendency among American lawyers, for example.

But these are both errors, and what is surprising is that they persist even though both civil and criminal law treat them as errors. Hiring someone as your agent increases your responsibility, rather than decreases it – that increased responsibility is, as it were, the price of the increase in your powers. And there is no reason to think that you are permitted to do something for someone else that you regard as unacceptable if done by yourself. We cannot lie, cheat or kill for others, simply because we are paid to do so. Talking about corporate moral responsibility obscures this fact.

At bottom, then, the issue of corporate moral responsibility, and corporate complicity, comes down to correcting those errors: seeing that we retain, indeed expand, the scope of our responsibilities in virtue of what our corporate enterprises do. If we seek to profit from exercises of corporate agency, then we ought to bear the moral costs, as well as the financial ones, of their ventures – those moral costs are all part of our return. The right question to ask is, can we regard ourselves as living ethically when we ask our corporate agents to gain profit at the expense of the vulnerable, or to share in the corruption of power, simply for our own gain? Asked in this way, the question whether the Fund will be a contributor, through investment, in future wrongdoing describes only one among a range of ways that the ultimate bearers of moral responsibility relate to that wrongdoing. If the question of Fund complicity is, at root, a question of citizen complicity, then the possible answers must – at least in principle – answer to the full range of ethical demands.

4.   Was the Graver Commission correct to focus solely on future complicity?

So now let us shift the ethical example slightly, towards the question before us. Assume now that it is not a family's wealth in question, but an investment fund. And the fund has discovered that one of its more profitable investments acquired a significant amount of its operating capital, and thus a basis for its contemporary market advantages, through active complicity in serious human rights violations in the recent past. (Let us say, for example, that it conducts mining operations in a region whose indigenous population was forcibly relocated by the host state, precisely with an eye to making the region more hospitable to mining interests.) The company now operates within strict ethical guidelines. The fund bought in recently, and had no reason to know at the time of purchase, based on reasonably available information, that the company was complicit in these wrongs. Nor has it reason to think the company will collaborate in, or take advantage of, future such abuses. But now it knows.

There is no question of fund blameworthiness or liability, to be sure. And in the legalistic sense of complicity, there is no issue either. But the issue of taint goes beyond mere guilt by association, for the profits from the current, ethically clean, enterprise stem from past wrongful acts. The fund is profiting from wrongdoing, now knowingly, even if not deliberately. If the ethical concern is that its beneficiaries be able to enjoy the profits of the fund without ethical concern as to their source, then the fund must clearly divest (and, to be extremely scrupulous, perhaps ought to donate any capital gain to charity). This is not a question of metaphysical or superstitious taint, such as one might feel towards a knife used in a killing, or a house in which crimes took place. It is, simply, a question whether one's own favourable financial position is a causal consequence of the culpable suffering of others.

Now a range of objections might be voiced here. First, why should the culpability of the company matter, now that it has reformed its actions? After all, profit-taking as a result of suffering need not be morally objectionable, so long as it is not exploitative. Pharmaceutical companies need not be convicted of complicity in the ravages wrought by the diseases they cure, nor construction companies in the damage done by the earthquakes whose rubble they restore. Yet we do distinguish between natural tragedy (including tragedy in which human failures play a role) and active human wrongdoing. The first is unfortunate, the second unjust. And only the second is a basis for ethical charges of complicity. Different reasons might be offered for this distinction, from a phenomenological aversion to marching hand in hand, as it were, with wrongdoers, to practical concerns with minimizing the scope of the deliberate and avoidable introduction of harm into the world. If one assumes, as I do, that the aim of the responsibility system is the guidance of conduct, not the allocation of metaphysical credits and demerits, then the pragmatic point has further purchase: what has ethical salience for us are acts, our own and others, not mere events in the natural world.

Second, and more compelling, are practical concerns, chief among them that an over-strict concern for the purity of one's associates would lead to a muddled, Dostoyevskean responsibility for the sins of the world. Given the complex intertwining of capital in a globalized economy, it is inevitable that any investment decision would link one to wrongdoing in some form, by predecessors of one's investment objects. Just as personal life would be disconsolately lonely – indeed impossible – were one to try to shun all wrongdoers, and to subsist only through products produced through a clean history of free labour and contract, so preclusion of all companies with wrongdoing in their past would make the very prospect of investment impossible. Indeed, the impossibility of insisting on purity renders the point one of principle as much as practice. Rather than subscribe to an impossible ideal of purity, we make our ethical lives by letting bygones be bygones, through collective forgetting as much as memory (as Ernest Renan reminds us). The Pension Fund's future-directed criteria reflect, in a stark form, this practical point. Moreover, if we did not let bygones pass, in investment or life, then there would be little incentive for wrongdoers to reform: once tainted, they could never be fit associates, and so would have no reason to desist from wrongdoing.

These points are powerful, and doubtless lay at the heart of the Graver Commission's views. Yet, like all practical principles, they too admit of a range of application. Concern for past wrongdoing need not be categorical, but neither must it simply be reduced to a basis for suspecting future wrongdoing. In the case of serious crimes of recent vintage, it would be bizarre for an investor to announce that that is history, while the investment future looks bright. One's own judgment about the importance of wrongdoing becomes subject to question when one replies with, effectively, indifference as to one's companions' wrongdoing, even if it is sustained by a set of practical considerations. The distinction between caring about past wrongdoing but according it no decisional weight (except as future-bearing evidence), and not caring about it at all, is very difficult to sustain. Such indifference also lends itself to the equally practical concern with 'greenwashing', whereby a company uses its profit stream to obscure problems in its history.[11] One might, instead, adopt intermediate principles, permitting the exclusion of investment in companies that can be shown, within a certain timeframe, to have been complicit in serious violations. Such principles would even be easier to apply than the future-directed injunction, which involves a calculation of risk of wrongdoing, rather than the amassing of forensic evidence of actual wrongdoing.

I do not mean to condemn Norway's impressive ethical venture from a standpoint of righteous purity. The more restrictive set of principles may well be superior overall, especially in light of further concerns relating to the viability of the Fund and the possibilities of mischief-making by competitors of the Fund's objects. I only mean to point out that the strict separation between past and future, like all strict separations in ethics, is not a function of clear principle, but must instead be defended on the basis of a balance of advantages. It also might well be rethought, as the Council's recommendations come to enjoy a deserved reputation for objective ethical analysis.

5. Responses to complicity: clean hands versus political agency

Whether or not the Fund's principles screen out complicity in a fully defensible way, I want now to consider the broader issue of ethical versus political concern. Substantial as the Fund's investments are,

---

[11] This is one reason, along with reputational concerns, that universities in the United States routinely reject gifts or cancel contracts with partners later found to have engaged in seriously wrongful acts.

its decisions to exclude can only have limited effects on international business.[12] The individual ethical concern I have focused on, which seeks to preserve the integrity of the individual beneficiaries of the Fund, must be consistent with the actual control individuals have over their lives. More importantly, taking individual responsibility seriously means recognizing its limits, and recognizing the need for much larger-scale, political solutions to the problems of corporate complicity.

There are really two issues here, one dealing with different aspects of individual responsibility, the other with the power or significance of the individual. First, the principle that it is as individuals that we must confront issues of responsibility must be consistent with recognizing that, as individuals, we confront these issues in different ways, in virtue of our different roles and our different forms of participation, and usually with very tiny degrees of influence. A CEO bears responsibility differently from a low-level employee, a large investor differently from a small one and a citizen of a state that benefits from the corporation's economic activity bears responsibility differently from a citizen at large in the world. We have layered responsibilities, in other words, in virtue of our different roles and relationships to the activity in question. As a matter of pure theory, all we can say is that these different layers, or identities, all bear on the question of responsibility. But it is, I think, basically indeterminate how one should reconcile these layers of responsibility, and how to act on them effectively. If expanded responsibility is a consequence of collective action, then the solution to that responsibility is collective as well, and has to come through specific collective decisions and actions.

This is the relevance of politics. Politics is the form through which we manage these collective ethical concerns. Once we focus on the individual as the unit of moral responsibility, a new set of problems emerge – what you could call problems of the core versus the periphery. The problem is that, taken one by one, it's hard to see how individuals have much responsibility for what their corporate agents do. If you didn't buy shares of Total Oil, someone else would have – someone with an interest in maximizing profits at the expense of human rights. Of course, if we all had an interest in pursuing human rights, there wouldn't be a problem – but as not everyone does, there is a problem: people who want to do good look like suckers. Even if we assume an ethical viewpoint – a

---

[12] The Fund's current value, as of 30 June 2010, is approximately US$432 billion (NOK 2,792 billion). Edwin M. Truman, *Sovereign Wealth Funds: Threat or Salvation?* (Washington, DC: Peterson Institute for International Economics, 2010), pp. 12–15.

desire to make sure our capital or labour is deployed unobjectionably – it can be hard to see why we should decline an investment opportunity if the harm would come about anyway, if someone else would make sure that rights weren't respected, or human rights were violated.

This means that one of the central tasks of politics is to make ethical life rational, to make sense of being good. In short, we need to work out ways for realizing our responsibilities, leveraging our powers and duties and individuals through institutions like the Pension Fund. Politics sets the limits within which our corporate agents operate, and it can create, through enforcement of certain ethical principles, assurance that we will not be suckers for the sake of our ideals. Politics, when it works, can do this in a couple of ways, first by raising the costs of being unethical – taxing or prohibiting unethical conduct by others so that, as a comparative matter, it becomes rational for us. This is why ethical guidelines cannot be purely voluntary, or matters of self-reporting: if they are, the race-to-the-bottom logic of collective action will drive the ethically minded from the field. This should be obvious: we are talking about responsibilities that arise in virtue of collective action, and politics is the mode by which we regulate and make rational that collective action. To talk about corporate complicity abstracted from political efforts risks making us feel better without offering any real hope.

As a further point, one promise of broad political reform is that it might enable a more modest and feasible form of social responsibility on the corporate side as well as on the investor side. There has been a gathering movement to encourage corporations to concentrate on the well-being of their stakeholders and the sustainability of their enterprises, in ways that go beyond (and potentially against) their profits.[13] The movement is admirable, especially given the often weak standards and underenforcement of law governing corporate operations. But as a general matter, corporations seem ideally suited to a different mission, namely the efficient deployment of capital in search of productive endeavours. Asking corporations to do social justice is like asking armies to build democracies – whether or not it works in theory, or even on particular occasions, it is not a systematic solution to the problems of serious injustice. Just as, in virtually all developed countries (with one notable exception), national healthcare has replaced a piecemeal system of employer-funded care, the broader project of building a just and sustainable future requires systematic national investment. Issues of global injustice need to be rectified by states operating through a

---

[13] A useful recent discussion of the movement can be found in José Allouche (ed.), *Corporate Social Responsibility* (New York: Palgrave, 2006).

range of institutions and practices, from trade barriers to technology transfers, and not just through expanding the missions of some particular set of corporate agents.

Here, perhaps, is a political parallel between corporations and individuals. It is a general theme in the political theory of liberalism that part of the role of the state is to ensure that individuals have space for private lives and private projects, against a backdrop of social justice. Politics, in other words, should make possible a distinction between public and private identities. In the individual case, this division is justified by the way it makes possible the private, sectarian relationships that give our lives particular meaning. In the corporate context, the justification is much crasser, in terms of efficiency. But in both cases, it points to the way in which ethical and political demands reinforce one another.

Norway's political act of endowing its Pension Fund with ethical principles is an important first step towards broader political solutions, and it is already far more than one might expect of political actors today. But it is only a first step, and will require the coordinated efforts of other large-scale investors, with meshing strategies, to bear the fruit we ultimately wish to harvest: not the purity of our consciences, but business conducted in good faith and with respect for the rights of all those affected. The ethical demands of our concepts and ideals may reach further than we can practically implement, and they may go much further than the law, with its distinct remedial purposes, will afford. But the demands they make are real, and we have only just begun to respond to them in a spirit of ethical honesty.

5   Attribution of responsibility to listed companies

Ola Mestad

1.   Introduction

In the modern globalized business world of complex corporate structures, violations of human rights and other unethical conduct related to multinational companies normally take place at a level very distant from the listed parent company. This creates several difficulties in analysis of corporate responsibility.

When assessing corporate responsibility from *an investor perspective*, the general problem concerns the relationship between the listed company in which the investor holds shares and the often very distant level on which the unethical conduct or the unacceptable production takes place. That problem is the reverse of the problem that faces *victims of corporate wrongdoings* wanting to hold a listed company liable for consequences of unacceptable conduct like violations of human rights. Both problems belong to the overall discussion on corporate social responsibility. The basic difference between discussions of investor divestment due to unethical behaviour, on the one hand, and suits against companies based on the same type of conduct on the other, is the perspective from which the analysis has to be undertaken.

What these two groups of problems have in common is the interest in the analysis of the link between the listed multinational company and the unethical, and even illegal, behaviour. To describe, analyse and discuss this link is the aim of this chapter. A better understanding requires a more detailed description of corporate structures than is usually given in the literature. I use the term *attribution* of responsibility to the listed company to describe the task of establishing the link.

To put the analysis of attribution into context, it can be said to concern one of the three groups of questions that relate to the link between an investor, the listed company, the subsidiaries or other related corporate actors and the unethical conduct, which may be undertaken by one of the corporate actors, or the state in which operations take place.

The first question, which will not be further discussed here, relates to *the participation of the investor* in the listed company. Is it sufficient to hold shares to be said to be ethically responsible? Or should the conduct be foreseeable from the investor's point of view? With respect to the Norwegian Government Pension Fund – Global, it is made clear in the preparatory work to the Guidelines that holding of shares is sufficient, no matter how small the holding is, as long as it is foreseeable that the company in which the shares are held may be complicit in grossly unethical conduct.[1]

The second question concerns the *attribution to a listed company* and will be discussed in the following. Sometimes, it is sufficient to solve these two questions, to establish the complete link between the investor and the conduct. That is so when the conduct takes place within the company structure, as is typically the case with respect to damages to the environment.

Often, and always in relation to human rights violations, there is a third question on how to establish the *link between the corporate actor in question and the human rights violations done by states*. Basically, under international law, only states can directly violate human rights. A specific analysis is needed to attribute to a company the violation made by a state. This question is the most discussed issue in the literature on business and human rights, and it is also discussed elsewhere in this book,[2] but it is not the topic of this chapter.

Discussion of the link between a listed company and the entity which does the unethical conduct or is complicit in the state's human rights violations is the main task of this chapter. It will be done based on materials from the Council on Ethics for the Norwegian Government Pension Fund – Global and from court cases under the United States Alien Tort Claims Act (ATCA). In section 2, I will briefly present the materials to be used and its normative basis. Use of ethical as well as legal materials will reinforce the analysis from both perspectives and, at the same time, sharpen the conceptual differences between the two tasks.

The discussion is divided into four parts. In section 3, I will analyse and discuss problems related to *ownership structures within company groups*. Special problems related to *joint ventures*, which are a mixture of ownership and contractual issues, will be analysed in section 4. Supply-chain issues and other contractual structures are the subject of section 5.

---

[1] See Norwegian Government White Paper, NOU 2003:22, p. 14: 'Even though the issue of complicity raises difficult questions, the Committee considers, in principle, that owning shares or bonds in a company that can be expected to commit grossly unethical actions may be regarded as complicity in these actions.'

[2] See Gro Nystuen, Chapter 2 above.

In section 6, I will discuss a related and smaller, but different question of attribution, i.e., attribution from within. When can a company claim that a *wrong-doing by its own employees* should not be attributed to the company? This will typically be the case with corruption charges, where the company will argue that an act of corruption has been undertaken by the employee on his or her own, and not on behalf of the company.

In section 7, some conclusions will be drawn and I will refer to the wider discussion of corporate social responsibility and companies' spheres of influence. Based on the analysis, I will submit that a concept of companies' *sphere of control* is better suited than a sphere of influence concept, at least related to the discussion of attribution.

2. The Ethical Guidelines of the Norwegian Government Pension Fund – Global and the US Alien Tort Claims Act

In the following discussions, I draw on materials from two sets of sources. First, I use cases where the Council on Ethics for the Norwegian Government Pension Fund – Global ('the Council on Ethics' and 'the Fund' respectively) has issued recommendations.[3] The cases from the Council on Ethics come from all areas of the scope of work of the Council, not only human rights violations. Second, I draw on cases involving companies and human rights violations decided under the US Alien Tort Claims Act (ATCA). These two sets of materials are, as far as I can see, the two most concrete official analyses of corporate wrongdoing worldwide.

The Ethical Guidelines for the Fund, which the Council is applying, have been presented in the introduction to this book.[4] Complicity is the core concept of the Guidelines with respect to assessing the link between the Fund and unethical conduct. In the English translation of the 2004 version of the Guidelines on the website, unfortunately it has been said that exclusion of companies shall be recommended 'because of acts or omissions that constitute an unacceptable risk that the Fund *contributes to*' a specified list of types of unethical conduct.[5]

---

[3] I have first-hand knowledge of these cases as a member of the Council on Ethics. However, the opinions expressed here are my personal ones and do not necessarily reflect an official position of the Council. Recommendations from the Council in the official Norwegian-language version as well as translations into English are published on the Council website and included in the Annual Reports of the Council (also on the website); see www.etikkradet.no.

[4] See Chapter 1 above.

[5] See Norwegian Government Pension Fund – Global: Ethical Guidelines 2004, para. 4.4 (emphasis added) (see Appendix 2 below). In the 2010 version of the

This translation is misleading. In Norwegian, the official wording is 'an unacceptable risk that the Fund "*medvirker til*"' the unethical conduct. This concept of '*medvirker til*', and the parallel noun, '*medvirkning*', is generally applied in Norwegian and Scandinavian criminal and tort law. It is much more related to complicity than to contribution. To give one pertinent translation is impossible since the common law and civil law systems probably are too different in this field.

In the preparatory work of the Guidelines, the Graver Committee addressed briefly the question of the relationship between the listed company and other related entities. It took as a starting point that it could be unethical to invest also in companies that are only indirectly involved in unethical practices, through 'controlling interests or ownership interests or other links'.[6] The Committee did not set up clear rules on how to handle such issues: 'It is not appropriate to set clear limits as to which links of this nature should result in exclusion and which should not result in exclusion. This must be assessed on a case-by-case basis. A guiding principle for the assessment should be whether there are factors that indicate complicity in an ethical sense or whether the use of alternative measures is appropriate.'

In practice, it is very rare that unethical acts investigated by the Council are undertaken by the listed company in which the Fund is invested. As a rule, one has to analyse the different links between the company and the unethical conduct, as I will do in the following.

The other set of sources to be used are cases on human rights violations against companies, decided under the US Alien Tort Claims Act (ATCA). An ATCA claim is roughly speaking a claim brought by foreigners in a US federal court, against private persons or against companies (or states), claiming monetary damages in tort due to violations of some rules of international law, typically international humanitarian law or gross violations of international human rights. ATCA is a special US feature, and worldwide the only important domestic remedy for trying human rights violations against multilateral companies in other jurisdictions than the one where the alleged violation occurred. This makes ATCA cases especially attractive as examples of thorough analysis of corporate wrongdoings, because they undergo all the complicated

---

Guidelines, the rule has been somewhat rephrased, but not on this point. In the English translation, the language is now 'if there is an unacceptable risk that the company contributes to or is responsible for' the unethical conduct (Section (2)3, see Appendix 1 below). This also is a translation of the Norwegian concept '*medvirker til*'.

[6] See Norwegian Government White Paper, NOU 2003:22, p. 35.

features of US law, especially related to questions of jurisdiction and of discovery. A word of caution on the use of ATCA cases is appropriate. Since the provisions of the act are old and very brief indeed,[7] and the act has been applied only since the late 1970s, most aspects of the law are still unsettled.[8] Particularly, this goes for the standards of complicity and liability to be applied should a case be found to fall within the ambit of ATCA.

Even if ATCA cases are solved based on law, and not on ethical considerations, the company structures in the cases before the Council on Ethics and under ATCA are similar. In some cases, even the companies are the same and some of the questions are parallel.

However, solutions differ. In principle, suits against companies come from the victims of the violations or somebody acting on their behalf. The plaintiffs have been at the receiving end. Violations have typically taken place in a country where courts do not function well, and by governments that definitely do not protect their citizens as they should. Companies that have been directly complicit in violations are often subsidiaries fairly remote from the parent company. They may be undercapitalized and registered in another jurisdiction than the host state, or the home state of the parent company. To succeed in a suit, the victims have to climb up the corporate ladder to get to the parent company with capital and presence in a jurisdiction where they can be sued. The possible outcome, the sanction, in these cases is compensation.

Analysis of whether divestment by an investor should be made, the task of the Council on Ethics, is undertaken from the opposite perspective, from the other end of the corporate ladder. The investor normally holds shares in the ultimate parent company. The investor's identification is with the company and the company group itself, and he finances the activities. He looks down the corporate ladder to see whether what goes on at the other end is acceptable, and to check with the listed company's management what it intends to do. His sanction is selling his shares.

---

[7] The wording of ATCA is: 'The district courts shall have original jurisdiction of any civil action by an alien for a tort only, committed in violation of the law of nations or a treaty of the United States.' For a broad presentation of the background and many current issues, see Ralph G. Steinhardt and Anthony D'Amato (eds.), *The Alien Tort Claims Act: An Analytical Anthology* (New York: Hotei Publishing, 1999).

[8] The famous *Sosa* case in the US Supreme Court solved some of the most debated issues, but not much related to companies' liability, see *Sosa* v. *Alvarez-Machain*, 542 U.S. 692 (2004).

3.   Complex ownership structures

International business is normally organized in complex manners. The legal structures which form the basis for shareholdings do not reflect what we can term the real economic unity or entities. Underlying reasons for this will differ from sector to sector and between different country traditions.[9]

In some sectors, like mining, oil and gas and other extractive industries, the participants often prefer to work jointly to share the huge investments and risks and pool their technologies and knowledge, or they are forced to cooperate with other companies, typically national state-owned entities. Limitation of liability, which means reduction of risk for the parent company, is also important. In other sectors, like large service-providing companies, many subsidiaries on regional or national levels are set up, partly to limit risks and partly to establish competitive structures within a company group. Other motives for creating complex structures can be tax optimization or national requirements of local registration to make efficient the functioning of national control systems. Combinations of structures of subsidiaries and joint structures are also common. Joint ventures will be discussed below in section 4. A company group often consists of a listed parent company and several subsidiaries which again very often have their own subsidiaries and legally form company groups in their own right. All of these examples relate to company *ownership structures* and the difficult issues are issues of ownership control and separate corporate entities.

In this section, I will first present and discuss the basic rule on ownership structures with respect to the Ethical Guidelines for the Norwegian Fund, before looking at three different examples: the company groups of Talisman, Freeport and Vedanta.

Under the Guidelines, the basic rule must be that ownership that gives the legal competence to instruct and control the acts of the subsidiary must be decisive when it comes to responsibility for unethical conduct at the level of the subsidiary. This suffices for exclusion of the company from an investment portfolio for complicity in unethical conduct as long as the other conditions are met.

What is said here is in line with the Graver report's comments on matters of ownership control: 'Where ownership is concerned, it is reasonable to require that the company has actual control over the

---

[9] For a brief overview, see Reinier H. Kraakman et al., *The Anatomy of Corporate Law* (Oxford University Press, 2004), p. 75.

entity involved in unethical action before complicity on the part of the Petroleum Fund can be invoked.'[10]

Generally, the control requirement is met when the parent company holds more than fifty per cent of voting shares in a subsidiary. It is no valid excuse that the subsidiary is a separate legal entity with its own responsibilities under the laws of the state of registration and the state of operation. This is different when liability under ATCA is the question. Incorporation of each subsidiary will normally be respected and piercing the corporate veil or vicarious liability may be necessary. Below, I will take a closer look at that in relation to the *Talisman* case.

Under most laws, fifty-one per cent voting rights in the subsidiary gives the power to direct the subsidiary's operations. In some cases, even smaller shareholdings than fifty-one per cent give a controlling interest. This may be the case in listed companies with dispersed shareholding and one big shareholder that holds, for example, thirty-five per cent due to the fact that many smaller shareholders never vote. In principle, this effect of the control rule should apply. But such cases will be rare with respect to control over companies where an investor holds shares in a listed company and that company holds a large part of the shares in another company. The other company – the subsidiary – is usually not of the type with one big shareholder and many other smaller ones. But in principle, it should be the test of controlling interest that is relevant when attributing responsibility and not the formal fifty-one per cent shareholding.

An example of complex, but quite normal, ownership can be found in the ATCA case against the oil company *Talisman Energy, Inc.*[11] Talisman, a Canadian corporation, was accused of complicity in human rights violations in southern Sudan. The alleged violations of international law were complicity in war crimes, crimes against humanity and genocide, all committed by the government of Sudan against some non-Arabic peoples in southern Sudan, living in prospective oil and gas areas. Some victims and others sued for compensation in tort.

A US district court in 2006 granted summary judgment in favour of Talisman. That decision was upheld in 2009 by the Court of Appeals for the Second Circuit and the plaintiffs have petitioned the Supreme Court for Writ of Certiorari.[12] I will not go into detail on the facts and

---

[10] Norwegian Government White Paper, NOU 2003:22, p. 36.

[11] See the decision on summary Judgment dated 12 September 2006, *Presbyterian Church of Sudan* v. *Talisman Energy, Inc.*, 453 F. Supp. 2d 633 (S.D.N.Y. 2006).

[12] See Opening brief for Plaintiffs-Appellants dated 26 February 2007, *Presbyterian Church of Sudan* v. *Talisman Energy, Inc.*, 582 F.3d 244 (2d Cir. 2009) dated 2 October 2009 and Petition for Writ of Certiorari dated 15 April 2010.

the terrible and complex situation in southern Sudan. What interests us here is the corporate structure of Talisman and the link between the unacceptable conduct and the listed company. These questions were at the core of the appeal, but the Court of Appeals based its decision mainly on a requirement of purpose for the standard of aiding and abetting in the Sudanese government's human rights violations.[13]

The corporate background was as follows: SPC (State Petroleum Company), a Canadian Corporation, in 1993 purchased the rights to three blocks in Sudan and entered into a production sharing agreement with the Sudan government. In May 1994, Arakis Energy Corporation, a Canadian Corporation, acquired SPC that became a wholly owned subsidiary. In November 1996, SPC established a consortium with three other companies: China National Petroleum Corporation (CNPC), Petronas Carigali Overseas SDN BHD (Petronas) and Sudapet Ltd (wholly owned by the government of Sudan). All these three are government-owned companies. A complicated set of agreements was established. The purpose was twofold: to conduct oil exploration and to build and operate a pipeline. SPC held twenty-five per cent of the interests.

The consortium members established the Greater Nile Petroleum Operating Company Limited (GNPOC) 'as the entity which would conduct operations for the Consortium Members under their agreement with the Government'. GNPOC was incorporated in Mauritius.

In 1998, Talisman entered the scene through acquiring Arakis, and establishing a complicated corporate structure. It transferred the interests in GNPOC to a separate company, Talisman (Greater Nile) B.V., which was a Dutch subsidiary of the Dutch company Goal Olie-en-Gasexploratie B.V., which again was owned by two subsidiaries of Talisman's own UK subsidiary. Talisman's involvement in Sudan lasted from 1998 to 2003 when it withdrew due to pressure from many directions, including important NGOs and the Canadian government.[14]

If assessed under the Guidelines of the Government Pension Fund, the chain of control would be in place from Talisman through all the four layers of subsidiaries. It cannot matter whether a subsidiary is held through two sister subsidiaries as long as all the companies are part

---

[13] Some issues on corporate structure are discussed in the Petition for Writ of Certiorari at pp. 6–7. The case also involves some questions related to joint ventures (consortia). Such questions are discussed below in section 4.

[14] For the background of the case as well as an analysis of the civil society campaigns against Talisman's engagement in Sudan and the political difficulties between the US and Canada, see Stephen J. Kobrin, 'Oil and Politics: Talisman Energy and Sudan', *New York University Journal of International Law and Politics*, 36 (2004), p. 425. Kobrin does not analyse the corporate structure of the engagement.

of the same group with Talisman as the ultimate parent. With respect to the twenty-five per cent participation in the consortium in Sudan, there is not enough information in the case report to say anything certain, but I assume that it raises the same type of problems that are discussed in section 4 below. Generally, joint ventures and consortia often have provisions that require unanimous decisions on important matters and qualified majorities for other decisions.[15] But if a case under the Guidelines had been raised now, Talisman could not be excluded since the company group's involvement in Sudan was terminated in 2003. A basic feature of the exclusion mechanism is that the Fund should not contribute to *future* violations, it is not a judge of previous violations.[16] But from the control perspective, the conditions seem to be fulfilled.

In the ATCA analysis of the District Court, the direct complicity in the violations were mainly committed by GNPOC, owned by the consortium in which Talisman, through four corporate layers, held twenty-five per cent, and by the consortium itself. Talisman's request for summary judgment that the case should not go to trial was accepted. The court did not find complicity on the part of Talisman Energy, Inc., the parent company that was party to the case. It was of the opinion that it was the GNPOC, the consortium's vehicle company, and the participants in the consortium that had the relevant knowledge and made the necessary decisions, not Talisman itself. Accordingly, Talisman succeeded in demonstrating that the different corporate layers under the law made it too distanced from the events to incur liability.

The plaintiffs also advanced three theories of liability to hold Talisman Energy, Inc. liable for the actions of GNPOC or of the joint venture partners (including the government of Sudan) through the ownership of Sudapet. First, the theory of alter ego (piercing the corporate veil); second, a theory of agency; and third, joint venture liability with Talisman as a direct joint venturer. Talisman opposed these theories on procedural grounds as being amendments of the case that were too late. The court found that the plaintiffs did not show good cause in coming forward with the amendment at such a late stage. However, it also found that the amendment 'appears to be futile'. In the opinion of the court,

---

[15] For the concrete involvement of Talisman in the Sudan GNPOC joint venture see ibid., p. 443: 'While Talisman Energy was only one of four partners in the GNOPC, it is clear that its participation was critical to the project's success. It provided funding and, more importantly, technical know-how and a great deal of expertise and experience in exploration and development.'

[16] See Ethical Guidelines 2004, para. 4.4 and Section (2)3 of the Ethical Guidelines 2010. See also Total Recommendation, 'Annual Report 2005', p. 40, para. 51, and Nystuen, Chapter 2 above.

these special liability issues had to be solved based on state, not federal, law, and it undertook a brief analysis of the matters based, *inter alia*, on New York choice of law rules. This took the court through questions of piercing the corporate veil under the laws of Mauritius, of England and of the Netherlands, as well as New York law on joint ventures.

The District Court would not accept theories of tort liability making the parent company liable for what had taken place in formally incorporated indirect subsidiaries unless the requirements of traditional theories which overturn the effects of incorporation were fulfilled. This is, as we have seen above, different from the basic rule of ethical corporate responsibility that has been followed by the Council on Ethics.

In the appeal, the appellants forwarded a general perspective that, if it had been accepted, would have made the two approaches much more similar. In the preliminary statement of the appeal brief, it was said:

Perhaps the central flaw in the District Court's analysis was its failure to recognize that a huge, multinational corporation like Talisman can only act through its employees, subsidiaries or agents. Talisman is liable for what its partners and agents, be they natural persons or corporations, did to facilitate the human rights violations committed against Plaintiffs.[17]

The appeal continued in offering analysis of Talisman's alleged direct involvement as well as expanding on theories of agency, etc. Further development of the *Talisman* case will be followed closely by everybody who has an interest in the relationship between multinational companies and human rights. At the core of the case for the time being is the requirement of purpose for aiding and abetting liability, but if a Writ of Certiorari is granted, it may come back to the issues regarding corporate structure, since the District Court judge seems to have accepted the existence and character of the alleged conduct.[18]

Another example of corporate structure is the organization of *Freeport McMoRan Copper & Gold Inc.*'s holding in the Grasberg mine in the Indonesian province of Papua. This company was excluded from the Norwegian Pension Fund due to severe environmental damages at the mine.[19] Freeport is a mining, energy production and copper refining

---

[17] Opening brief for Plaintiffs-Appellants dated 26 February 2007, pp. 2–3.

[18] In the ATCA Apartheid cases, the US District Court for the Southern District of New York has recently ruled that the plaintiffs may proceed on a theory of vicarious liability based on corporate agency, see US District Court for the Southern District of New York, in re. South African Apartheid Litigation, 8 April 2009, pp. 82–7, available at www.business-humanrights.org/Categories/Lawlawsuits/Lawsuitsregulatoryaction/LawsuitsSelectedcases/ApartheidreparationslawsuitsreSoAfrica.

[19] Council on Ethics, 'Recommendation on Freeport McMoRan Copper & Gold Inc.', and 'Annual Report 2006', p. 36. In 2008, Rio Tinto Plc. and Rio Tinto Ltd were excluded from the Fund due to participation in the same mining operation.

company with headquarters in the USA. Its mining operations in Indonesia are organized through a subsidiary, PT Freeport Indonesia, which owns and runs the Grasberg mine. Freeport McMoRan has a (direct and indirect) 90.64 per cent stake in PT Freeport Indonesia, the Indonesian state holds the remaining 9.36 per cent. In 1995, PT Freeport Indonesia again formed a joint venture with Rio Tinto PLC, giving the latter a share of the profits from the Grasberg mine.

This case also demonstrates a parent–subsidiary structure which is clear-cut from a corporate control perspective even though the Indonesian state holds a minority position in the subsidiary. The joint venture agreement between two parties only, related to the expansion of the mine, does not complicate the matter when assessed under the Guidelines of the Norwegian Government Pension Fund.

The third example is the British company *Vedanta Resources Plc*, listed on the stock exchange in London. It was excluded from the Norwegian Pension Fund due to severe environmental damage as well as human rights violations.[20] The basis for exclusion was activities in four of Vedanta's subsidiaries in India, Sterlite Industries Ltd, Madras Aluminium Company Ltd (MALCO), Bharat Aluminium Co. Ltd and Vedanta Alumina.[21] Both Sterlite and MALCO are separately listed companies in India, but Vedanta Resources Plc holds seventy-six per cent and eighty per cent respectively of the shares. There was no doubt expressed about the attribution to the listed parent company of the responsibility for the violations even if two of the involved subsidiaries were listed themselves.

Vedanta has another interesting feature from a corporate structure perspective. The London-listed Vedanta Resources is itself a subsidiary of the privately held Volcan Investments Ltd which holds fifty-four per cent of the shares in Vedanta Resources.[22] This does not complicate the control structure below the level of Vedanta Resources which itself is a company group.

A corporate structure like the one in Vedanta, where the listed company in which the investor holds shares is itself a subsidiary of another company, also raises a question whether unethical conduct by or related to the ultimate parent company could be attributed to the listed subsidiary where the ethically concerned investor holds shares. This issue

---

[20] Council on Ethics, 'Recommendation on exclusion of Vedanta Resources Plc.', (Vedanta Recommendation) and 'Annual Report 2007', p. 34.

[21] Vedanta Alumina may not be incorporated as a subsidiary but only an operation within Vedanta Resources.

[22] On the relationship between Volcan and Vedanta, see the company's own corporate governance report: 'Vedanta, Investor Relations, Corporate Governance Report'; www.vedantaresources.com/corporategovernancereport.asp.

is not unimportant since such structures are also known in company groups where the ultimate parent is a 100 per cent state-owned company with a listed subsidiary.

Attribution to a subsidiary of responsibility based on acts or omissions by, or attributed to, the ultimate parent would be turning upside down the corporate pyramid and corporate structures. Corporate control goes from the top and downwards. Therefore, as a starting point, such attribution should not be undertaken. Special concrete circumstances could change the assessment, for example if the legal boundaries between the parent and the subsidiary are not respected or the corporate control structures are very special. In most cases it is improbable that erasing of the company boundaries could be established as long as the subsidiary is listed on a well run and controlled stock exchange which would monitor the conduct of the parent as a majority shareholder in relation to other shareholders.

With respect to corporate structures and the general discussion of corporate social responsibility, it is clear from the analysis above that different approaches apply whether one takes the perspective of the ethically concerned investor or of the victims of corporate misconduct, respectively. From the investor perspective, corporate control should be decisive. And that could even apply on a lower threshold than ownership of fifty per cent. From the perspective of the victims of human rights violations seeking to hold a parent company liable under law, it seems as if formal company entities will be respected. Being in control of the operation is not sufficient. That has however been challenged in the *Talisman* case. At least, that challenge has not yet been successful.

4.   Joint ventures involving listed companies

Companies in which an investor holds shares may be engaged in activities through long-term unincorporated joint ventures. This is typical for the oil and gas industry with large investments, large risks and need for the most advanced technology, as well as in many sectors where mandatory national participation often is organized through a joint venture with one or a few multinational companies. Other sectors also have joint ventures, like the weapons industry, as we shall see below. Joint ventures raise other questions of attribution than limited companies with normal control through majority participation.

The term joint venture is used in different meanings and has not one settled international legal meaning. Here we address unincorporated joint ventures that typically have similar features as partnerships, especially unlimited liability. The core of most joint ventures is that there are few participants and all are supposed to take active part in the activities. Sometimes the form is also used to establish cooperation with some parties participating financially only, and others participating through other activities as well as financially.

In relation to attribution of responsibility, the main question is whether unethical conduct on the part of the joint venture, or, on the part of another joint venture partner, should be attributed to the listed company that takes part in the joint venture, or, that normally is the parent company of its participating subsidiary, even if the participating interest is below fifty per cent.

If we take the principle of control as the starting point, joint ventures are usually different from limited liability companies. Joint ventures do not have limited liability, and usually very few participants, typically between two and six. All participants are normally jointly liable for the full economic activities of the joint venture.[23] Accordingly, minority participants have more to say than in limited liability companies. Often decision rules of a joint venture agreement require unanimous decisions, or at least a qualified majority.

Applying the principle of control on typical joint ventures implies that also participants with a smaller interest than fifty per cent could be said to exercise control. As long as unanimous decisions are required, any participant is capable, at least legally, of blocking activities of the joint venture. This gives even a small participant a position that can block basic joint venture decisions.

I will here look closer at two examples of joint venture issues; first, the European defence joint venture MBDA and, second, and more thoroughly, the oil and gas joint venture related to the Yadana gas field in Burma which involved Unocal and Total. In section 3 above, I have already commented somewhat on the joint venture that involved Talisman in southern Sudan.

The *MBDA* joint venture was involved in a case from the Council on Ethics which led to exclusion of the English company BAE Systems Plc and the Italian company Finmeccanica SpA from the Norwegian Government Pension Fund.[24] The joint venture was at the core of a

---

[23] This can differ between individual joint venture agreements and between jurisdictions.

[24] Council on Ethics, 'Recommendation on the exclusion of companies that are involved in production of nuclear weapons' and 'Annual Report 2005', p. 25. EADS had already been excluded due to its involvement in production of cluster munitions, see Council on Ethics, 'Recommendation on the exclusion of companies that are involved in the production of cluster munitions' and 'Annual Report 2005', p. 19. These exclusions were based on the weapons criteria under the first sentence of para. 4.4 of the Ethical Guidelines 2004 (Appendix 2 below).

comprehensive European defence industry cooperation.[25] There were (and are) three participants: BAE Systems Plc (37.5 per cent), EADS (37.5 per cent) and Finmeccanica SpA (25 per cent). The exclusion was based on this participation and MBDA's involvement in production of nuclear weapons which took place in a subsidiary of MBDA in France. On the issue of participation, the Council on Ethics stated in its recommendation:

> It is not clear whether BAE and Finmeccanica play an active role in the development and production specifically of ... [the nuclear weapon component] ... other than being partners in MBDA. This is in any event not decisive, as the Council will base its recommendation on the fact that both companies are active owners of MBDA and thus directly contribute to the production of key components to nuclear weapons.[26]

This statement by the Council was based on the assumption that the three joint venture partners, even Finmeccanica with its twenty-five per cent, all had decisive votes in decisions on the strategy of the joint venture as well as economic interests in all the underlying subsidiaries.

A more complicated joint venture structure is involved in the *Unocal* case and the *Total* recommendation. These two cases are closely related because both the ATCA case against Unocal and the Total recommendation of the Council on Ethics were based on participation in construction of the Yadana gas pipeline in Burma.

The Unocal case in US Federal courts is probably the most well-known of all ATCA cases involving corporations. It was decided by the Court of Appeals for the Ninth Circuit in 2005.[27] After the summary judgment of the District Court had been reversed by the Court of Appeals, Unocal settled with the plaintiffs. Accordingly, no final court decision was necessary. The settlement amount is unknown.[28]

The basic human rights issue of the cases concerns the clearing of the site for construction of the pipeline where Burmese military forcibly evicted the village people out of the areas and used many village people as forced labour. Should responsibility for these serious human rights violations be attributed to Unocal and Total?

Organization of oil and gas activities in the military dictatorship of Burma (Myanmar) is at the core of the case. Myanmar Oil and Gas

---

[25] Sometimes by the participants also called a partnership.
[26] Council on Ethics, 'Annual Report 2005', p. 30.
[27] *Doe I* v. *Unocal Corp.*, 403 F.3d 708 (9th Cir. 2005).
[28] Later, Unocal was denied summary judgment for insurance coverage for the compensations that had been agreed, *Unocal Corp.* v. *Lexington Insurance Co.*, CV05–01857, C.D. Cal., filed 15 March 2005.

enterprise (MOGE) is a 100 per cent state-run corporation owned by the Ministry of Energy. MOGE is responsible for oil and gas extraction and gas supply, including construction of gas pipelines, and is the regime's tool for control over production of the country's oil and gas resources. Foreign companies wishing to engage in petroleum production in Burma need to establish collaboration with MOGE, the only state corporation entitled to enter into such contracts in the petroleum sector.

Between Total Myanmar, a subsidiary of Total S.A., and MOGE, a production sharing contract was entered into before Unocal entered the project. The contract provided that MOGE '*shall ... supply* [] *or mak*[*e*] *available ... security protection* ... as may be requested by [Total Myanmar and its assigns]'.[29]

In 1992, Unocal acquired from Total a twenty-eight per cent interest in the project. Unocal's chosen corporate structure for the project was as follows: Unocal's interest in the gas *production* part of the project was held by the Unocal Myanmar Offshore Company, which from 1999 was a wholly owned subsidiary of Unocal Global Ventures, Ltd, a Bermuda corporation, which was a wholly owned subsidiary of the Unocal International Corporation, a Delaware corporation, which again was a wholly owned subsidiary of the Union Oil Company of California, one of the defendants in the case and again a wholly owned subsidiary of the ultimate parent, the Unocal Corporation. Unocal's interest in the gas *transportation* part of the project was held by the Unocal International Pipeline Corporation, which from 1998 was owned by the Unocal Global Ventures, Ltd. The gas production in the Yadana project was organized as a joint venture while the gas transportation was organized through a separate Gas Transportation Company, and, disputably, also through a joint venture.

Unocal argued in court that it was 'not vicariously liable for the Myanmar military's torts because the pipeline was constructed by a separate corporation' (p. 14222 n. 30) and that there was no basis to pierce the corporate veils. This did not convince the Court of Appeals. It stated that 'there is evidence allowing a reasonable fact-finder to conclude that the Unocal Pipeline Corp. and the Unocal Offshore Co. were alter egos of Unocal, and that any actions by the Unocal Pipeline Corp. or the Unocal Offshore Co. are therefore attributable to Unocal.' The evidence pointed to was undercapitalization of the companies and the direct involvement in the project by the Unocal President, the Unocal CEO and other officers and employees of Unocal. This line of reasoning

---

[29] *Doe I* v. *Unocal Corp.*, 403 F.3d 708 (9th Cir. 2005) (emphasis added).

cut through the defence based on the individual limited companies involved in the case, in contrast to the District Court's opinion in the *Talisman* case, as we have seen above.

The court also emphasized that it did not find Unocal vicariously liable for the torts of the Myanmar military, but 'we find that there is sufficient evidence to hold Unocal liable based on *its own actions* and those of its alter ego subsidiaries which aided and abetted the Myanmar Military in perpetrating forced labour. These actions include the employment of the Myanmar Military to provide security and build infrastructure along the pipeline route, and the use of photos, surveys, and maps to show the Myanmar Military where to do this. Unocal took these actions with the knowledge that the Myanmar army was likely to use and did in fact use forced labour "on behalf of the project".'

Joint venture liability as a principle of US federal law was explicitly discussed by Judge Reinhardt in his concurring opinion since he held that federal common law, not international law principles, should apply as the standard of third party liability. On joint venture liability, he stated that '[i]t is well-established as a federal law principle that a member of a joint venture is liable for the acts of its co-venturers' (p. 14257). He further pointed to joint liability as a general principle of law and said that it 'is fundamental to "major legal systems"' (p. 14258). He would hold that 'plaintiffs may recover on a federal common law theory of joint liability if they can prove both that the forced labour violations occurred and that Unocal was a co-venturer with the Myanmar military, which perpetrated the violations' (p. 14258).

On the factual question of whether there was a joint venture with respect to the pipeline part of the project which would have to be decided at the trial stage, Judge Reinhardt stated: 'Rather, a reasonable jury could conclude that Unocal freely elected to participate in a profit-making venture in conjunction with an oppressive military regime – a regime that had a lengthy record of instituting forced labour, including forced child labour' (p. 14529).

The different standards of liability to be applied as well as the sources of such standards under ATCA are contested and may be decided by the US Supreme Court in the recent apartheid case.[30] The final solution

---

[30] In the very contested apartheid ATCA case, *Khulumani v. Barclay National Bank, Ltd*, 504 F.3d 254 (2d Cir. 2007), decided 12 October 2007 by the Court of Appeals for the Second Circuit, Judge Hall, in his concurring opinion, laid out the theory that in his opinion should be followed in applying a federal common law standard of aiding and abetting. He gave three examples, one which directly related to the allegations made in the *Unocal* case: 'The second [type of aiding and abetting liability] is designed to cover circumstances where the alleged aider and abettor is accused of having purchased

of these questions under US law is not what interests us the most here. The *Unocal* case demonstrates different types of legal argument to hold companies responsible for violations of human rights committed within the range of their own activities.[31] In relation to responsibility for activities in joint ventures, the most important point is that a joint venturer normally under the law is liable for the actions of the joint venture, even if he does not hold a majority position. Based on ethical considerations, each joint venturer has not only liability, but also so much influence in the joint venture that it is reasonable to attribute acts of the joint venture also to participants that do not hold a majority.

The *Total* case of the Norwegian Government Pension Fund was based on the same facts and agreement on the ground in Burma as the Unocal litigation, except that the Total corporate organization followed a simpler pattern.[32] Even so, exclusion of Total was not recommended by the Council on Ethics because the Council found that the risk of *future* contribution to human rights violations was acceptable. This conclusion was based on Total's changed attitude after the period of laying the pipeline. On the other hand, the Council is fairly clear when it comes to attribution of responsibility to Total for the previous violations related to the construction of the Yadana pipeline. The Council stated: 'Hence it is likely that Total knew of the accusations of gross abuses perpetrated by the security forces. Moreover, it is likely that they were aware, for example that forced labour was directly employed in connection with the construction of the pipeline.'[33] If the case had come up during the construction work, it appears as if Total would have been recommended for exclusion.

security services with the knowledge that the security forces would, or were likely to, commit international law violations in fulfilling their mandate' (p. 62). The other judge of the majority based the aiding and abetting standard on international law. The decision was petitioned for a writ of certiorari by the defendants (approximately fifty multinational corporations) but the case could for procedural reasons not be decided by the US Supreme Court. Accordingly, the decision of the Court of Appeals was upheld. The basic reason for the petition was the argument that accepting jurisdiction would have a strong negative effect on US foreign relations with the Republic of South Africa. The source and standard of liability were also challenged, see Petition for a Writ of Certiorari dated 10 January 2008, pp. 22–33, available at www.scotusblog. com/wp/wp-content/uploads/2008/01/SA.pdf. The case has continued in the District Court where the court on 8 April 2009 ruled partly in favour of the plaintiffs and partly in favour of the defendants. It has now been narrowed down to more specific claims and fewer parties, see US District Court for the Southern District of New York, in re. South African Apartheid Litigation, 8 April 2009.

[31] Court cases, like the US ATCA cases, are also valuable sources of information about facts. This is especially so with respect to cases from countries with broad discovery procedures.

[32] Total Recommendation and 'Annual Report 2005', p. 40.

[33] Council on Ethics, 'Annual Report 2005', p. 51, para. 4.

A related issue to joint venture responsibility in the Yadana project where Unocal and Total participated, concerns the *production sharing agreement* between Total, initially, and the military government's corporation, MOGE. This agreement stipulated that MOGE would provide 'security protection'. In my experience, this is a fairly unusual contract clause. Normally, a production sharing agreement is a contract on the distribution of produced oil and gas, or the proceeds from such production, between a host government, or a host government corporate entity, and one or more foreign oil companies. The actual production is managed and executed by the foreign company(ies). If a production sharing contract has a similar clause as the one in the Yadana project, and human rights violations take place as part of the 'security protection', this would be a fairly clear-cut case of violations that could be attributed to the oil company. If a more ordinary production sharing agreement is entered into, without a specific security clause, then the case requires a closer examination of the facts allegedly linking the oil company activities to violations by the government.

Under an ethical assessment, a listed company could be said to be complicit in the activities of a joint venture even if it does not hold a majority interest in the venture, like we have seen in the case regarding the MBDA joint venture. This is due to the fact that the issue of control in a joint venture is different from control in limited liability companies because of specific decision-making processes, allocation of benefits and unlimited liability and active participation by the participants. But in principle, the individual organization has to be examined. With respect to liability towards the victims, the joint liability of the joint venturers gives a cause of action against each participant. However, normally, at least the foreign participants would be subsidiaries held by the listed company through chains of companies. This implies that the problems discussed in section 3 above also have to be solved.

A broader theory of joint venture liability may help to overcome that difficulty, as we have seen hinted at in the Unocal case. If one considers the whole corporate setup as one joint venture between the listed parent company on the one hand and the host government on the other, it seems to be possible under US federal law to argue a case of liability even without formally undertaking an analysis of piercing the corporate veil through every corporate layer.[34]

---

[34] Such an analysis, if successful, would at the same time solve both the second and third group of questions presented in the Introduction (section 1 above).

5.   Supply chains and attribution through contracts

Attribution of responsibility based on *contractual structures* between the direct wrongdoer and a listed company group is different from the questions related to ownership structures we have looked at above. The issue is often referred to as a question of responsibility for conduct in the supply chain of the company group. The alleged wrongdoings take place within companies different from the listed company, and there are no ownership ties which establish formal corporate control. The supplier companies are separate and, from an ownership perspective, independent. The core question is whether the listed company still is so powerful in relation to the supplier that it has a possibility of changing its conduct, and therefore should be held responsible.

Questions of responsibility based on contractual links are dominant in some consumer goods sectors, like clothing and personal equipment, shoes and in semi-industrialized agriculture. Responsibility for human rights violations in the supply chain, or at contractors' facilities more generally, is a hotly debated topic in criticism of multinational companies.

A concept of control is also useful when analysing these sectors. They raise questions of control through contractual relations and, more generally, through dominating positions. The control concept will cover both actual control, as well as contractually agreed formal competences on the buyer side. In this section, I will look at the preparatory works of the Norwegian Ethical Guidelines, at the recommendation by the Council on Ethics which led to the exclusion of Wal-Mart from the Fund, and discuss some other ways of organisation of production.

The Graver Committee discussed briefly problems related to suppliers' unethical conduct. It took as a starting point that unethical conduct at a supplier is not enough to exclude the buyer company from the Fund, but in some cases it would be different:

Even if a company has unethical sub-contractors, it may be sensible to refrain from excluding investment unless there is a pattern where the company uses the sub-contractors with dubious practices without seeking to influence the situation. The situation will come closer to complicity if the customer relationship is long-term or repeated after the unethical practices have been identified.[35]

The Committee pointed to a possible pattern of using unethical suppliers, and to the company's knowledge of the situation as well as the duration of the contractual relationship. The company should also seek

---

[35] Norwegian Government White Paper, NOU 2003:22, p. 36 (with my rephrasing of a part of the Ministry of Finance translation).

to influence the situation. A requirement of influencing the situation implies that the company in question must have some power or control in relation to the supplier.

In the *Wal-Mart* case, the Council on Ethics made a recommendation with respect to human rights violations in the supply chain.[36] It found serious, even 'very serious', and systematic violations of human rights in several Wal-Mart supplier factories in different developing countries.[37] How could these be attributed to Wal-Mart? The Council held:

> Where the reported patterns of violations in the supply chain are concerned, the Council assumes that Wal-Mart is largely aware of them and largely refrains from seeking to prevent them. The Council also recognises that Wal-Mart wields substantial influence in regard to the working environment, wages etc., particularly in relation to manufacturers which the company itself describes as direct suppliers. This is due not least to the company's size and widespread presence in many countries, and thus to its engagement in a large number of suppliers.[38]

The Council attributed to Wal-Mart violations that took place in companies fully owned by others, due to Wal-Mart's knowledge of the violations and the control that Wal-Mart exerts over many of its suppliers. Wal-Mart's strong purchasing power in the relevant markets and the contractual arrangements it uses is basis for that control. In 2005, Wal-Mart was the world's largest retailer and was considered as the single largest buyer of goods from China.[39] For many suppliers Wal-Mart is the dominating buyer.

There is a particular issue concerning whether Wal-Mart seeks to influence the conduct of its suppliers. Wal-Mart has a contractually based monitoring regime that its suppliers must accept. The monitoring regime is allegedly designed to ensure acceptable working conditions at the direct suppliers as well as monitoring some indirect suppliers. It includes standards as well as inspection procedures.[40] One may see this regime either as window dressing or as a serious initiative to control and improve the conditions in the supply chain. Anyhow, the Council on Ethics found that the regime was not efficient in remedying the violations.[41]

---

[36] Wal-Mart Stores Inc. Recommendation and 'Annual Report 2006', p. 14.
[37] Council on Ethics, 'Annual Report 2006', pp. 19–24 and 31.
[38] Ibid., p. 30.   [39] Ibid., pp. 15 and 24.
[40] Ibid., p. 20. The monitoring regime seems today (July 2010) to be part of Wal-Mart's Sustainability Program, see: walmartstores.com/sites/sustainabilityreport/2010/default.aspx.
[41] Council on Ethics, 'Annual Report 2006', pp. 20–1 and 30.

Wal-Mart is not alone in having established a monitoring regime. Monitoring programmes appear to be fairly common among large multinational companies. The United Nations Special Representative of the Secretary-General, John Ruggie, found in a study of the Fortune Global 500 firms that it is 'relatively common' that these large companies have a form of supply-chain monitoring.[42] No matter whether a monitoring system is considered as being basically for marketing purposes or really to control and change the conduct of the suppliers, the existence of and publicity related to the regime, must be indicative of some sort of responsibility.

In its recommendation, the Council on Ethics focused on Wal-Mart's dominating position and its contractual arrangements. The strong impact of Wal-Mart's regulation on its suppliers' conduct is demonstrated from another perspective in a recent study by Larry Catá Backer.[43] He argues that:

Wal-Mart ... has in place a system of supplier norms that it has imposed on its global supplier base. These uniform international standards specify certain basic conduct norms imposed on all suppliers. These norms are made part of the contractual relationship between Wal-Mart and its suppliers. Failure to comply with the behaviour norms could lead to contractually-imposed sanctions, from suspension of the contract to its termination. In addition, the contract permits Wal-Mart to require suppliers to undergo training in business conduct and ethics, and requires all suppliers to conduct their operations with a certain large degree of transparency – permitting Wal-Mart to audit and inspect the supplier.[44]

Imposition of norms is a key notion in Backer's analysis. It demonstrates precisely the power that Wal-Mart typically exerts in its supply chain. And it supports the idea that Wal-Mart has a strong degree of control over many of its suppliers.[45]

Other sectors may have even more severe violations of human rights related to working conditions than in the *Wal-Mart* case, where violations mainly took place in factories (in developing countries). In

---

[42] John Ruggie, 'Business and Human Rights: Mapping International Standards of Responsibility and Accountability for Corporate Acts. Report of the Special Representative of the Secretary-General (SRSG) on the Issue of Human Rights and Transnational Corporations and Other Business Enterprises', UN Human Rights Council, UN Doc. A/HRC/4/035 (9 February 2007), para. 72.

[43] Larry Catá Backer, 'Economic Globalization and the Rise of Efficient Systems of Global Private Law Making: Wal-Mart as Global Legislator', *Connecticut Law Review*, 39 (2006–7), p. 1739.

[44] Ibid., pp. 1783–4.

[45] In my opinion, Backer seems to overestimate the efficiency, or, at least, the use of Wal-Mart's monitoring system, but that issue is a little besides his main analysis. And he is aware of the risk of suppliers 'cheating' under the system, see ibid., p. 1781.

industrialized agriculture, the worst forms of child labour are often reported. Can, and should, such violations be attributed to listed multi-national companies? That must depend on the specific facts of each case. How production is organized is important. Farmers who make their own children work hard and not attend school is a sad situation, but it cannot be unethical for an international company to buy products from the farm.

Other modes of production require much more organization from the buyer's side. Some types of seed production offer examples where the agriculture company may provide to the growers or to middle men, plants, financing, fertilizers, pesticides and quality control, and require the right to buy the full production. At the same time, the work may be 'better suited' for children than adults because it can be an advantage to be short and have smaller hands. Elements like these may consti-tute grounds for attribution of responsibility for violations to the multi-national company. Overall control of the production is in the hands of the company.

Another example can be large plantations where people live and work on the plantation under quota regimes with production quotas impos-sible to fulfil for the formally employed or engaged male worker. He needs to bring his children with him for long hours, and the work may be dangerous for children involving use of chemicals or sharp tools. This could be an example of indirect child labour directly caused by the company's organization of the production. Proximity of the organiza-tion of the work to the company's own direct operations may even make this an example of violations within the company's own structure.

Attribution of responsibility for conduct on the supplier side to a listed multinational company raises difficult questions because one cannot follow traditional legal rules on corporate control. A more com-plex and more specific analysis has to be undertaken. The supplier–customer relationship is contractual. In functioning markets with many buyers and sellers and short-term relations, it is hard to say that a buyer is responsible for the conduct on the supplier side. Elements that could transform contractual relations into cases where responsibility would seem appropriate, relate to the market situation and to the type of con-tract with respect to duration as well as content. A basic precondition is knowledge on the part of the multinational company of the unethical conduct.

With respect to the market situation, the important factor is whether the buyer is dominant in the relevant market. Is the buyer a 'term setter' or 'rule maker'? Such dominance makes it possible for the buyer to impose his conditions. This condition is fulfilled in the case of Wal-Mart which is a huge corporation and dominant in many sub-sectors. In other smaller sectors, also much smaller companies could fulfil the condition. The type of market is decisive. If it is specialized, it can be difficult for suppliers to get out and then they are stuck with the dominant buyers.

Long-term contracts can also speak in favour of responsibility. When a long-term contract has been entered into it changes the relationship between supplier and buyer. Besides the formal binding contract with its obligations, investments by the supplier in the sector, or even customer-specific plant and machinery, may also tie the parties together.

Many contracts contain mechanisms that establish power on the customer side. These can have been imposed by a dominant buyer or follow from other characteristics of the sector or contract tradition. It could be formal competences on the buyer's side in respect of appointing personnel on the supplier side, accepting the work sites to be used or even instructing the performance of the work. The production could in fact be dependent on supply of specific factors of production from the buyer's side. Or it could be remuneration systems or quotas that lead to human rights violation because labourers' children need to be involved to fill the quotas. Other elements could relate to financing from the buyer of the supplier's investments, tying up the relationship even longer than the formal contract duration. And, as we have seen in the *Wal-Mart* case, it could be monitoring regimes with standards and inspections that are accepted by the supplier.

The different elements outlined above draw partly on market theory and traditional competition law analysis and partly on contract law analysis. Only combined analysis of actual economic and legal factors can establish a satisfactory test of corporate responsibility in the supply chain, as long as the ethical analysis is more advanced than just requiring multinational companies to shun away from goods or services where unethical conduct has been present in the production.

6.   Non-attribution to company of conduct by an employee in corruption cases?

A special question of attribution concerns the *relationship between company and employee*. All acts by a company are done by employees or persons in the company's governing bodies. Should all unethical acts by employees be attributed to the company?

In law, a company is liable for its employees' conduct in contract as well as in tort, with very few exceptions. From an ethical perspective, this may be different. Corruption gives a good example. Who is actually committing the corrupting acts? Is it only the employee who engages a well-paid agent to assist in getting a contract that will increase the turnover in his department? Increased turnover will probably benefit the company, and definitely demonstrate the employee's managerial skills. Should this also be attributed to the company itself?

Typically, a company accused of corruption will contend that the corrupting acts cannot be attributed to the company because they have been undertaken by employees on their own. No instruction or acceptance has been given by the 'company' as such. Most companies would point to corruption as a violation of company policy and state that company management has not had any knowledge of what has been going on. Pointing to company policy is in my view not a sufficient defence. But what if sensible company policies are in place and control mechanisms appear to have been working? Is it still fair to hold the company responsible? In countries with rules on corporate criminal liability, this question is parallel to the criminal law question of whether the company should be fined in corruption cases, together with a criminal finding against the persons actually committing the wrongdoings. Evidence is difficult in such cases since acts of corruption by their very nature are secretive because they are criminal offences. This makes it difficult to establish whether management actually knew about them. In principle it must be possible for a company to demonstrate that the governing bodies and management have done what was sufficient to try to avoid corruption, and thereby avoid attribution. The actual employee may have acted outside the control of the company. But if the company has profited from the corruption it should carry the burden of proof.

Is this problem particular for cases of corruption? That may be so because of their secretive and criminal nature. Other types of unethical conduct will typically be much better known within the company as well as externally. That is the case with respect to working conditions and other human rights issues, environmental damages and the situation for individuals in war and conflict, to mention the other specifically listed types of unethical conduct from the mandate of the Council on Ethics. All these types are recurring acts, generally for everybody to observe.

7.   Conclusion: Some reflections on responsibility and spheres of control

Description, analysis and discussion of the link between a listed multinational company and unethical conduct undertaken by others than the listed company itself have been the aims of this chapter. The examples discussed have shown that multinational enterprises are organized in complex corporate ownership structures and take part in contractually advanced supply arrangements. That raises different issues of attribution of corporate wrongdoings to a listed company, as demonstrated above. A common factor of all the analyses is the extent of *control* by the listed company over the entity where the unethical acts or omissions take place as a requirement for ethical responsibility. With respect to corporate ownership structures as discussed in section 3, use of a control concept is relatively straightforward and it is much applied in the legal and economic literature. In joint ventures, the concept is less used, but the analysis in section 4 demonstrates, in my opinion, that it is a useful tool here, too. The same applies to the analysis of supply chains in section 5. It does not seem appropriate to attribute unethical conduct in the supply chain to a listed company on the customer side unless the company exerts some kind of control over the supplier. Even with respect to the special issue of attribution of an employee's wrongdoings to his employer company, it can be seen as a question of company control. Generally, the analyses show that a useful tool when assessing corporate ethical responsibility is the concept of *companies' sphere of control*. I will return to this shortly.

The parallel discussion of ATCA cases on corporate economic liability for human rights violations shows that a control requirement is not sufficient to establish liability. A control requirement is not sufficient because of the respect for corporate structures with limited liability under the law. Limited liability has been a basic defining feature of company law over more than a century. It is applied in 'virtually all economically important jurisdictions'.[46] The principle of limited liability, also within corporate structures, is central to the development of modern capitalism, but the precise extension of the application of the principle may be discussed further. That is not the task here.

Discussing in parallel recommendations from the Council on Ethics and cases under ATCA gives a basis for a better understanding of both discourses. The basic difference between investor disinvestment due to unethical conduct like human rights violations and suits against companies based on the same types of conduct is the perspective from which the analysis has to be undertaken. Suits against companies come from victims of violations done by subsidiaries, taking place typically in a

---

[46] See Kraakman et al., *The Anatomy of Corporate Law*, p. 5, stating that limited liability is one of the five 'core structural characteristics' of the business corporation. The other four are legal personality, transferable shares, centralized management under a board structure, and 'shared ownership by contributors of capital'.

country where courts do not function well. To succeed in a suit the victims have to climb up the corporate ladder to get to the parent company with capital and presence in a jurisdiction where they can be sued.

Analysis of whether disinvestment by an investor should be made is undertaken from the opposite perspective. The investor normally holds shares in the ultimate parent company. His identification is with the company and the company group itself, and he finances the activities.

Difference in perspective does not always result in different analyses. An analysis of *ethical responsibility* concerning the link between the listed multinational company and the unethical conduct could be very similar from both perspectives. The important elements from the victim's as well as from the investor's perspective would be: who controls the activity (including who initiated it) and who profits from it? Since the activities are within the corporate sphere, all these ethical questions involve legal issues. The right to control company matters in the sense of initiating and stopping or directing activities on the parent company level itself as well as on lower levels, is a question of company law. The same applies, at least partly, to the right of profiting. This means that the victims would have a legitimate 'right' to *blame* the controlling parent company for violations that follow from the company group's activities. But blameworthiness does not give a cause of action under the law.

An analysis of *legal responsibility* – liability – is different. If the investor suffers loss caused by the parent company he can sue the company in his capacity as investor. His rights belong on that level. If the victims of human rights violations suffer losses through company group activities undertaken formally by a subsidiary, they are, at least as a starting point, bound to relate to – to sue – the company which directly was complicit in the violations. Moreover, company law in all countries does, as we have seen, respect the rules on limited liability of a company. Under the law, it is difficult to get through to the one that from an ethical point of view is to blame.

The characteristic features of the two different tasks, ethical assessment from an investor perspective and legal assessment from a victim's perspective, are that the first is top-down and forward-looking, while the other is bottom-up and backwards-looking.[47]

If we consider the overall discussion on corporate social responsibility, a much discussed concept has been the companies' 'sphere of influence'. Not much consensus has been reached on the more precise

---

[47] To be forward-looking is a requirement of the Guidelines for the Norwegian Government Pension Fund.

content of the concept.[48] Its most prominent use is in the preamble to the United Nations' Global Compact principles, where it is stated: 'The Global Compact asks companies to embrace, support and enact, *within their sphere of influence*, a set of core values in the areas of human rights, labour standards, the environment and anti-corruption.'[49] The Global Compact principles are also one of the international basic documents for the Ethical Guidelines of the Norwegian Government Pension Fund – Global.[50] Due to the uncertainty, one of the six tasks listed in the mandate for the Special Representative of the UN Secretary-General, John Ruggie, is the clarification of the concept, alongside that of the concept of 'complicity'.[51]

I have concluded above that a concept of companies' *sphere of control* is useful when assessing companies' ethical responsibility. It establishes a helpful general criterion for attribution of responsibility. In my opinion, the concept of sphere of influence is not workable in this context. The idea of a corporate sphere is apt and points in the right direction, but the notion of influence is too vague. It could cover all types of possible impact. John Ruggie in his interim report also commented negatively on the use of the 'sphere of influence' concept as a basis for binding obligations.[52] In the context of the preamble of the Global Compact, it functions well because what the preamble does is only set out some types of activities that companies shall do. They are asked 'to embrace, support and enact' a set of core values within the sphere. As long as positive action is the only requirement, it is less important that it is impossible to delineate the relevant area. In one sense, the further the good effect of the companies' action reaches the better. I will suggest that to establish a workable concept for the analysis of attribution, the concept should be the *company's sphere of control*. This can be generalized. As long as one wants to assess consequences of unethical conduct, the more precise concept of control should be applied.

---

[48] See Urs Gasser, Chapter 6 below.   [49] Emphasis added.

[50] See Norwegian Government White Paper, NOU 2003:22, pp. 19–20. Through reference to the Global Compact the concept has even become part of the Ethical Guidelines of the Fund. It is one of the two sets of norms that form the basis for the exercise of ownership rights, which is undertaken by the Central Bank of Norway, see para. 3.1 of the Ethical Guidelines 2004 (Appendix 2 below).

[51] John Ruggie, 'Interim Report of the Special Representative of the Secretary-General on the Issue of Human Rights and Transnational Corporations and Other Business Enterprises', UN Human Rights Council, UN Doc. E/CN.4/2006/97 (22 February 2006), para. 1.

[52] Ibid., para. 67, commenting on the use of the concept in the draft 'Norms on the responsibilities of transnational corporations and other business enterprises with regard to human rights', see paras. 56–69.

Even if the concept of control also can be, and has been, given different interpretations, it is a concept known from company and contract law as well as competition law.[53] That demonstrates that it is possible to apply in normative analysis. Moreover, it is linked to the exercise of corporate power which is at the core of what we are discussing. In my opinion, the discussions above have demonstrated that a control concept is an appropriate tool in the analysis both of corporate and contractual structures.

---

[53] In company law, control is a widely used concept that does not need references. In contract law, a well-known example is Article 79 of the Vienna Convention on the sale of goods which provides that a party is not liable for a failure to perform a contract if the failure is 'due to an impediment *beyond his control*'. See more generally on theories of spheres of control in contract, Friedemann Nassauer, *'Sphärentheorien' zu Regelungen der Gefahrtragungshaftung in verträglichen Schuldverhältnissen* (Marburg: Elwert, 1978).

6   Responsibility for human rights violations, acts or omissions, within the 'sphere of influence' of companies

Urs Gasser in collaboration with
Silke Müller, LL.M. and James Thurman

1.   Introduction

This chapter approaches the question of corporate social responsibility for acts and omissions of business entities outside the ownership sphere but possibly within the 'sphere of influence' from a *law and regulation* perspective.[1] Here, the term 'regulation' is used in the broad sense of the New Chicago School and includes soft law-oriented forms of regulation such as internal corporate policies, best practice principles and purely aspirational guidelines. Within this thematic context, the chapter addresses four issues. The first section provides a sketch of the genesis of the 'sphere of influence' concept, provides in a nutshell a summary of the current state of the debate regarding its concretization and specification, and comments on its legal status and relevance under current law. The second section briefly identifies – against the backdrop of the current debate – some of the characteristics that make it particularly challenging to define the notion of 'sphere of influence'. The third section of the paper then outlines two basic strategies to overcome the definitional problem: a 'top-down' approach where the criteria to decide whether or not an act or omission is within a company's sphere of influence is decided authoritatively – focusing on third-party liability as the furthest reaches of indirect liability; and a 'bottom-up' approach

---

[1] Please note that this paper was originally researched and written in 2007. In recent years, the concept of 'sphere of influence' has been taken up in a number of international venues, including via the work of the Special Representative for the Secretary-General on Human Rights and Business, the ISO, the GC and elsewhere. We have partially adapted the text to reflect these developments. The section focuses on the SRSG's mandate and recent findings has been updated to reflect the current state of play; the case law analysis and 'bottom up' research remains mostly untouched. The author thanks Caroline Nolan and Seth Flaxman for their advice and help on the update.

that looks at companies' human rights policies in order to explore their actual reach and potential for taking effective measures. The fourth and final section offers some reflections on the question of the virtue of the 'sphere of influence' concept – despite its relative vagueness.

2.   What is the legal status of the 'sphere of influence' concept?

2.1   *Genesis of the 'sphere of influence' concept*

The 'sphere of influence' concept evolved in the political environment. It was introduced into the corporate social responsibility discourse by the UN Global Compact Nine Principles in July 2000[2] and gained importance through the adoption of the 'Norms on the responsibilities of transnational corporations and other business enterprises with regard to human rights' on 13 August 2003 by the United Nations Sub-Commission on the Promotion and Protection of Human Rights.

Both sources originate from a time period in late 1999 and early 2000. The UN Global Compact with its ten principles was instigated by former Secretary-General Kofi Annan in an address to the World Economic Forum on 31 January 1999. It was intended as a 'learning forum'[3] for corporate social responsibility of multinational corporations. Harvard Professor John Ruggie described it as a 'voluntary initiative intended to induce corporate change by identifying and promoting good practices'.[4] It started its operational phase on 26 July 2000, when several dozen business leaders joined in an international initiative that brought companies together with UN agencies, civil society and other stakeholders to advance universal social and environmental principles. The UN Global Compact principles use the term 'sphere of influence' in its preamble: 'The Global Compact asks companies to embrace, support and enact, within their sphere of influence, a set of core values in the areas of human rights, labour standards, the environment, and anti-corruption.'

---

[2] John Ruggie, 'Interim Report of the Special Representative of the Secretary-General on the Issue of Human Rights and Transnational Corporations and Other Business Enterprises' (Interim Report 2006), UN Doc. E/CN.4/2006/97 (UN Human Rights Council, 22 February 2006), para. 40. A tenth principle concerning corruption was added later. See UN Global Compact Office, 'Transparency and Anti-Corruption: Results of the Consultation Process on the Introduction of a Principle against Corruption'; www.unglobalcompact.org/docs/issues_doc/7.7/result_consultation.doc.
[3] John Ruggie, 'The Theory and Practice of Learning Networks', *Journal of Corporate Citizenship*, 5 (2002), p. 32.
[4] Ibid., p. 35.

Roughly during the same time a process started that later resulted in the adoption of 'The Norms on the responsibilities of transnational corporations and other business enterprises with regard to human rights' ('The Norms'). On 3 August 1999 the former Sub-Commission on Prevention of Discrimination and Protection of Minorities[5] established a Sessional Working Group on the Working Methods and Activities of Transnational Corporations consisting of five members, which compiled a draft document that also made reference to the term 'sphere of influence'.[6] David Weissbrodt, a distinguished international human rights law scholar, was drawing upon this term in his May 2000 Working Paper 'Draft Human Rights Code for Companies' from the Global Compact Principles when he described the general obligations in a draft of section 6 for 'The Norms':

While Governments have the principal responsibility to respect, ensure respect for and promote internationally recognized human rights, companies shall also respect, ensure respect for and promote international human rights within their respective spheres of activity and influence.[7]

Representatives of business, unions, non-governmental organizations (NGOs), the scholarly community and other interested persons were involved in reshaping the document through both public hearings and meetings that took place between the years 2000 and 2003[8] until the Norms were finally adopted on 13 August 2003 by the United Nations Sub-Commission on the Promotion and Protection of Human Rights.

The adoption of the Norms was generally considered to be a landmark step since they represent the shift that is at the core of this book, i.e., the shift towards holding private actors accountable for human rights abuses instead of strengthening human rights only against governmental violations.[9] However, the Norms induced several contentious issues, for instance regarding the binding nature of the act itself,[10] or the scope

---

[5] Sub-Commission Decision 1999/101, Sub-Commission on the Promotion and Protection of Human Rights, E/CN.4/SUB.2/DEC/1999/101.

[6] Karsten Nowrot, 'The 2006 Interim Report of the UN Special Representative on Human Rights and Transnational Corporations: Breakthrough or Further Polarization?', *TELC Policy Papers on Transnational Economic Law*, 20 (2006).

[7] David Weissbrodt, 'Business and Human Rights', *University of Cincinnati Law Review*, 74 (2005), p. 22.

[8] Ibid., p. 67.

[9] David Weissbrodt and Maria Kruger, 'Norms on the Responsibilities of Transnational Corporations and Other Business Enterprises with Regard to Human Rights', *American Journal of International Law*, 91 (2003), p. 901.

[10] Corporate Europe Observatory (CEO), 'Shell Leads International Business Campaign Against UN Human Rights Norms', *CEO Info Brief* (March 2004), www.corporateeurope.org/norms.html.

of the responsibilities described by the 'sphere of influence' concept[11] –
a term neither defined in the text of the Norms nor the Commentary.

Against this backdrop, Professor John Ruggie was appointed Special
Representative of the Secretary-General (SRSG) on the issue of human
rights and transnational corporations and other business enterprises.
His mandate, among other things, included research into the concept
of 'sphere of influence' in order to clarify the implications for business
and commercial activities in general.[12] To date, this research has not
been finalized, and the 'sphere of influence' concept is still very much
up for discussion.

2.2   Interpretations of the 'sphere of influence' concept

Against the backdrop of this brief history, the next paragraphs seek to
investigate how the 'sphere of influence' concept has been interpreted
by UN representatives, leading international human rights scholars
and the International Organization of Standardization (ISO). Before
doing so, let us start with the concept's basic functions first – a topic
we will revisit later in this article. In a 2005 report by the UN High
Commissioner, the following functions of the 'sphere of influence' concept were outlined:

The notion of 'sphere of influence' could be useful in clarifying the extent to
which business entities should 'support' human rights and 'make sure they
are not complicit in human rights abuses' by setting limits on responsibilities
according to a business entity's power to act. Importantly, 'sphere of influence' could help clarify the boundaries of responsibilities of business entities in
relation to other entities in the supply chain such as subsidiaries, agents, suppliers and buyers by guiding an assessment of the degree of influence that one
company exerts over a partner in its contractual relationship – and therefore
the extent to which it is responsible for the acts or omissions or a subsidiary
or a partner down the supply chain. At the same time, 'sphere of influence'
should help draw the boundaries between the responsibilities of business and
the obligations on States so that business entities do not take on the policing
role of Government. Finally, the notion of 'sphere of influence' could ensure
that smaller business entities are not forced to undertake over-burdensome
human rights responsibilities, but only responsibilities towards people within
their limited sphere of influence.[13]

---

[11] 'Report of the United Nations High Commissioner on Human Rights on the
Responsibilities of Transnational Corporations and Related Business Enterprises
with Regard to Human Rights', UN Doc. E/CN.4/2005/91 (OHCHR, 15 February
2005), para. 52e.
[12] 'Resolution 2005/69 of Economic and Social Council' (UN Commission on Human
Rights, 15 April 2005), UN Doc. E/CN.4/2005/L.87 (appointment of John Ruggie).
[13] OHCHR Report 2005, para. 38.

As a starting point for future research, the United Nations High Commissioner on Human Rights provided a brief and tentative sketch of the meaning of the concept:

[It] tends to include the individuals to whom it has a certain political, contractual, economic or geographic proximity. Every business entity, whatever its size, will have a sphere of influence; the larger it is, the larger the sphere of influence is likely to be.[14]

This description of the concept's function and meaning links back to the definitional questions. In this regard, the two reports of the Special Representative of the Secretary-General (SRSG) on the issue of human rights and transnational corporations and other business enterprises deserve particular attention. In the Interim Report of February 2006, Professor Ruggie characterized 'sphere of influence' as a non-legal concept,[15] but wasn't in the position at that time to give much guidance regarding the definition of the term. In Professor Ruggie's second – and what was originally intended to be the final – report of February 2007, he concluded that further work is necessary to test the 'sphere of influence' concept as a policy tool.[16] According to the report, the SRSG and his team have thus far focused on producing a solid and objective evidentiary foundation, while additional time is needed to further explore the term in detail. The rest of the 2007 report concentrates on mapping the current international standards and practices regarding business and human rights.[17] In this context the SRSG notes that surveys have been conducted that, *inter alia*, reflect how corporations rank their own 'sphere of influence':

The survey asked the FG500 firms to rank order the stakeholders their human rights policies or practices encompass – in effect, to indicate the companies' conception of their 'sphere of influence.' Employees were ranked highest (99 percent); suppliers and others in their value chain next (92.5 percent); then the communities in which companies operate (71 percent); followed by countries of operation (63 percent). The only significant variations are that the extractive sector ranks communities ahead of suppliers, while US and Japanese firms place communities and countries of operations far lower than European companies.[18]

In the 2008 Report, Professor Ruggie stated that the sphere of influence represents 'a useful metaphor for companies in thinking about their

---

[14] Ibid., para. 37.   [15] Ruggie, Interim Report 2006, para. 67.

[16] John Ruggie, 'Business and Human Rights: Mapping International Standards of Responsibility and Accountability for Corporate Acts. Report of the Special Representative of the Secretary-General (SRSG) on the Issue of Human Rights and Transnational Corporations and Other Business Enterprises' (Report 2007), UN Doc. A/HRC/4/035 (UNHRC, 9 February 2007), para. 9.

[17] Ibid., para. 5.   [18] Ibid., para. 68.

human rights impacts beyond the workplace and in identifying opportunities to support human rights ...'[19] Yet while seeming to suggest that the concept was ill-suited for providing concrete guidance with respect to the scope of corporate responsibility.[20]

In fact, over the past two years since this article was written, Professor Ruggie has concluded that the Norms are 'a deeply flawed formula' and that he 'would not base [his] mandate's work on it', stating that 'the Norms sought to impose on companies, directly under international law, essentially the same range of human rights duties that States have adoped for themselves – to respect, protect, promote, and fulfill human rights. The two sets of duties were separated only by the slippery distinction between States as primary and corporations as secondary duty bearers, and by the elastic concept of corporate spheres of influence, within which companies were said to have those duties.'[21] Predictably, the SRSG 2010 Report takes the final step in moving away from the sphere of influence concept, eliminating even a single reference to it.

In the meantime, several international human rights scholars and experts have also given their tentative interpretations of the 'sphere of influence' concept. Nicholas Howen of the International Commission of Jurists, for instance, commented on the term in 2005 during an international business and human rights seminar.[22] He recommends that companies adhering to the Norms take a rather precautious approach and 'look for warning signs'. Further, he suggests a rather broad interpretation of the concept outside the zone of legal enforceability:

> The closer you are to victims, the more you have a responsibility to watch out for the impact of your actions. The closer you are to those who commit the violations, the greater the danger. And the more systematic the nature and scale of the violations, the more dangerous they are .... Do not be limited by the law. The law is a vital test of accountability and will give clarity to what is acceptable and unacceptable behaviour. But we're all forced to swim in a much

---

[19] John Ruggie, 'Promotion and Protection of all Human Rights, Civil, Political, Economic, Social and Cultural Rights including the Right to Development. Protect, Respect and Remedy: A Framework for Business and Human Rights – Report of the Special Representative of the Secretary-General on the Issue of Human Rights and Transnational Corporations and Other Business Enterprises', UN Doc. A/HRC/8/5 (UNHRC, 7 April 2008), para. 67.

[20] Ibid., paras. 67–72.

[21] Keynote Address by SRSG John Ruggie, 'Engaging Business: Addressing Respect for Human Rights' was sponsored by the US Council for International Business, US Chamber of Commerce and International Organization of Employers. Hosted by The Coca-Cola Company in Atlanta on 25 February 2010.

[22] The 2005 Business and Human Rights Seminar on the topic 'Exploring Responsibility and Complicity' was held under the auspices of Mary Robinson, who held the honorary chair. It took place in London on 8 December 2005.

rougher and more profound sea of morality and public policy, and that's how it should be.[23]

Margaret Jungk of the Danish Institute for Human Rights, in contrast, formulates a rather restrictive interpretation of possible positive responsibilities of business in relation to human rights when implicitly addressing how to possibly fill in the concept of 'sphere of influence'.[24]

First, ... businesses should act like a government in relation to the workers who are, in effect, their 'citizens', and promote, protect and secure their rights.

Second, businesses have a duty to ensure that their products are not used in the violation of human rights. This comprises responsibility to take reasonable measures to prevent both the intentional misuse, and the unintentional wrongful use of the product .... [However,] this responsibility must be limited. It is suggested that responsibility should only extend to what a business could legitimately be expected to foresee as a potential wrongful use or misuse of its products, to avoid the imposition of unrealistic responsibilities. Third, a business should assume positive responsibilities in relation to anyone residing on its land. Fourth, companies should incur positive duties when they *de facto* replace the government.[25]

The 'sphere of influence' concept is also the foundation for the ISO 26000's definition of social responsibility.[26] The ISO offers its own broad interpretation, articulating that an organization's 'sphere of influence' goes beyond its activities and the activities of those with whom it does business, arguing that organizations are also responsible for taking action in support of human rights when feasible:

In addition to being responsible for its own activities, there are situations where an organization has the ability to influence the decisions or behaviour of those with whom it has a relationship (see 5.2.3). Influence will depend on a number of factors, including physical proximity, scope, length and strength of the relationship. In promoting social responsibility, there will be situations where an organization's ability to influence others will be accompanied by a responsibility to exercise this influence. An organization derives influence from sources such as: ownership and governance – this includes the nature and extent of ownership or representation, if any, on the governing body of the associated organization; economic relationship – this includes influence based on the level of economic dependency involved: the greater the interest or dependency, the greater the influence; legal/political authority – this is based, for example, on provisions in legally binding contracts or the existence

[23] Nicholas Howen, quoted in Matt Shin (ed.), 'The 2005 Business & Human Rights Seminar Report: Exploring Responsibilities and Complicity' (London, 8 December 2005), p. 15.

[24] Margaret Jungk, 'Defining the Scope of Business Responsibility Abroad', *Human Rights & Business Project* (Danish Centre for Human Rights, 2005), p. 8.

[25] Ibid., 8ff.   [26] ISO/DIS 26000, clause 5.2.3.

of a legal mandate granting the organization the ability to enforce certain behaviours on others; and public opinion – this includes the ability of the organization to influence public opinion, and the impact of public opinion on those it is trying to influence.[27]

Stepan Wood of Osgoode Hall Law School provides a robust defence of ISO 26000, arguing that the ISO is right to assert that companies should be held responsible for human rights abuses that they can control and also for abuses committed by those that they can influence.[28]

Acting responsibly within an organization's own workplace is the least of the problems facing social responsibility (not that it is a small problem). The real challenge of social responsibility lies in an organization's relationships with contractors, suppliers, customers, local communities and end users. Organizations often have substantial influence over the decisions and actions of these actors ... the problem of human rights abuses cannot be solved by allowing organizations simply to wash their hands of abuses perpetrated by actors with whom they have a significant relationship and over whom they have a significant degree of influence. Only by affirming that a firm's responsibility varies with its ability to influence decisions and actions will social responsibility standards galvanize the sort of changes that are needed to improve respect for and realization of human rights.[29]

In sum, the exact meaning of the 'sphere of influence' concept remains uncertain at this point in time. Neither the materials, the SRSG, nor leading international law scholars offer a definition or clear-cut test of what acts or omissions are within the 'sphere of influence' of a company.

2.3   Case law analysis

In order to identify possible direct or indirect references to the 'sphere of influence' concept in courts, the team at the Research Center for Information Law at the University of St. Gallen has conducted a rather extensive case law review as of 2007. The search was conducted mainly within two areas: one area being what can be referred to as 'international law' and the other focusing on jurisprudence from the US, Switzerland and Germany as national jurisdictions with which the author of this chapter is most familiar.

---

[27] Ibid., clause 7.3.2.
[28] Stepan Wood, 'In Defense of the Sphere of Influence: Why the WGSR should not follow Professor Ruggie's Advice on Defining the Scope of Corporate Social Responsibility', submitted to the Working Group on Social Responsibility (WGSR) of the International Organization for Standardization (ISO) (Copenhagen, 17–21 May 2010), p. 5.
[29] Ibid., pp. 5ff.

With regard to *international case law*, several electronic sources have been researched. A search in the international case law collections by the Business & Human Rights Resources Centre,[30] the Danish Institute for Human Rights[31] and the University of Minnesota Human Rights Library,[32] for instance, yielded no results in response to the search terms 'sphere of influence', 'sphere of influence' AND corporate AND 'human rights', or 'transnational corporations' AND 'human rights'. Similarly, searches in the international case law catalogues of other law databases such as Westlaw for cases with reference to and application mainly in international law did not produce any explicit references to the 'sphere of influence' concept within the human rights context.[33] Finally, recent literature on transnational corporations (TNCs) and human rights was scanned for references to case law featuring the term 'sphere of influence'. This effort also met with no success.

With respect to *national* case law, roughly the same procedure was applied: resource collections were consulted and legal databases were tested for case law on 'sphere of influence'. Again, the search terms described above were run. Under Swiss Law and German Law, no relevant case law has been identified. Searches of US case law turned up few relevant results. Yet, there is an emerging body of case law under the Alien Tort Claims Act which likely represents the broadest attempts to apply liability to transnational corporations for company-related activities transpiring abroad.[34] But the incidents that have been

---

[30] Business & Human Rights Resources Centre; www.business-humanrights.org.

[31] Danish Institute for Human Rights; www.humanrights.dk/.

[32] University of Minnesota Human Rights Library online; www1.umn.edu/humanrts/.

[33] Searches included the search terms 'sphere of influence' at Westlaw and Beckonline, as well as Swisslex.

[34] For examples of cases filed, see *Aguinda* v. *Texaco, Inc.*, 303 F.3d 470 (2d Cir. 2002); *Mujica* v. *Occidental Petroleum*, No. 03–2860, 2005 WL 1962635 (C.D. Cal. April 24 2005); *Bowoto* v. *Chevron Texaco Corp.*, 312 F. Supp. 2d 1229 (N.D. Cal. 2004); *Presbyterian Church of Sudan* v. *Talisman Energy, Inc.*, 244 F. Supp. 2d 289 (S.D.N.Y. 2003); *Wiwa* v. *Royal Dutch Petroleum Co.*, No. 96 Civ. 8386, 2002 WL 319887 (S.D.N.Y. 28 February 2002); *Doe* v. *Exxon Mobil Corp.*, No. 01-CV-1357 (D.D.C. 19 June 2001) (Westlaw, DOCK-ALL); *Doe* v. *Unocal Corp.*, 110 F. Supp. 2d 1294 (C.D. Cal. 2000), aff'd in part, rev'd in part, 395 F.3d 932 (9th Cir. 2002), vacated and reh'g en banc, 403 F.3d 708 (9th Cir. 2005), *Flores* v. *S. Peru Copper Corp.*, 414 F.3d 233 (2d Cir. 2003); *Beanal* v. *Freeport-McMoran, Inc.*, 197 F.3d 161 (5th Cir. 1999); *Maugein* v. *Newmont Mining Corp.*, 298 F. Supp. 2d 1124 (D. Colo. 2004); *Sarei* v. *Rio Tinto*, 221 F. Supp. 2d 1116 (C.D. Cal. 2002), *Bano* v. *Union Carbide Corp.*, 273 F.3d 120 (2d Cir. 2001); *Bigio* v. *Coca-Cola Co.*, 239 F.3d 440 (2d Cir. 2000); *Villeda Aldana* v. *Fresh Del Monte Produce, Inc.*, 305 F. Supp. 2d 1285 (S.D. Fla. 2003), aff'd in part, vacated in part, 416 F.3d 1242 (11th Cir. 2005); *Sinaltrainal* v. *Coca-Cola Co.*, 256 F. Supp. 2d 1345 (S.D. Fla. 2003); *Doe* v. *The Gap, Inc.*, No. 01-CV-0031, 2001 WL 1842389 (D.N. Mar. I. 26 November 2001); *Arias* v. *DynCorp*, No. 01-CV-01908 (D.D.C. 11 September 2001) (Westlaw, DOCK-ALL), *Abdullahi* v. *Pfizer, Inc.*, No. 01-CV-8118, 2002 WL 31082956 (S.D.N.Y., 17 September 2002), vacated in part,

subject to US adjudication[35] do not generally raise the question whether an act should have been prevented based on the 'sphere of influence' concept because in most cases, US corporations were alleged to have directly cooperated with army or paramilitary units in unlawful acts. For instance, in the Drummond Case 'the families of three deceased Colombian labour leaders filed suit against Drummond Company, Inc. and its wholly-owned subsidiary Drummond Ltd. in the US Federal court. The plaintiffs alleged that Drummond hired Colombian paramilitaries to kill and torture the three labour leaders in 2001. In March 2007, the court ruled that the case against Drummond Ltd. (the subsidiary) would go to trial, but dismissed the case against Drummond Company (the parent company). In June of 2007, the district court judge dismissed the wrongful death claims but allowed the plaintiffs' war crimes allegations under the ATCA (summary execution) to stand. The trial was held in July 2007. The jury acquitted Drummond finding that the company was not liable for the deaths of the three murdered labour leaders.[36] Other cases are: *Wiwa* v. *Royal Dutch Petroleum Co.* (2000) (discussing the alleged complicity in imprisonment, torture and murder of political activists in Nigeria) or *Bowoto* v. *Chevron Texaco Corp.* (2004) (alleging complicity in the deaths of protesters at the Chevron Parabe Oil Platform).

The outcome of our case law research correlates with two other analyses of case law on 'sphere of influence'. In August 2006, Arthur Robinson Allens published a 'Brief on Corporations and Human Rights in the Asia-Pacific Region' prepared for the SRSG. It reported to have not been able to identify case law within the jurisdictions of Australia, India, Indonesia, Myanmar, New Zealand and Papua New Guinea that dealt with the 'sphere of influence' concept.[37] Similarly, in his Interim Report of February 2006, the SRSG declares to have found no case law on 'sphere of influence'.[38] The 2007 Report of the SRSG likewise cites no case law on 'sphere of influence'.[39]

---

77 F. App'x 48 (2d Cir. 2003), *Deutsch* v. *Turner Corp.*, 317 F.3d 1005 (9th Cir. 2003); *Iwanowa* v. *Ford Motor Co.*, 67 F. Supp. 2d 424 (D.N.J. 1999).

[35] Based on the collection of case law by the Business & Human Rights Centre; www.business-humanrights.org/Categories/Lawlawsuits.

[36] See Business & Human Rights Resources Centre; www.business-humanrights.org/Categories/Lawlawsuits/Lawsuitsregulatoryaction/LawsuitsSelectedcases/DrummondlawsuitreColombia.

[37] Arthur Robinson Allens, 'Brief on Corporations and Human Rights in the Asia-Pacific Region', prepared for Prof. John Ruggie UN SRSG for Business and Human Rights (2006), p. 92; www.reports-and-materials.org/Legal-brief-on-Asia-Pacific-for-Ruggie-Aug-2006.pdf.

[38] Ruggie, Interim Report 2006, para. 67.   [39] Ruggie, Report 2007, para. 34.

2.4   Conclusion

The exact status of the 'sphere of influence' concept and its legal relevance are the subject of an ongoing (and controversial) debate among stakeholders. A legal perspective suggests that the concept – at least at this point in time – is a *non*-legal or potentially what we might call a *pre*-legal ('vorrechtliches') concept. The 'sphere of influence' concept was introduced into the corporate social responsibility discourse by the UN Global Compact and is now most prominently mentioned in ISO 26000, which were developed outside the legal system and evolved in the political environment. The fact that neither national nor international courts to date seem to have adjudicated on the concept within the corporate responsibility context (as extensive case law searches suggest) also speaks for its non-legal character – although, of course, the notion of 'influence' as such plays an important role in many areas of law (including corporate liability law). Similarly, experts have not been able to find definitions or explicit references to the concept in national legislation (with the exception of one reference in Indonesian environmental law).

However, the qualification of the 'sphere of influence' concept as non-legal does not mean that it is entirely irrelevant from a legal perspective. Even without having a clear legal meaning or being suited to serve as a basis for establishing binding obligations, the notion of 'sphere of influence' is itself likely to influence, to some degree or another, the reasoning of law-/policy-makers and courts alike. Cases such as *Doe* v. *Unocal* (2002) on corporate complicity may serve as early examples in that respect. In addition, a possible future incorporation of the 'sphere of influence' concept in, for instance, international treaty law or at the level of national legislation would apparently change the current qualification.

3.   What makes it so difficult to define the notion of 'sphere of influence'?

The 'sphere of influence' concept is not defined by international human rights standards. In fact, a consensus about the definition has yet to be reached. Although the use of vague terminology is by no means new or foreign to law in general and international law in particular, some commentators have expressed frustration with the continued lack of concrete meaning assigned to key terms in documents such as the UN Norms or Global Compact. Yet, the slow emergence of substantive discussion of the 'sphere of influence' concept may also be linked to the supposition that the definition of each company's 'sphere of influence' depends on a *highly fact-specific evaluation* of that company's operations. As the OHCHR Briefing Paper states, each company's 'sphere of influence' is in part a function of its political, contractual, economic and geographical proximity to individuals. It also follows that larger companies will generally have a larger 'sphere of influence', since they will share proximity with a larger number of individuals.[40] Additional factors that may impact on the determination of a particular company's 'sphere of influence' are the exact nature of the company's operations, the industry or industries it engages in, as well as its corporate structure. In this way, there is not only a quantitative aspect to a company's 'sphere of influence' that may be measured in miles or numbers of individuals, but also a qualitative aspect.

It may be useful to take a look at a *case study* to illustrate how subtle the factual differences with potential (legal and ethical) significance might be for the question of a business's 'sphere of influence'.

For example, in 2006 and 2007, Cisco, Yahoo!, Microsoft and Google were all implicated with alleged complicity in human rights violations perpetrated by the Chinese government.[41] While the challenges faced by at least three out of the four US corporations are similar – Yahoo!, Microsoft and Google alike have to deal with issues of individual security and government control of internet content in China – and although the situation with regard to the 'sphere of influence' might appear to be comparable at first glance, the analysis gets much more complicated if one takes a closer look at some of the elements mentioned before, including, for instance, the different *ownership structures* of the three internet service companies – as reported in news media – with regard to their Chinese business operations:[42]

- Yahoo!, for instance, formed a long-term strategic partnership in China with Alibaba.com, a Chinese company that owns the Yahoo! China business. According to statements by Yahoo! executives, Yahoo! held one of the four Alibaba.com board seats, but did not have day-to-day control over Alibaba's Yahoo! China division.[43]

---

40 Allens, 'Brief on Corporations and Human Rights', p. 4.
41 See, e.g., 'The Internet in China: A Tool for Freedom or Suppression?', Joint Hearing Before the Subcommittee on Africa, Global Human Rights and International Operations, & the Subcommittee on Asia and the Pacific (House Committee on International Relations, 15 February 2006); www.foreignaffairs.house.gov/archives/109/26075.pdf.
42 Note that this section was drafted based on the situation at the time of writing the article and has not been updated; the differences listed below are still illustrative, however. See also footnote 1 above.
43 Jeffrey MacDonald, 'Congress's Dilemma: When Yahoo in China's not Yahoo', *Christian Science Monitor* (14 February 2006); www.csmonitor.com/2006/0214/p01s04-usfp.html.

- Microsoft's China portal has been operated by a local entity, Shanghai Alliance Investment Ltd (SAIL), through a joint venture agreement. SAIL has reportedly been operated by the Chinese government, while the servers which deliver Microsoft's Chinese services apparently have not resided in China, but rather in the United States.[44]
- As for Google, it evidently had operated its 'google.cn' business under a licence owned by a local company, Ganji.com.[45] The precise nature of the presumably merely contractual relationship between the two entities, however, had not been made public.

What are the consequences of these rather small, but in our context important differences with regard to the 'sphere of influence' analysis? Naturally, we can only speculate about it at this point, but a few questions might illustrate some of the issues up for discussion.

- To what extent, for instance, did the corporate separateness between Yahoo! and Alibaba.com, which operates Yahoo!'s China businesses, limit Yahoo!'s 'sphere of influence' compared to other instances where Yahoo! had direct control over a subsidiary located elsewhere? What does it mean for the 'sphere of influence' analysis that Yahoo! held one seat out of four on the board of the local partner?
- How was Microsoft's sphere of influence affected if Reuters' reports were correct and the Chinese government in fact operated Microsoft's joint venture partner, Shanghai Alliance Investment Ltd?
- To what extent was Google's 'sphere of influence' vis-à-vis the Chinese government larger or smaller given its model of a relatively loose contractual relationship with a local partner – as compared to alternative approaches taken by its competitors?

All of these factors, among many others, weigh into the determination of each company's 'sphere of influence'. Therefore, the meaning of 'sphere of influence' for each company must be analysed in detail and on a *case by case basis* with a holistic view of the company, its partnerships and relationships with other entities and governmental agencies,

---

[44] David Temple, 'China's Search Engine Landscape', Multilingual Search (6 January 2006); www.multilingual-search.com/china-search-engine-landscape-article/06/01/2006, and Committee on International Relations House of Representatives, 'The Internet in China: A Tool for Freedom or Suppression?' (US House Committee on International Relations, Serial No. 109–157, 15 February 2006), p. 169; http://commdocs.house.gov/committees/intlrel/hfa26075.000/hfa26075_0f.htm.

[45] Testimony of Michael Callahan, in 'The Internet in China', p. 117; and Danny Sullivan, 'Google License To Operate In China Questioned; Will Disclosure Have To Go?' (21 February 2006); http://blog.searchenginewatch.com/060221–091709.

its legal structure and organization as well as its physical property and operations.

It is this highly fact-specific nature of the 'sphere of influence' concept that makes it so challenging to define in general terms and on an abstract level. This conclusion leads to the next question: What are possible approaches to the definitional problem given the outlined characteristics of the 'sphere of influence' concept?

4.   Approaches to the definitional problem

4.1   *Top-down approach*

Essentially, one might distinguish between two approaches aimed at giving the concept a clear meaning. A *top-down* approach seeks to address the definition problem authoritatively (or quasi-authoritatively) by introducing a set of criteria such as the size of a company, and/ or to provide a typology of situations that allows the determination of whether an act or omission is within a business entity's sphere of influence or not. A top-down approach along these lines was taken by ISO 26000 and was apparently envisioned in the Human Rights Resolution 2005/69 by the Commission on Human Rights, where it included in the mandate of the Special Representative (on the issue of human rights and transnational corporations and other business enterprises) the task 'to research and clarify the implications ... of concepts such as "complicity" and "sphere of influence".'

This leaves open, however, the ways in which criteria or constitutive elements can be identified. One common way to deal with such situations – at least seen from a legal perspective – is to analyse frameworks dealing with structurally similar problems or issues in previous situations and other areas of law, and to derive criteria from these discourses based on their similarities. Such an *analogy* has recently been proposed in the aforementioned brief from Arthur Robinson Allens on corporations and human rights in the Asia-Pacific region. The authors of the report argue that the *doctrine of duty of care* as used in the realm of corporate civil liability is analogous to the concept 'sphere of influence'.[46]

The duty of care concept in the common law tradition (we refer to US law in the following paragraphs as one leading proponent of such a tradition) entails the full scope of liability for negligence. In the context of this study, we are concerned with the extension of liability to

---

[46] Allens, 'Brief on Corporations and Human Rights', p. 13.

business enterprises due to the commission of a tort on the part of a third party – what may be termed third party liability. Generally, liability may be based on principles of agency or where the organization may be deemed to share an enterprise with the tortfeasor – i.e., where the organization and the tortfeasor are 'cohorts' or joint venturers.

In terms of agency-based theories of liability, we focus on the liability of organizations for the tortuous acts or omissions of independent contractors or other agents who do not fall within the scope of an employee relationship. Traditionally, an employer could not be held liable for the acts or omissions of an independent contractor.[47] This traditional rule, however, represented a retreat from earlier decisions which had held the employer liable for torts committed by an independent contractor.[48] Yet, the pendulum began swinging back the other way in the United States in the twentieth century. Today, most if not all US jurisdictions recognize a number of exceptions to the rule.

For instance, it is generally accepted in the United States that an employer may be held liable for failing to exercise reasonable care in the *selection* of independent contractors.[49] Thus, the employer may generally be regarded as having a duty to ensure that the contractor has the necessary competence and qualifications to perform the work in question.[50] To the extent that the employer maintains any degree of control over the work of the contractor, the employer may also be held liable for negligence in exercising or failing to exercise that control appropriately.[51] For instance, if the employer supplies equipment for the performance of the contractor's work, the employer may be held liable for injuries resulting from the use of the equipment where that equipment is faulty or inadequate or otherwise creates a foreseeable risk of harm.[52] Additionally, liability has been extended to employers for the failure to stop practices on the part of the contractor that create a dangerous condition where the employer has actual or constructive knowledge of such practices.[53] Moreover, courts throughout the US have adopted an exception where the work to be performed by the independent contractor is 'inherently dangerous' (see Restatement (Second) Torts section 427) or likely to be 'peculiarly dangerous' (see Restatement (Second)

---

[47] See, e.g., *Laugher* v. *Pointer*, 1826; *Blake* v. *Ferris*, 1851; *Hilliard* v. *Richardson*, 1855.
[48] *Bush* v. *Steinman*, 1799; *Lowell* v. *Boston & Lowell R. Corp.*, 1839.
[49] See, e.g., *Ozan Lumber Co.* v. *McNeely*, 1949; *Joslin* v. *Idaho Times Publishing Co.*, 1939; *American Coated Fabrics Co.* v. *Berkshire Apparel Corp.*, 1972.
[50] See, e.g., *Western Stock Center, Inc.* v. *Sevit, Inc.*, 1978.
[51] See, e.g., *Everette* v. *Alyeska Pipeline Service Co.*, 1980; *Dowell* v. *General Telephone Co. of Michigan*, 1978; *Franklin* v. *Puget Sound Tug & Barge Co.*, 1978.
[52] See, e.g., *Risley* v. *Lenwell*, 1954.
[53] See, e.g., *Kuhn* v. *P. J. Carlin Construction Co.*, 1935, *Kojic* v. *New York*, 1980.

Torts section 416).[54] Some of the examples of activities that have been deemed to be inherently dangerous are the construction of reservoirs, handling of vicious animals, work involving electric wires, blasting, the production of firework exhibitions and crop dusting.[55]

More generally, under agency principles, liability is imputed to the principal where the agent has actual or implied authority to act on behalf of the principal. Additionally, liability has sometimes been applied where the particular circumstances, actions and representations on the part of a principal would lead a third party to reasonably believe that the agent has the authority to act on behalf of the principal.[56] Thus, agents who may not (clearly) fall into the category of employee or independent contractor may still incur liability for a principal company under such circumstances. In addition, liability has also been extended in cases where deceit is involved (see, e.g., *Cellucci* v. *Sun Oil Co.*, 1974).

Joint enterprise liability may represent an analogy developed from partnership liability.[57] Where a joint enterprise has a common business or commercial purpose the enterprise is generally deemed to be a 'joint venture' and partnership liability principles apply. Thus, both venturers would be jointly and severally liable for the tortuous acts or omissions of either venturer. The mutual agreement to share profits and losses is also a particularly significant factor for the finding that an enterprise represents a joint venture.[58] In some instances, even joint action on the part of two parties without a commercial arrangement has been deemed to constitute a joint venture.[59] In the case *Ruth* v. *Hutchinson Gas Co.*, the Supreme Court of Minnesota stated that a joint enterprise exists 'where all the parties have a community of interest in the purposes and objects of the undertaking and an equal right in its control and management'.[60] In that case, the Court deemed that a hunting party consisting of mutual friends might constitute a joint enterprise and that if such a finding were made, all members of the party would be agents of the enterprise and negligence on the part of one could be imputed to all.[61]

---

[54] See also *Western Stock Center, Inc.* v. *Sevit, Inc.*, 1978.
[55] William Prosser, *Prosser and Keeton on Torts*, 5th edn (St. Paul, MN: West Publishing, 1984), p. 513, with references.
[56] *Foley* v. *Allard*, 1988, citing *Hockemeyer* v. *Pooler*, 1964.
[57] Prosser, *Prosser and Keeton on Torts*, p. 516.
[58] See ibid., p. 517, and Jersey M. Green, 'The Imposition of Vicarious Liability Through Joint Venture', *Trial Talk*, 38 (1990); reprinted at www.preeosilverman. com/CM/Articles/Articles29.asp#_ednref1.
[59] See, e.g. *Ruth* v. *Hutchinson Gas Co.*, 1941.   [60] Ibid.
[61] Ibid., citing *Murphy* v. *Keating*, 1939.

This brief overview of the duty of care doctrine in the US suggests that it is worthwhile to further explore the merits of the proposed analogy and take a closer look into the common law concept of duty of care and its doctrinal counterpart in the civil law system. The rich body of case law on corporate liability for acts and omissions of subsidiaries, for instance, provides a tentative list of criteria and factors that might be considered in the context of the human rights 'sphere of influence' concept. These criteria include, among other things:

- profit sharing,
- contributions towards financing the subsidiary,
- degrees of oversight and/or joint control, or
- masterminding a venture,
- etc.

Similarly, case law on third party liability in the context of *joint ventures* sets forth criteria that may be useful in the corporate social responsibility context. Among the criteria are:

- shared common interest in the subject matter of the venture;
- shared profits and losses; and
- joint control or the joint right of control over the venture.

Although the proposed analogy might prove to be helpful to further develop and clarify the 'sphere of influence' concept, the analogy should in my view *not be overstretched*. In particular, further research is needed to determine to what extent duty of care mechanisms are normatively appropriate to assess the potential scope of a corporation's *legal* 'sphere of influence' in the human rights context as proposed by the authors of the above-mentioned brief on corporations and human rights in the Asia-Pacific Region.

4.2   Bottom-up approaches

An alternative type of approach aimed at clarifying the meaning of the notion 'sphere of influence' would not operate top-down, but *bottom-up*. Outside the legal realm, *corporate policies on human rights issues* are the key drivers of such an approach. As pointed out in the interim report by the Special Representative, nearly eight out of ten Fortune Global 500 companies report to have an explicit set of principles or management practices regarding the human rights dimensions of their operations.[62]

---

[62] Ruggie, Interim Report 2006, para. 33.

These policies usually also encompass third parties such as suppliers, contractors, distributors and joint venture partners.

For illustrative purposes, we have reviewed a random sample of over 120 statements on human rights by corporations as of 2007. The documents have been collected by the Business and Human Rights Resource Centre.[63] Within a sample of 122 policy statements, 40 corporations actually used the term 'sphere of influence' to describe the scope of their responsibility. The majority of the policies, according to our tentative analysis, did not use the term 'sphere of influence' at all or only made implicit references to it. Within the group of corporations that directly or indirectly referred to the 'sphere of influence' concept, three categories can be distinguished:

• *Implicit references*: Some policies do not use the term 'sphere of influence' but clearly address the issue of human rights abuses by third parties. In several cases, this interpretation can be based on the fact that the companies declare elsewhere their support for the Global Compact.[64]

> Example:

> 'Aviva also has influence – via its fund management or purchasing activities (see Group Purchasing policy) – over other companies and their approach to human rights in the way they conduct their business both internally and with their suppliers. This influence should be identified and applied consistently around the group.'[65]

• *Explicit references, but no interpretation*: The majority of the statements refer to the UDHR or the Global Compact. Most corporations only mention the 'sphere of influence' without giving further details on how the concept is interpreted.

> Examples:

> BASF: 'We are committed to high standards both within the company and in the societal environment. In keeping with our role as a good corporate citizen, we strive to contribute to the protection and wide recognition of human rights in our spheres of influence.'[66]

---

[63] See www.business-humanrights.org/Documents/Policies.
[64] Aviva PLC, 'Corporate Social Responsibility Report 2007', 'UN Global Compact Communication in Progress'; www.aviva.com/csr07/index.asp?pageid=143.
[65] Ibid., 'Human rights', Appendix 1; www.aviva.com/index.asp?pageid=312.
[66] BASF, 'Corporate Report 2005: Our Values to Social Responsibility'; www.berichte. basf.de/en/2005/unternehmensbericht/02_unternehmen/10_werte/?id=V00-BJ.5GAzq2bir1dv.

Marriott: 'Marriott's Human Rights Policy reflects the Company's commitment to conduct its business in a manner consistent with these principles and to protect human rights within the company's sphere of influence.'[67]

Novartis: 'We seek to promote and protect the rights defined in the Universal Declaration of Human Rights of the United Nations within our sphere of influence. We do not tolerate human rights abuses within our own business operations.'[68]

Roche: 'As a company that depends on the creativity, initiative and commitment of all its employees, Roche supports, respects and believes firmly in the universal human rights proclaimed by the United Nations. It enforces these rights within its sphere of influence and takes immediate action against any infringement of these rights.'[69]

• *Interpretation of the concept*: A few of the surveyed corporations have elaborated in greater detail on what they consider to be their 'sphere of influence'. This ranges from commitments to avoid becoming complicit in human rights abuses within their 'sphere of influence' to the attempt to restrict the scope of responsibility.

Examples:

Nexen: 'Nexen Inc. will strive to ensure its contractors, suppliers and partners will respect these fundamental standards of human rights through consultation, training or contractual requirements.'[70]

ABN AMRO: 'We strive within our sphere of influence to uphold and promote human rights, take full responsibility for our own operations. While we do not have a direct influence over our business partners' operations, we recognise that our engagement with them creates an indirect impact on our human rights performance. So we will only engage with our business partners who are deemed responsible and share our belief in human rights. In situations where national laws differ from our own standards, we

[67] Marriott International, Inc., 'Human Rights Policy Statement' (2006); http://ir.shareholder.com/mar/downloads/HumanRightsStatement.pdf.

[68] Novartis, 'Policy on Corporate Citizenship' (2001), p. 1; www.corporatecitizenship.novartis.com/downloads/managing-cc/02_2003_policy_on_corporate_citizenship.pdf.

[69] Roche, 'Human Rights' (2006); www.roche.com/sus_emp-hum.

[70] Nexen, 'Nexen Human Rights Policy' (2003), p. 2; www.nexeninc.com/files/Policies/Human_Rights_Policy.pdf.

engage and work with our business partners to assess a course of action to foster and protect human rights.'[71]

In some instances, corporations have expressed more concrete commitments, such as Occidental Petroleum which indicates that social impact assessments have been incorporated into its standard business processes and that human rights-related provisions have become a standard part of its business contracts with third parties.

Occidental Petroleum: 'The Company is committed to being attentive to concerns raised by stakeholders, including with respect to the needs of the communities in which it operates, and to working with stakeholders to support Human Rights within the spheres of the Company's activity and influence. ... Occidental's commitment extends to persons and entities beyond its Employees. For the communities in which the Company operates, such commitment includes observing the laws of the countries in which it operates, respecting the cultural values of such communities, including indigenous peoples recognized by applicable law, giving appropriate regard to the self-sufficiency, sustainability, health, safety, and the environment of such communities, and conducting business as a responsible member of society. Before beginning operations in any foreign jurisdiction, the Company will perform a social impact assessment to understand local issues as well as security risks and, to the extent consistent with applicable law, will seek the pre-approval of legitimate local communities affected by the Company's business operations in order to minimize negative impacts on such communities and the Company's operations.

With respect to its contractors and suppliers, Occidental's commitment includes promoting respect for ethical conduct and Human Rights with the contractors and suppliers and demonstrating a preference for working with those who share the Company's values. With limited exceptions, all contracts between Occidental and any third party (other than a foreign government) concerning the Company's activities in a foreign jurisdiction must contain provisions with respect to the observance of Human Rights, including Human Rights training. For detailed information about the Company's commitment to

---

[71] ABN AMRO, 'Sustainable Development' (2006); www.abnamro.com/com/about/sd/sd_policies.jsp.

Human Rights, reference should be made to OPC Policy No. 06:55:00, Human Rights.'[72]

> In other instances, corporations attempt to delineate between the corporation's own responsibility and the responsibility of other parties – including governments. At the same time, these corporations might recognize that corporate action may sometimes be called for even where direct responsibility does not apply.

Shell: 'Where the operating company does not have complete control, that is, when the issue relates to incidents which did not take place on their site or where the company has limited legal or actual influence, the capacity to influence events is clearly diminished. However that does not mean that the issue can be ignored.

In such cases, the company should tailor its approach according to its capacities and its view of how best to achieve policy aims. For example, the obligation to express support for fundamental human rights within the legitimate role of business does not necessarily mean public statements of support. It may be that expressions of view behind closed doors are more effective in achieving the desired goal. If, in the judgement of the responsible executives, that is the case, then that approach should be taken. The emphasis must be on achieving a result which upholds the human rights standards of the Group's business principles.

The public relations aspect must, as in every other business decision, be taken into account, but it is not the primary consideration. When the operating company feels that the issue has ramifications which may be detrimental to other parts of the Shell Group the matter should be referred to those other affected companies.

Operating companies also have a responsibility to identify existing and potential human rights issues which may arise in their area of operations. Where the company feels it has the capacity to handle the issue itself it should, as far as is practicable, do so. However if significant doubts exist as to capacity to resolve the issue, the matter should be referred to the responsible Business.

Shell companies must work in the real world in which, tragically, many human rights abuses occur. Our capacity to

---

[72] Occidental Petroleum, 'Occidental Petroleum Corporation, Code of Business Conduct' (amended 2004 and 2007), p. 26; www.oxy.com/PUBLICATIONS/PDF/ code.pdf.

mitigate these is in many cases limited. However, individually and collectively, as a Group of Companies, we can make our own contribution to upholding human rights standards.'[73]

British American Tobacco: 'Statement of Business Principles: Last year's commitments: Develop and publish a Statement of Business Principles covering a wide range of areas including human rights, community relations, supply chain, employment, and environmental, health and safety standards;

Consult with stakeholders during development of the Business Principles, with the aim of establishing more clearly the extent of our responsibilities and spheres of influence as a commercial organisation, and those areas for which we cannot be responsible.

Employment Principles: What are we responsible for?

Our primary relationships and influences are with employees at our core operations. Our aim, in these Principles, is to develop goals in the field of employment appropriate to our own situation. We do, however, also recognise our potential to influence business partners in our supply network – and our responsibility to enter into dialogue with those within our sphere of influence. When dealing with such wide-ranging and complex employment-related issues, responsibility is divided amongst different sections of society. National governments have the primary responsibility to raise their own local standards of employment legislation, requirements and compliance.'[74]

BHP Billiton: 'In broad terms there are two levels of influence as they apply to BHP Billiton sites:

- Direct control and responsibility for human rights, such as for employees and contractors.
- Influencing and contributing to the realisation of human rights in conjunction with others, such as suppliers.

It is recognised, however, that in certain circumstances it may also be appropriate to contribute to the promotion of human rights, with, for example, host governments.'[75]

---

[73] Shell, 'Business and Human Rights: A Management Primer', p. 23; www.shell.com/static/envirosoc-en/downloads/management_primers/business_and_human_rights_primer.pdf.

[74] British American Tobacco, 'Social Report' (2001/2002), p. 111; www.corporateregister.com/a10723/bat02-soc-uk.pdf.

[75] BHP Billiton, 'Sustainability Report' (Full Report 2006), p. 32; http://sustainability.bhpbilliton.com/2006/documents/BHPBillitonSustainabilityReport2006.pdf.

A thorough analysis, evaluation and multi-stakeholder discussion of this evolving body of norms – especially of the third type of statements (i.e., policies with interpretations of the 'sphere of influence' concept) – could ultimately result in broadly accepted industry best practice standards, which may serve as 'testing ground' for further norm-setting projects, for instance in the context of the UN Global Compact initiative.

The *structural advantage* of such a bottom-up approach is straightforward: Emerging industry standards based on respective corporate policies would be grounded in 'real world scenarios' and more likely to reflect the *actual reach* of the businesses involved. Further, businesses are arguably better suited to identify and analyse criteria aimed at clarifying the abstract concept of 'sphere of influence', either by introducing substantive criteria or developing procedural obligations that would ensure that they take into account the scope of their human rights responsibilities while planning and executing their operations. On the other hand, of course, such a bottom-up approach carries an inherent risk that companies aim for the lowest common denominator rather than realistic and best practice-oriented definitions and assessments of their respective 'sphere of influence', or that a consensus cannot be reached at all.

Our Google, Microsoft and Yahoo! example is instructive on that score. In the intervening years since this article was first written, these three companies have come together with leading human rights organizations, academic institutions, socially responsible investors and others to form the Global Network Initiative.[76]

Alternatives to a corporate-policy-driven approach to the 'sphere of influence' concept include, among others, *civil litigation* over corporate human rights violations. The promises of this alternative type of bottom-up approach largely depends on the question of whether the notion of 'sphere of influence' itself enters the legal arena or not – for instance in the context of legally binding obligations. While litigation-based mechanisms of making abstract concepts more concrete over time are obviously well-known in law in general and statute-based jurisdictions in particular, this approach has significant drawbacks from the perspectives of some stakeholders (including corporations), because it naturally creates legal uncertainty and bears no guarantee that, in fact, important interpretative issues will ultimately be clarified by courts. In addition, it might be difficult to distill shared criteria and common standards from the jurisprudence of various courts that operate in different jurisdictions and legal cultures.

---

[76] www.globalnetworkinitiative.org/.

5.   'Sphere of influence': virtue despite vagueness?

Given the discussed uncertainty regarding the contours of the 'sphere of influence' concept and its questionable feasibility in the legal context, does that mean it lacks *any* virtue? In the view of the research group involved in producing this chapter, the answer to this question is no. The reason is at least twofold.[77]

First, we can observe considerable activity in the development of actual models and *practical tools designed for monitoring conduct of corporations* towards human rights, as it has been recommended by the UNHCHR,[78] that are at least in part built upon the 'sphere of influence' concept. The UN Global Compact, for instance, provides such a model[79] that distinguishes among six spheres: employees/contractors, local communities, suppliers, security forces, business partners and government. Another tool is developed by the Office of the High Commissioner for Human Rights in close collaboration with the United Nations Global Compact Office, and with assistance from the United Nations System Staff College: The Human Rights and Business Learning Tool.[80] This tool identifies five spheres of influence: workplace, supply chain, marketplace, community and government. Along the same lines, the Human Rights & Business Project of the Danish Institute for Human Rights has developed a monitoring tool called the Human Rights Compliance Assessment (HRCA). Its description is illustrative:

The HRCA is a diagnostic tool, designed to help companies detect potential human rights violations caused by the effect of their operations on employees, local residents and all other stakeholders. The tool runs on a database containing approximately 350 questions and more than 1,000 corresponding human rights indicators, developed from the Universal Declaration of Human Rights and over 80 other major human rights treaties and ILO conventions. The interactive web-based computer programme allows each company to select questions in the database to suit their type of business and area of operations. When a questionnaire is complete, the computer programme generates a final report identifying areas of compliance and non-compliance in the company's operations. Numeric scores are included in the report to help the company report, improve and track its performance from year to year.[81]

---

[77] Stepan Wood identifies in a recent article eight good reasons why 'sphere of influence' should not be abandoned, see Wood, 'In Defense of the Sphere of Influence', pp. 5ff.

[78] OHCHR Report 2005, para. 52f.

[79] Also referred to as the Human Rights 'Sphere of Influence Model', BHP Billiton 2006, p. 416.

[80] Can be found at www.unssc.org/web/hrb/Default2.asp.

[81] Danish Institute for Human Rights; www.humanrightsbusiness.org/040_hrca.htm.

But the 'sphere of influence' concept has not only what we might call a 'factual' or 'empirical' dimension that – toolbox-like – may help in monitoring corporate behaviour and detect human rights violations, but also an important – probably an even more important – *discursive* function. From such a normative perspective, the 'sphere of influence' concept is not only the expression, but also among the *drivers* of the seismic shift from a state-oriented paradigm of human rights to a broader, holistic approach aimed at ensuring and fostering human rights (among private actors). In this respect, it may not only prove useful for corporations in contemplating best practices, but may also serve investors in guiding their investment decisions – the Council on Ethics, for instance, references the UN Compact in its Ethical Guidelines for the Norwegian Pension Fund – Global. The debate among the stakeholders about the concept's status, its concretization and its institutional and procedural implications at various policy levels suggests that the concept of 'sphere of influence' has indeed 'taken on a life of its own' as expressed in the Special Representative's interim report,[82] although it remains to be seen in what direction this evolutionary process will take us.

[82] Ruggie, Interim Report 2006, para. 40.

7   Human rights investment filters: a defence

Andreas Follesdal

> ... to gain money we must not lose our souls ... We are ... to gain all we can without hurting our neighbour.
>
> John Wesley, 'On the Use of Money'[1]

1.   Introduction

Do investors have an obligation to not invest in corporations that contribute to human rights violations? – even when such divestment neither causes changes in the corporations, nor prevents the violations? These questions go to the heart of what over the last forty years has become known as 'Socially Responsible Investing' (SRI).[2]

This name may be new, but both divestment and such worries about the practice are old. Appeals to divest from multinational corporations go back to the seventeenth century, against one of the earliest forms of economic globalization: the international slave trade. The present reflections address questions that have accompanied SRI since this very first case. Is there a justification of divestment that holds up even in the face of general breaches of the norms? Can such a justification avoid reliance on controversial religious views? And are there any grounds to believe that such divestment may be effective against human rights violations, even in the absence of a powerful hegemon that sanctions violations of the norms?

The affirmative answers below draw on theories of legitimacy and distributive justice that regard SRI as part of a response to the challenges of globalization. Section 2 frames the issues, drawing on the discussions among Quakers on divesting from the slave trade in the

[1] Iris Marion Young, 'Responsibility and Global Labor Justice', *Journal of Political Philosophy*, 12 (2004), pp. 365–497.
[2] Some of these arguments were presented at the Conference on Complicity and Human Rights hosted by the Council on Ethics. I am also grateful to Professor John Ruggie and the Mossavar-Rahmani Center for Business & Government at the Kennedy School of Harvard University, who provided an excellent environment for writing during 2007.

eighteenth century. Sections 3 and 4 provide a normative defence for some minimal human rights filters on investments under economic globalization. Section 5 addresses several objections.

2.   Historical background

Multinationals, their human rights violations and protests against such abuses have a very long common history. The Dutch East India Company, established 1602 – the first corporation to ever issue shares – profited from slave trade across oceans. In 1696 and 1698, the Philadelphia Yearly Meetings of Friends warned against involvement in the slave trade as a business venture. Quaker protests in America and Britain in effect blacklisted several prominent multinational corporations of the day.

By Quaker lights all these corporations should be shunned as inconsistent with the will of God, against minimal standards of justice and in violation of the golden rule. This is not to say that the Quakers or other groups always had seen slavery as problematic. As so many other Colonial Americans, many Quakers kept slaves and accepted slavery 'as part of the natural order of things'.[3] But they objected to investment in the slave trade, and eventually came to also condemn the holding of slaves. They exercised such social sanctions against their fellow believers as they could. In 1758 the Philadelphia Yearly Meeting agreed to also exhort slave-holding Friends to mend their ways, and the Yearly Meeting urged 'to exclude anyone who bought or sold slaves from participation in the business affairs of the church'.[4]

The challenges of this early case of SRI remain to this day: how are we to respond to the coordination quandaries that arise in the absence of a common authority? While the Quakers refused to trade in slaves, they saw that other traders moved into the market, 'over whom we have no gospel authority'.[5] William Southeby, the vocal opponent of slavery, dismissed this objection. Quakers should still move forward, to 'be exemplary to other places, and not take liberty to do things because others do them'.[6] The religious moral view of the Society of Friends might allow them to bypass such arguments of ineffectiveness. We must still ask whether there are more broadly acceptable justifications of SRI that support disinvestment even under non-ideal circumstances where many others are known to violate the best normative standards. Are

---

[3] Thomas E. Drake, *Quakers and Slavery in America* (Gloucester, MA: Peter Smith, 1965), p. 4.
[4] Ibid., p. 61.   [5] Ibid., p. 65.   [6] Ibid., p. 28.

there such justifications that avoid controversial premises – religious or otherwise?

The long fight to outlaw the slave trade also illuminates a second topic that remains crucial today. What are the necessary enabling conditions, if divestment is to help end such condemnable practices? It would seem that divestment by single actors is irrelevant, since it would take a powerful hegemonic global authority to establish reasonably effective human rights screens on investments. Someone must stand to gain by enforcing such principles and norms against other central players in the system. Thus Stephen Krasner argues that

The abolition of the slave trade across the Atlantic, a precursor to full emancipation, was a product of principles and norms that were supported by the most powerful states in the international system, especially by the dominant naval power in the nineteenth century, Great Britain.[7]

Today, those who favour SRI look in vain for a hegemon strong enough to enforce a human rights regime against states or multinational corporations. There may be no reason to believe that SRI may be more than a moral washing of hands, unlikely to help eradicate the harms. Indeed, SRI may even be counterproductive. Is SRI a waste of activists' efforts and resources that should instead address the root causes: the fundamental rules of the global economy that engender great social and environmental harm? The following sections address these concerns.

3.   A social contract theory for business obligations regarding human rights

This section outlines a justification of human rights filters on investments that seeks to avoid overly controversial normative premises shared by only a few normative theories.

3.1   *The multiple contributions of institutions*

Institutions serve many functions and have several features that make them valuable for the promotion of human interests, and warrant normative scrutiny. Social institutions and the organizations that operate within them, such as markets, corporations, arrangements for political decision-making and the media shape our lives in profound and inescapable ways. They are instruments and social creations that affect

---

[7] Stephen Krasner, 'Structural Causes and Regime Consequences: Regimes As Intervening Variables', *International Organization*, 36:2 (1982), p. 152.

not only what we get, but also our interests and aspirations, even more so when they are global in reach. We are dwellers in this complex web of institutions, but also its weavers, in that we jointly participate in maintaining this social basic structure. Indeed, our rule-governed practices *constitute* institutions such as money and the rules of transfer and property more generally.

Consider how legal regulations create both opportunities and constraints. They frame our interactions and exchanges, as individuals and groups. Some of these we are coerced into, such as taxation and legal obligations. Institutions also affect the option range for our voluntary choices, alone and with others.

Consider also how domestic and global legal rules frame practices that constitute corporations and markets. The constitutive role of legal regulations is especially obvious for the case of corporations.[8] A corporation is a legal entity with a separate legal personality – with its own set of legal rights, powers, obligations and immunities. A corporation can sue and be sued, own property and sign contracts. And unlike many other cooperative projects, legal rules grant corporations *limited liability*: shareholders' responsibility for the company's debt is limited to the value of their share. Investors become members of the cooperative project that is the corporation when they buy shares in the corporation, and they stop being such participants when they transfer that share to others.

The market is similarly constituted by rules of many kinds, including regulations about what may be bought and sold. Such property rights, the rules of contracts and ownership and so forth are social creations in a certain sense: An individual who owns something has acquired it according to public rules regulating entitlements and transfers. Insofar as she has complied with these rules, the object is clearly hers, and not anybody else's. But her claim of ownership is only true – indeed, it can only be made sense of – because a particular set of rules of ownership is publicly known and generally complied with by those who participate in that practice. The owner enjoys certain Hohfeldian powers and immunities, but only insofar as others generally abide by these rules of ownership. Likewise, money exists only as part of a social practice regulated by rules that define 'legal tender', where it is common, public knowledge that all accept the currency in return for goods and services.[9]

---

[8] See Christopher Kutz, 'Acting Together', *Philosophy and Phenomenological Research*, 61:1 (2000), pp. 1–31, and Amitai Etzioni, 'A Communitarian Note on Stakeholder Theory', *Business Ethics Quarterly*, 8 (1998), p. 681.

[9] James Coleman, *Foundations of Social Theory* (Cambridge, MA: Harvard University Press, 1990), p. 119.

Rules such as those of limited liability, of ownership and of market transfers were established with certain effects, many of them intended by their creators. In particular, the rules governing corporations and markets have profound beneficial impact on the ability to gather and invest capital and promote value creation. Such regulations clearly could be otherwise: the rules of contract may allow certain transfers but not others.[10] Most notably, corporations could once legally buy and sell human beings, but no more. But even today corporations can buy and sell goods made under conditions that violate basic human rights, rights that most governments have committed to respect.

Institutions thus play many important roles. Firstly, purely instrumentally, since they allow individuals to pursue their existing interests. Secondly, the institutions affect the choices available to the participants. Institutions not only allow, but also create certain choices, and they hinder others – be it to establish corporations with particular business objectives, or to engage in trade of shares without concern for damages beyond the share's value. Thirdly, institutions considered as a whole also have profound impact on participants' values and preferences, aspirations and life plans.

This is why the philosopher John Rawls calls attention to what he called the 'Basic Structure': 'the way in which the major social institutions distribute fundamental rights and duties and determine the division of advantages from social cooperation'.[11] This basic structure not only facilitates and shapes our existing options, but also helps create and shape our starting points in life, our hopes, resources, rewards and responsibilities. It determines not only what we own but also what we can hope to acquire, our levers of political influence, career opportunities and life plans generally. These insights are not new: the economist and moral philosopher Adam Smith recognized that several aspects of the labour market are endogenous to the market. Workers' values and preferences not only operate within a market, but are also its effects. The workplace conditions that form part of the market shape workers' aspirations and preferences profoundly.[12]

For our concerns it is important to insist that many of these background institutions are global in reach.[13] State borders cluster and

---

[10] Anthony Kronman, 'Contract Law and Distributive Justice', *Yale Law Review*, 89 (1980), p. 472.

[11] John Rawls, *A Theory of Justice* (Cambridge, MA: Harvard University Press, 1971), p. 7.

[12] Debra M. Satz, 'Liberalism, Economic Freedom, and the Limits of Markets', *Social Philosophy and Policy*, 24:1 (2007), p. 139.

[13] See Thomas Pogge, *World Poverty and Human Rights* (Cambridge: Polity Press, 2002).

constrain the rules of political and economic interaction. But state borders no longer limit these rules completely. Rather, the rules of domestic and international institutions jointly now structure how benefits and burdens are distributed globally, according to the rules and practices of this 'Global Basic Structure' ('GBS'). Of particular concern here is that part of the GBS that forms the international order, aptly described by David Held thus:

The international order involving the conjuncture of: dense networks of regional and global economic relations which stretch beyond the control of any single state (even of dominant states); extensive webs of transnational relations and instantaneous electronic communications over which particular states have limited influence; a vast array of international regimes and organizations which can limit the scope for action of the most powerful states; and the development of a global military order, and the build-up of the means of 'total' warfare as an enduring feature of the contemporary world, which can reduce the range of policies available to governments and their citizens.[14]

Many of the rules of the GBS are part of private and public international law, ranging from the World Trade Organization to the laws that define sovereignty. Our GBS thus enables mutually beneficial global cooperation, for instance in the form of much international trade or respect for borders. But it also contributes to burdens, e.g., in the form of unfair trade practices or unjustified invasions. Importantly, these rules could be otherwise. Alternative rules could effect other distributions, with other divisions of benefits and burdens among individuals. An obvious normative question is therefore how this set of global and domestic rules should be arranged: which normative objectives and standards should they secure as a whole?

I submit that the rules of the present GBS appear to fall far short of any defensible standards of normative legitimacy – witness such data as UN reports of widespread undernourishment, extreme mortality rates for under-five-year-olds, extensive severe poverty and continued practices of forced and compulsory labour.

Even faced with these calamities, it is not obvious how to change the norms of the GBS. Of particular concern to us, the choice of norms that should regulate investors remains unclear. Investors play one small part within corporations, each of which has limited opportunities within this GBS. The situation of individual investors prompts at least two important issues that must be distinguished: Firstly, what rules should regulate investors as part of a just GBS, when most others act as they should? Secondly, what rules should investors follow when other actors

---

[14] David Held, *Democracy and the Global Order* (Cambridge: Polity Press, 1995), p. 20.

cannot be expected to do their share according to such just rules, but instead abide by the unacceptable rules of the present GBS?

The present reflections focus on one particular modification from the present set of rules that concern rules of divestment and screening. Should concerned shareholders require that the corporations they invest in respect some minimum human rights of its employees and of its subcontractors, and perhaps even protect and promote their rights? Should shareholders, as a last resort, be morally – and perhaps even legally –required to disinvest from corporations that contribute to violate such human rights?

3.2   *Bringing social contract theory to bear*

I shall suggest that there are good reasons why a contractualist normative theory offers a fruitful perspective to argue about these issues of human rights filters on investment. The GBS shapes its subjects, is maintained by them – and is sometimes partly under their control. The social contract tradition in political philosophy expresses and ties together several of these normatively salient features.[15]

Contractualism addresses the question what normative standards we must require of this global patchwork of practices. How must the set of institutions affect constraints and opportunities, benefits and burdens, if it is to be defensible to all participant human beings as social and political equals? For those of us with some political influence over the GBS, these normative questions are as inescapable as the basic structure itself.[16] I shall argue that the normative aims must be twofold, both to avoid moral complicity in the worst consequences of the present GBS, and to promote its longer term improvement toward a set of coercive institutions that can be justified to all its subjects as political equals.

Insofar as the present structures violate those minimal standards of justice, we must then ask what changes justice requires, both in the shorter and longer run. Who must take responsibility for such changes, when state governments and borders no longer limit or buffer the impact of global economic forces sufficiently to secure the basic interests of all – and when individual states or corporations can hardly be held solely responsible for the rules they make and maintain especially

---

[15] Jean Hampton, 'Contract and Consent', in Robert E. Goodin and Philip Pettit (eds.), *A Companion to Contemporary Political Philosophy* (Oxford: Blackwell, 1993), pp. 379–93.

[16] See Charles R. Beitz, *Political Equality* (Princeton University Press, 1989), p. 23, and Thomas M. Scanlon, *What We Owe to Each Other* (Cambridge, MA: Harvard University Press, 1998).

not when highly mobile corporations shop among states for favourable terms.

Several aspects of the GBS counsel that Contractualism is an appropriate normative stance with regard to these issues. Firstly, the institutions and the categories they establish are created by human beings: they are not natural, but creations of human coordinated interaction. This discovery was central to the Quakers' protests against the slave trade.

Secondly, the institutions serve a variety of functions, and their benefits and burdens can contribute to – or confound – a variety of goals we pursue within the complex collective project that is the GBS. For instance, some of us choose to avail ourselves of markets for investment opportunities. Then we plan around and contribute to maintain certain organizations, in pursuit of these projects within this basic structure.

Thirdly, this GBS could be otherwise: the background institutions could be constructed differently, with quite different consequences for the lives of those who maintain them, those who use them and those who are their subjects.

Fourthly, some of these background institutions are – albeit to varying degrees – subject to conscious, intentional and successful control and modification. To hold such political power is a great value, especially given the profound impact of the GBS.

Fifthly, while no one can avoid being subject to the rules that constitute the GBS, some of us are not only subjects, but also privileged as co-authors of parts of these background institutions, and actors within them. As citizens with democratic rights within states, and as market actors with some economic influence over powerful multinational corporations, we may affect domestic, international and global rules. As active citizens of democracies, as consumers or as stock holders, we may exert some – albeit limited – intentional influence on which opportunities and powers the GBS will make available, and what will be the consequences. As co-authors of particular projects within the GBS and of the GBS, we render ourselves accountable, and morally complicit in the objectives and consequences of those parts – and of the whole.[17] Contractualism frames our situation in this way, and focuses on certain crucial normative questions:

How should the GBS be shaped, given its profound and inescapable impact on human beings who are at the same time inescapably its subjects, and at the same time required to maintain these institutions?

---

[17] For a sophisticated elaboration of this sense of complicity in collective action, see Christopher Kutz, 'Acting Together', *Philosophy and Phenomenological Research*, 61 (2000), pp. 1–31.

For the domestic case, this is been one of the central questions of political legitimacy. Answers from the social contract tradition including Locke, Rousseau and Kant have provided influential support for several basic moral human rights.

Many earlier contributors to this tradition were concerned with domestic institutions. Our questions concern the larger object of the GBS as a whole: what objectives and normative standards must the domestic and global basic structures combine to honour, in order to treat all those who are its subjects with due respect? And insofar as the existing GBS falls short of those standards, how can we, as its co-authors and contributors, honour our obligation to its victims to improve on it – while continuing to act within it?

The social contract tradition offers one way to specify these questions in ways that may facilitate substantial, reasoned answers: how must the GBS as a whole be designed and improved upon, to ensure that it is defensible toward all as members of equal moral standing within it?

To express the respect we owe each other as social and political equals, this contractualist tradition asks whether the justification for proposed standards of legitimacy is one we have reason to expect all to agree to on a footing of equality.

A central feature of this contractualist approach is that it centres on justification of our actions and our participation, rather than only on the effects of these actions – though these effects are often crucial. For instance:

Since human beings have reason to avoid pain, they could reasonably reject principles that allowed others to inflict pain on them without good reason, or to fail to relieve their pain when they could easily do so.[18]

While the effects such as pain matter in these normative arguments, we have more weighty grounds for objecting to someone inflicting pain, than to someone who refrains from alleviating it. The central relation of morality on this view is what T. M. Scanlon calls 'a relation of mutual recognition':

living with others on terms that they could not reasonably reject, acting in accord with principles that others (similarly motivated) could not reasonably reject.[19]

One reasonable ground for rejecting a proposed principle of action is if it allows more severe burdens to be put on someone than would be allowed by another proposed principle. A decisive objection in favour

---

[18] Scanlon, *What We Owe to Each Other*, p. 181.   [19] Ibid., p. 162.

of the alternative principle is on behalf of those who are asked to be subject to the burdens imposed by the first principle proposed, since the alternative would not subject anyone to such a great sacrifice. Such considerations favour principles for the GBS that rule out sets of institutions that place burdens of greater severity on *someone*, than other sets of institutions would impose on *anyone*.

Our central concern is whether some have such reason to rule out certain permissive principles for investments, in favour of rules that require disinvestment from corporations that contribute to human rights violations. The argument would be that less permissive standards better honour their interests in the long run, and don't impose an equally burdensome impact on anyone else.

3.3 Normative standards for the GBS: Respect for Vital Human Interests

What standards must the GBS as a whole satisfy to be normatively acceptable in this contractualist sense, that no one should have good reasons to reject them? Applications of this Contractualist commitment must explicate such central terms as 'severity', 'burden' and 'greater than'. I submit – there is no space for a detailed justification – that for our purpose, we may focus on the protection of subjects' vital interests against what we may think of as standard social threats. I submit a minimum principle of legitimacy akin to Mill's Harm Principle is the *Principle of Respect for Vital Interests*.[20] It requires of us that:

The institutional structure we maintain must not impose avoidable threats to the vital interests of any of those persons who maintain it.

These vital interests include at least basic physical and mental subsistence needs necessary for survival, and integrity of person.

That is: if we are to treat each other as equal participants in the institutional structure, it must *at least* satisfy this condition. At least three features of this principle are worth noting for our purposes. First, while the content of 'vital interests' is vague, with a broad grey zone, this principle lays down not only procedural conditions, but substantive requirements. Martha Nussbaum offers one well-known account and defence of such interests. She identifies certain 'basic capabilities' to life, health, bodily integrity, senses, emotions and practical reason.[21] They are valued across a broad range of normative life views, and are

[20] John Stuart Mill, *On Liberty* [1859], Mary Warnock (ed.) (Glasgow: Collins, 1962).
[21] Martha C. Nussbaum, *Sex and Social Justice* (New York: Oxford University Press, 1999).

therefore suitable as grounds for weighty claims among us, about how to order our common institutions. Persons have reason to value such capabilities, and the vital interests they give rise to:

the kinds of goods that virtually anyone capable of living a rationally self-directed worthwhile life has at least prima facie reason to care about. The elements of this list will consist of items such as 'not experiencing chronic pain,' 'not being hungry,' 'being healthy,' 'being safe from attack,' 'having shelter from the elements,' and so on.[22]

Secondly, the contractualist argument is that this principle *overrides* most other norms for the general regulation of institutions in cases of conflict. One example of a less weighty principle is a norm that sanctions individuals' pursuit of their own well-being. Central to the argument is that more is at stake for those whose vital interests are violated or seriously threatened when the Principle of Respect for Vital Interests is overruled, than anything at stake for those who pursue their own well-being beyond such vital interests. Each of the latter persons has less to gain, than each of the former stand to lose.

Thirdly, note that the *scope of application* of this principle is quite limited, in at least three ways. It is silent on important cases when vital interests unavoidably are at stake – i.e., when they are at risk under all sets of institutional rules. Furthermore, this principle only requires that each agent *respect* others' vital interests in the 'mild' sense that their own actions and projects do not impose threats to vital interests. It does not require that each also has a duty to protect vital interests from threats from nature or third parties. Whence this distinction? I submit that one central normative difference lies in the burdens others may reasonably reject. The Principle of Respect for Vital Interests rules out institutional arrangements that we might otherwise establish or use to further our own ends, if these arrangements are detrimental to others' vital interests. The principle thus explicates the 'Kantian' concern, to not use others merely as means to our own ends in ways that fail to recognize them as social and political equals. The burden we ask of each other is a constraint on our options when pursuing our own interests, so that we do not thereby worsen the plight of others. A more stringent principle might require that each of us not only aim at our own concerns, projects and objectives, but also aim to protect and promote the vital interests of others against threats we bear no responsibility for. This is not the place to discuss the plausibility of some such principle of

---

[22] Rahul Kumar, 'Reasonable Reasons in Contractualist Moral Argument', *Ethics*, 114 (2003), pp. 6–37.

beneficence; for our purposes it must suffice to point out that objections to that would be stronger, since it requires a higher level of (collective) concern for others' well-being.[23] Many normative traditions – among them many religions – include such requirements of varying stringency, and many such arguments seem plausible. But in order to build on relatively unobjectionable grounds, we limit ourselves here to the Principle of Respect for Vital Interests.

The final constraint on the scope of the Principle of Respect for Vital Interests is that it applies to institutional structures, rather than to individuals or single organizations or institutions. This underscores that institutions are to be assessed as collective projects with certain objectives that express sufficient respect for all those coerced to take part.

When we ask for the institutional implications of this principle, it is helpful to start by considering the role of states, and human rights constraints on them. Historically, Contractualism has focused on precisely the obligations that states have, especially given their authority and power to create and maintain a domestic basic structure. Think of a state characterized by centralized monopoly on political authority, with means of legitimate coercion. It has great value if it lives up to its main justifiable objective: to protect and promote the interests of its subjects as political equals. But such states also create new threats. One avoidable threat to citizens' vital interests is precisely that a powerful government with such monopoly does not pursue its legitimate objectives, but instead does nothing to protect individuals against potential violators – or becomes such a violator itself. The government, regarded as a complex of social institutions, thus carries the primary responsibility to not subject citizens' vital interests to standard threats, not only from other powerful actors, but from the government itself. The obligations of governments are both to *respect* these interests – i.e., not harm them – and to *protect* these interests from harm done by others.

These obligations of governments are often phrased in terms of human rights. The legal human rights found in international conventions provide some such safeguards. They specify how state power may and may not be used, and some of the strategies and objectives the government should pursue to adequately *respect*, *protect*, and *fulfil* vital needs.[24] This

---

23 Scanlon, *What We Owe to Each Other*, p. 29.
24 For these tripartite obligations of states, see A. Eide, 'Report on the Right to Food as a Human Right', United Nations Sub-Commission on the Promotion and Protection of Human Rights, UN Doc. E/CN.4/Sub.2/1987/23. Shue uses the terms 'avoid depriving', 'protect from deprivation' and 'to aid the deprived'; H. Shue, *Basic Rights: Subsistence, Affluence and US Foreign Policy* (Princeton University Press, 1996), p. 87.

justification most obviously supports various civil, social and economic rights.

As an example of the obligations of states to protect individuals against the threats of third parties, consider ILO conventions. They promote decent working conditions and social safety nets by setting and supervising international labour standards. States commit to establish national policies that ensure workers economic support during unemployment. This would be a typical state task. But ILO conventions go beyond this, and require the signatories to prevent corporations from the use of compulsory or forced labour (ILO No. 105) and from maintaining hazardous working conditions (e.g., ILO conv. No. 155). States must also secure workers' rights to organize and bargain (ILO No. 87, 98) – which serves to reduce power inequities to ensure fair compensation enough to secure basic needs.

The Principle of Respect for Vital Interests would support the view that corporations have obligations to comply with such human rights requirements not actively to harm the vital interests of anyone. But corporations may have no further moral obligation to *protect* the vital interests of all persons generally against the actions of third parties.

This might appear as an unstable position: why should corporations have any obligation to respect vital interests at all? If we consider a business corporation, its objective is usually not taken to be constrained thus. Instead, its aim is to promote the economic interest of its investors, with no intentional concern to respect or protect the interests of others. Below, I argue that the best defence of this view fails to hold under present conditions. Globalization makes it difficult to square the institutionalized pursuit of self-interest by corporations with the contractualist requirement of being justifiable to all. The main reason is that states are no longer able to bear the brunt of the obligations required by the Principle of Respect for Vital Interests. Corporations must also shoulder this responsibility.

4.   Investors' obligations under globalization

Theories of normative legitimacy have traditionally addressed domestic governments, largely with regard to their domestic policies. Within a system of sovereign states this may seem plausible and appropriate. Governments are the dominant actors, and state sovereignty is thought to provide sufficient authority and immunity to protect most citizens against other powers. Each government may be held responsible for maintaining and changing the domestic basic structure so as to respect, protect and fulfil citizens' best interests to the extent required by principles of justice.

For several reasons commonly referred to as 'globalization', questions of normative legitimacy and distributive justice must now be asked of the Global Basic Structure as a whole: how the set of global and domestic background institutions should pattern the distribution of benefits and burdens among those required to maintain it. Even the authority, power and hence obligations of governments must be assessed anew, especially since the ideal type of the 'system of states' fails to capture the varieties of states and other powerful actors around us. The upshot for our purposes is that corporations and their investors may have more moral responsibilities.

4.1   The Global Basic Structure as topic

The definitions, extent and impact of globalization are contested.[25] For our purposes, globalization describes the increased interdependence among individuals globally, without a common government. Our actions and practices systematically affect others across territorial borders, due to

the stretching and deepening of social relations and institutions across space and time such that, on the one hand, day-to-day activities are increasingly influenced by events happening on the other side of the globe and, on the other, the practices and decisions of local groups or communities can have significant global reverberations.[26]

Such globalization *per se* is not new. The old trade routes, including the slave trade, played important political and economic roles in previous centuries. What is new is the density, speed and the impact of global interdependence, due to several factors: the digital economy, globally integrated financial markets and large transnational corporations. The impact on individuals of this cross-border interdependence requires us to consider the distributive justice of the GBS as a whole.

One profound change to the global order is that economic globalization has shifted power and policy options from states toward corporations. The mechanism is not new: in 1776, Adam Smith observed that:

A merchant, it has been said very properly, is not necessarily the citizen of any particular country. It is in a great measure indifferent to him from what place he carries on his trade, and a very trifling disgust will make him remove

---

[25] David Held and Anthony McGrew (eds.), *The Global Transformations Reader: An Introduction to the Globalization Debate* (Oxford: Polity Press, 2000).

[26] Held, *Democracy and the Global Order*, p. 20.

his capital, and together with it all the industry which it supports, from one country to another.[27]

The global mobility of capital forces governments to compete to attract and keep multinational corporations that demand cheap resources and labour. Many critics worry that the volatility of markets feeds governments' uncertainty further. The result may be a race to the bottom for wages as well as environmental, health and safety standards and human rights protections.

These risks are greater under the current form of economic globalization than before. Until now, governments in many economically developed states have been able to protect their social protection schemes against the disadvantages of economic globalization.[28] Governments could create and maintain a 'grand social bargain' to share the adjustment costs when they opened domestic markets to international competition. Crucial instruments for governments to 'embed' liberalism in this way were their ability to buffer the impact of international competition, by means of tariffs and exchange rates, and their ability to finance social investments and safety nets.[29] Economic globalization removes or weakens these instruments. Governments have less de facto control over tariffs, monetary policies and taxation levels. No longer can a single state 'embed' economic liberalism.[30]

A central cause of states' reduced control is the mobility of capital and corporations. Their power has increased relative to states. Corporations with global reach and economic clout have more political influence: they not only act within the GBS, but can shape its rules deliberately. The states are no longer primarily the policy makers, nor are companies merely policy takers. Individual states peddle policies, while

---

[27] Adam Smith, 'How the Commerce of the Towns Contributed to the Improvement of the Country', in *An Inquiry into the Nature and Cause of the Wealth of Nations* [1776] (New York: Random House, Inc., 1937), Book 3, ch. 4.

[28] Fritz W. Scharpf, 'The Viability of Advanced Welfare States in the International Economy: Vulnerabilities and Options', *Journal of European Public Policy*, 7 (2000), pp. 190–228.

[29] John G. Ruggie, 'International Regimes, Transactions and Change: Embedded Liberalism in the Postwar Economic Order', *International Organization*, 36 (1982).

[30] John G. Ruggie, 'Promotion and Protection of Human Rights – Interim Report of the Special Representative of the Secretary-General on the Issue of Human Rights and Transnational Corporations and Other Business Enterprises' (Interim Report 2006), United Nations Human Rights Council, UN Doc. E/CN.4/2006/97 (22 February 2006) and Ruggie, 'Promotion and Protection of all Human Rights, Civil, Political, Economic, Social and Cultural Rights including the Right to Development. Protect, Respect and Remedy: A Framework for Business and Human Rights – Report of the Special Representative of the Secretary-General on the Issue of Human Rights and Transnational Corporations and Other Business Enterprises', United Nations Human Rights Council, UN Doc. A/HRC/8/5 (2008).

corporations are, if not policy makers, vocal policy shoppers. They know to use their economic power in pursuit of the financial interests of their investors. The upshot is that governments are less able to protect citizens' vital interests, even within developed states – not to mention citizens in developing countries and weak states, whose governments may never have been able to provide such buffers.

As regards developed welfare states, these threats are sometimes overdrawn,[31] and states sometimes seek to regain influence, such as when they agree international regulations, e.g., within the European Union. Yet many collective action problems remain, particularly for economically less developed states and states that cannot credibly commit to uphold such regulations. That is, the uncoordinated actions of each state leaves all worse off than if they had been able to agree to a common policy.

One normative implication of these power shifts concerns the obligations to respect vital interests. Within a global order where legally sovereign and quite autonomous states play dominant roles, they may be the prime actors charged with the main obligations to respect vital interests and to protect citizens against third parties. But states can no longer live up to those requirements. We must therefore reconsider how the global institutional structures we jointly maintain can be changed to avoid threats to the vital interests of any of those who maintain it. I submit that one such change concerns the obligations of investors. We must reconsider the distribution of responsibilities that traditionally have justified the insulation of corporations and their investors from considerations of distributive justice and human rights.

The traditional distribution of moral responsibility no longer holds, and this renders global markets and corporations' single-minded pursuit of their investors' economic interests in need of justification. This is even more appropriate since it is investors' increased cross-territorial impact through their corporations that reduces the governance capacities of many governments.

4.2   Changing the obligations of corporations

Considerations of justice underdetermine institutional design, and likewise underdetermine the choice of how to improve on existing injustice. To illustrate, several alternative GBSs could conceivably secure the vital interests of all: a global democratic and constitutional state, various forms of federations or confederations of regional states, or a system of

---

[31] Paul Pierson, *The New Politics of the Welfare State* (Oxford University Press, 2001).

states like the present but with more distributive obligations and less immunity from humanitarian intervention. I here leave the strategy of supranational regulation aside, and pursue another path of reform that focuses on changes in the moral obligations of corporations and their investors. This need not be an alternative to such more profound changes to the states system, but may be a permanent or interim supplement.

One reason to explore this venue is that we need not only focus on the changing role of states, but can also consider the obligations of investors and their corporations. The GBS as a whole does not have state-like central authorities to ensure that corporations respect the vital interests of those they impact on; nor does the GBS secure a fair redistribution of the benefits that corporations bring. Attempts at arguing for a distribution of responsibility fail, especially in developing countries with weak states. Workers are not protected, third parties are affected without compensation, governments cannot protect vital interests against attacks, and educational opportunities and other important public provisions are poor or non-existent. Where the distribution of responsibility fails, so does corporations' licence to ignore the Principle of Respect for Vital Interests.

We must therefore reconsider the obligations of investors. They, as do the rest of us, participate in the complex collective acts that are the GBS. This GBS currently violates the Principle of Respect for Vital Interests. Investors are the co-authors of the present GBS, and face reasonable and decisive objections from those whose vital interests are threatened, be it workers or third parties. Insofar as other parts of the GBS do not provide reliable protection against violations of vital interests, global markets and their major players cannot avoid responsibility for the violations of vital interests that they commit. Investors in corporations that violate the vital interests of their workers or of third parties choose to engage in projects that sacrifice the vital interest of some members of the global basic structure in order to maximize their own economic profit. In their actions and their projects, these investors fail to respect others who are involved in the common project as their moral equals. These victims suffer avoidable harm insofar as a GBS with somewhat different rules would impose stricter regulations on corporations to ensure the vital interests of all, without engendering comparable harm on anyone.

This account supports the position that corporations must respond responsibly to this 'governance gap'.[32] Norms that prohibit individual

---

[32] Ruggie, Interim Report 2006 and John Ruggie, 'Business and Human Rights: Mapping International Standards of Responsibility and Accountability for

corporations from violating vital interests and other forms of Socially Responsible Investing (SRI) may be part of such requirements of justice, especially under economic globalization without legitimate political structures of governance in place. Only when corporations take on such moral obligations can the investors claim that the actions and projects they pursue, including the GBS they maintain, respect the vital interests of all participants.

4.3   Why target corporations and investors?

Critics may object that this is a *non sequitur*: the conclusion does not follow. The normative imperative to re-allocate obligations under economic globalization underdetermines the solution. Even though the present GBS is unjust, the normative argument at most shows a shared responsibility among all who participate in it – that is, all of us. At least two questions remain open: *which* of several changes should be put in place, and *who* should be charged with more moral, and even legal, obligations than at present. For instance, the moral obligation might instead be primarily placed with states, to resolve their coordination problems vis-à-vis corporations, or with other actors such as consumers.[33] Five responses merit mention.

Firstly, it may well be that several actors must take on further obligations: neither legal nor moral responsibility is a zero-sum game.

Secondly, I submit that investors carry a *prima facie* heavy burden of justification, possibly heavier than consumers. Multinational corporations often contribute valuable resources to the countries where they work. But some of these corporations are also morally complicit in the new threats to vital interests. Through their corporations, investors contribute to, and sometimes actively exploit, the incapacity of states to protect citizens' vital interests.[34] Even governments of good will dare not always enforce requirements that would secure a decent economic floor, human rights protections and a safe work environment for workers and third parties, from fear that such constraints will lead

Corporate Acts. Report of the Special Representative of the Secretary-General (SRSG) on the Issue of Human Rights and Transnational Corporations and Other Business Enterprises', United Nations Human Rights Council, UN Doc. A/HRC/4/035 (9 February 2007), para. 82.

[33] For the role of consumers, see Andreas Follesdal, 'Political Consumerism as Chance and Challenge', in Michele Micheletti, Andreas Follesdal and Dietlind Stolle (eds.), *Politics, Products and Markets: Exploring Political Consumerism Past and Present* (New Brunswick, NJ: Transaction Press, 2004), pp. 3–20.

[34] See Young, 'Responsibility and Global Labor Justice', p. 385; and Kutz, *Complicity*, p. 67.

multinationals and capital to exit. Corporations are crucial cogs in the mechanism within the global economy that prevents states from protecting their citizens' human rights. Therefore, multinationals carry a special responsibility.[35]

Thirdly, investors are more morally complicit in these wrongdoings than many other actors. The objective of investors who invest in corporations is to benefit from them. When investors chose to participate in these collective projects, they become morally complicit in the damages that arise, and investors therefore owe those harmed an account for their collective acts. This burden of justification remains even when the wrongs technically are performed by the managers of the corporation, at least insofar as those managers act strategically in the pursuit of investors' interest in maximal returns. In particular, I submit that investors' moral complicity is especially salient when the violations of vital interests are part and parcel of the corporation's strategy to maximize returns, rather than an unintended consequence which does not impact on the bottom line.

Fourthly, the interest at stake for the investor is often less urgent, morally speaking – of less impact also than many interests of consumers, and clearly of less moral significance than the income required for the vital interests of many of the workers and third parties. The marginal reduction in yield of investors' capital constitutes a normatively significant gain. But this gain to them, larger though it may be in monetary terms, counts morally for less than the violation of vital interests.

Fifthly, the investor can avoid such complicity, since feasible alternatives are available without a comparable sacrifice. While the GBS is inescapable, investors may avoid the exploitation of its normative flaws when they pursue their economic interests at the expense of others' vital interests. Investors in corporations that harm workers or third parties can choose at least two main feasible alternatives, even in the short run. An investor can instruct the managers of corporations they co-own that company policies should respect the vital needs of workers and third parties, rather than contribute to human rights violations. Or investors can divest from those companies that contribute to such violations, so as to ensure that the investor does not violate the Principle of Respect for Vital Interests. Both of these options would prevent investors' moral complicity in the wrongdoing. Both options amount to taking on some moral responsibility, in response to the changing opportunities and powers of corporations and their investors within the present unjust GBS.

[35] Kutz, *Complicity*.

5. Objections considered

Several possible objections to this conclusion should be addressed.

5.1 The investor does not intend such violations of vital interests

This account of the obligations of investors may be criticized for ignoring their intentions. To describe them as intentional participants in projects that violate vital interests is misleading. Investors are not blameworthy, because they are often not conscious of these aspects of what corporations do. Indeed, these violations are therefore at most unintended consequences. And '[i]t would be unfair, whether we are considering a result produced by more than one person's action or by a single person, to blame a person for a result that he or she did not intend to produce'.[36] Thus Christopher Kutz notes that:

Many investors do not regard themselves as participants in any collective venture. Rather, they may think of themselves as gamblers simply 'playing the market,' attempting to maximize the return on their investments. For these investors, a stake in a given company means no more than an entry in their portfolio.[37]

In response, note that the question is not one of *blameworthiness*, but rather one of moral justifiability and *accountability*: whether such investment projects are justifiable to all those who are forced to contribute to it. The issue of blame does seem to require conditions of knowledge and will, but that is beyond the topic of concern here.

Furthermore, I submit that claims of investors' ignorance are now disingenuous, given the increased attention paid to SRI. Thus John Ruggie reports that:

many, if not most of the world's major firms are aware they have human rights responsibilities, have adopted some form of human rights policies and practices, think systematically about them and have instituted at least rudimentary internal and external reporting systems as well. None of this could have been said a decade ago.[38]

Thirdly, Kutz' rebuttal seems sound, when he claims that whether investors psychologically regard themselves as participants in such

---

[36] Stephen Sverdlik, 'Collective Responsibility', *Philosophical Studies*, 51 (1987), p. 68.
[37] Kutz, *Complicity*, pp. 247–8; see also E. Kelly, 'The Burdens of Collective Liability', in D. K. Chatterjee and D. E. Scheid (eds.), *Ethics and Foreign Intervention* (Cambridge University Press, 2003), pp. 118–39.
[38] Ruggie, Interim Report 2006, para. 38.

projects is beside the point. Their investments, aimed at maximal profit, make them part of these complex collective projects. Indeed, they are the principals of these projects, whose objectives determine the corporations' policies. These projects have as their guiding object-ive to maximize the investors' return, within whatever legal and moral constraints there are. A project that sacrifices someone's vital interests as means for this objective fails to accord the victims due respect as participants of equal standing. Those who take part in this collective project – and even more so, those whose objectives shape these policies, cannot absolve themselves of that responsibility.

5.2   *This is amoral self-indulgence: if I don't invest, someone else will*

One reason against self-imposed investment filters is that they are inef-fective under partial compliance. Recall that even the Quakers noted that their divestment from the slave trade would not stop the trade as long as other investors and sellers stepped in to meet the demand. So their divestment would leave them worse off, but would not improve slaves' welfare at all. Generalizing this point, it seems unreasonable and even irrational to refrain from profits by divesting, if the only effect of unilateral divestment is that others reap those profits – while harm to vital interests continue. Moral considerations, so this objection goes, cannot support a requirement of unilateral divestment, since the harm is 'overdetermined', or 'preempted' beyond the control of the individ-ual actor.

Observe that this objection draws on a moral perspective that not only urges consideration of consequences – most plausible views do that – but which seems to exclude all other concerns. On such moral views, bad things are equally bad regardless of how they are brought about or who does them. The fact that I, rather than someone else, con-tribute to cause this harm, or whether the harm is an intended part of a project or an unintended side effect, are distinctions with no moral difference. On this view, such 'agent relative restrictions', unless instru-mentally useful, are irrational and indefensible, and should not affect whether I have a moral reason to divest or not. An agent might think that morality requires divestment, but then perhaps only on the basis of a controversial, mistaken theological doctrine.

In response, I submit that a broad range of moral theories holds that other aspects than consequences may also be morally relevant. In particular, this holds for the considerations of *agency*, that it matters who brings these outcomes about. Christine Korsgaard, writing in the Kantian tradition, holds that 'the subject matter of morality is not what we should bring about, but how we should relate to one another'.[39]

The contractualist approach sketched above allows precisely such considerations – recall the formulation that we should be 'acting in accord with principles that others (similarly motivated) could not reasonably reject'.[40] This approach centres on justification of our actions, rather than on their effects. Consider the Principle of Respect for Vital Interests: even though the bad effects on vital interests are important, we have stronger reasons to object to rules that would allow others *to bring those harms about*, than rules that *allow someone to fail to alleviate harms* committed by others. Thus I violate the Principle of Respect for Vital Interests only when I bring those harms about. Such a breach is contrary to the contractualist motivation – even if others would have committed the harm had I not.[41]

The upshot for our purposes is that there are apparently plausible normative theories that may require such divestment practices, even under partial compliance when other investors or corporations will continue to harm the vital interests of employees and third parties. These theories, many within a Kantian tradition, cannot easily be dismissed as based on particularly controversial religious world views.

Problems still remain if divestment detracts from other short-term strategies, or if it hinders longer-term fundamental improvements of the GBS.

5.3   A focus on divestment drains attention and other resources from obligations to prevent harm

One important worry is that the practice of divestment might conflict with other moral obligations not addressed in these reflections, such as obligations to protect people against harms by third parties. Consider two such dilemmas. Firstly, there might be tensions between investors' two alternative strategies, to instruct managers to change policies and to exit from the corporation. The likelihood of convincing managers to change might diminish if they know that a concerned investor is more likely to choose to exit the more stubborn they appear: the plausibility of exit may reduce the impact of the investor's voice.[42]

---

[39] C. M. Korsgaard, *Creating the Kingdom of Ends* (Cambridge University Press, 1996), p. 275; and see Rahul Kumar, 'Defending the Moral Moderate: Contractualism and Common Sense', *Philosophy and Public Affairs*, 28 (1999), p. 284.

[40] Scanlon, *What We Owe to Each Other*, p. 162.

[41] See Kelly, 'The Burdens of Collective Liability'.

[42] Albert O. Hirschman, *Exit, Voice, and Loyalty* (Cambridge, MA: Harvard University Press, 1970).

In response, I submit that this hypothesis awaits empirical confirm-ation – as do alternative mechanisms that may work in the opposite direction. Especially in the present corporate climate, managers of many corporations are concerned to avoid reputation costs, including that of well-publicized, reasoned divestments by credible investors. So strategies of engagement and shareholder dialogues may actually gain impact if they occur in the shadow of credible risks of divestment.

A second dilemma concerns 'moral myopia' or 'normative fatigue' that may lead concerned investors to focus their attention and resources unduly on divestment, instead of on shareholder activism, or on efforts to protect vulnerable individuals from harms by others. In response, while the risks of exhaustion and scarce resources are real, they are not obviously a greater risk concerning divestment than any other norma-tive requirement. Also, divestment is only one of the obligations that follow from the Principle of Respect for Vital Interests, and this obli-gation may be less demanding over time. The Principle of Respect for Vital Interests clearly requires changes to the GBS itself. Not only do investors and corporations violate vital interests, but so does the GBS as a whole, regarded as a common project. The only morally defensible response therefore seems to be to seek to modify the GBS, in such ways that it treats all members as moral equals. As co-authors with some influence through our democratic governments, and as consumers, we have a moral obligation to seek to change the rules that regulate cor-porations and global trade regimes. If better rules were in place and generally complied with, the need for divestment would diminish or disappear, leaving more resources for other moral obligations.

6.   Conclusion

This chapter has laid out a defence for the view that investors have an obligation to exclude corporations from their portfolios, based on human rights conditions. I argued that a justification is available from a broadly 'Contractualist' normative perspective that takes account of the impact of globalization on the changing opportunity spaces and obligations of states and corporations. The present world order is one where the role of the state is 'recalibrated'[43] from one that lays down and sanctions rules, to one where the state's main task may be to con-tribute to set credible standards, monitor and adjudicate corporations'

---

[43] John Ruggie, 'Taking Embedded Liberalism Global: The Corporate Connection', in David Held and Mathias Koenig-Archibugi, *Taming Globalization* (Cambridge University Press, 2003).

compliance and to reframe the issues in credible ways. This account does not rely on as controversial religious assumptions as the first case of divestment – that of Quaker refusal to invest in slave ships. To invest in corporations that participate in human rights violations in order to maximize profit, is akin to investments in the slave trade of yore. Just as the Quakers in the past, investors and states that refuse to participate in human rights violations today may thereby avoid moral complicity in evil, and at the same time contribute to its eradication.

8 The moral responsibilities of shareholders: a conceptual map

Helene Ingierd and Henrik Syse

1. Introduction

The catchphrase for investments that both safeguard the financial assets of the funds under management and show proper concern for the communities and the environment affected by those investments is 'responsible investing' (RI) or 'socially responsible investing' (SRI). While such phrases until recently were reserved for funds that have a strict screening policy, they are increasingly becoming part of the self-understanding of large, broadly invested, mainstream funds.[1]

When we use such phrases, however, we should also be careful to clarify their meaning, in this case not least the meaning of responsibility. What is implied by the claim that someone is responsible? What kinds of responsibility are there? And which of these are relevant to a modern institutional investor?

A very basic way to explain what responsibility is focuses on the ability to *give a response*: If someone were to complain about the conference venue where this paper was first presented, and they came with their complaint to us, there is no reasonable way in which we, as authors or presenters, could be expected to respond to the complaint. We are in no position to respond, in terms of our competence, our knowledge, or our position. If they, on the other hand, lodged a complaint about the quality of the lectures at the conference, we might well be expected to give a response. And if the complaint especially surrounded the last lecture before lunch (ours!), then we would indeed be the ones from whom to expect a justifying or excusing response.

But what if someone complains about the behaviour of one of my children? What is my responsibility then (given that the child also has

---

[1] An important development in this regard is the publication of the United Nations Principles for Responsible Investment; UNEP Finance Initiative and UN Global Compact, *Principles for Responsible Investment* (New York: United Nations Environmental Program, 2006).

156

another parent and its own free will)? Or if someone complains about the rude behaviour of Norwegians generally? Where do we fix the limits of *my* or *our* responsibility vis-à-vis that of others?

Responsibility – both legally and morally – is judged according to the connection between actor and act, and admits of degrees and different kinds. There is, however, more to it than the causal connection between actor and act. One may be responsible without being a direct, physical cause of something. This can happen through inaction, such as negligence, or through participation in intention.

We also need to ask *towards whom* one has or holds responsibility. I obviously have more of a responsibility towards my own children than towards my neighbour's, but not in the sense that I have no responsibility for the latter. Circumstances dictated by my opportunity and by others' negligence will affect whether and to what extent I also have responsibilities towards individuals who are normally situated outside the scope of my responsibility. Also relevant is the extent to which I take advantage of or benefit from my interaction with others. If I do, it is also reasonable to say that my responsibilities towards these people increase or widen, since in that case it is more likely that I will actively continue to pursue the course of action that provides me with the benefit – a course of action that has effects, positive or negative, for the people in question who are essentially the means to my benefit (but not thereby, of course, to be *treated* merely as means).

We will venture the claim that large institutional investors, the main focus of this chapter, have a wide range of responsibilities, and that some of them pertain to more than merely the direct causal connections.

The most obvious responsibility of investors, in the sense of asset managers, is towards those whose money or capital one manages; this is the basic meaning of fiduciary responsibility. But in addition, indeed for the sake of one's fiduciary responsibility, investors take part in numerous dealings with other parties – among them the companies in the portfolio, political and other regulatory authorities and other investors – and thus enter into positions of potential responsibility towards these and, *ipso facto*, towards a wide range of stakeholders. These responsibilities differ in degree – and, one could say, in kind – and they are to a varying extent shared with others. Yet, some of them can and should properly be analysed as responsibilities of investors.

We may summarize these as (a) the responsibility an investment company (asset manager) has *to its owners* (i.e., to the owners of the investment capital, or the fiduciaries), and (b) the responsibility an investment company (asset manager) has *as an owner* (i.e., as owner (on behalf of its fiduciaries) and manager of capital in the investment objects).[2] We look at various aspects of these in the following.

The aim of the following reflections is two-fold: firstly and most importantly, to investigate various perspectives on responsibility that are of relevance to a large institutional investment organization; secondly and derivatively, to suggest how these perspectives help us understand the responsibilities of the investor towards – and compared to – other actors in the investment and business chain. We build on the work of others who have investigated responsibility – among them, the American philosopher Christopher Kutz – but by applying this specifically to the world of investors, we hopefully add new insights into the debate, with relevance for both theory and practice.

We distinguish in the following between two main perspectives on responsibility:[3] (1) causal responsibility and (2) role responsibility. As a subset of the first, we discuss the category of complicity, and as a subset of the second, we discuss what we call attitude responsibility, and also add some thoughts on the principal/agent distinction. They address different aspects of the overall moral and legal responsibilities that an investment organization can reasonably be said to have.

The primary aim of our analysis is to organize and investigate the kinds of moral responsibilities that large institutional investors can reasonably be said to have. While our approach, therefore, is analytical in its concentration on concepts and definitions, our aim is also normative. In other words, by laying out this conceptual map we also want to argue that these are responsibilities that a large investment organization *should* take seriously.

2.   Causal responsibility

Causal responsibility is essentially backward-looking (from effect to cause) and assigns responsibility and liability for acts that have been

---

[2] We owe this formulation to Professor Alexander Cappelen of NHH Business School in Bergen.

[3] We should note here that we employ a *broad* concept of moral responsibility. The distinction between strict and broad responsibility pertains to the range, intensity and content of responsibility according to two dimensions: first, what we may call the 'horizontal' dimension, which concerns the group of beings encompassed, e.g., whether responsibility is only to one's immediate associates (in this case, one's fiduciaries) or whether it is (at least in some cases) wider and more all-encompassing; and second, what has been named the 'vertical' dimension, which concerns how far responsibility extends in the temporal direction; see D. Birnbacher, 'Philosophical Foundations of Responsibility', in A. E. Auhagen and H. W. Bierhoff (eds.), *Responsibility: The Many Faces of a Social Phenomenon* (New York: Routledge, 2001), pp. 14–15. A broad concept of responsibility implies that we are in some way responsible to those affected by our actions and choices, even if the connection is not intimate and direct, physically or temporally.

carried out (or, if forward-looking, stipulates what the causal connections will be in regard to future effects). In short, causal responsibility stipulates that A is responsible for X because A's contribution can be identified in the causal chain leading up to X. In determining the responsibility of shareholders from this perspective, we need to consider the actual effects of ownership.

It is useful to distinguish between the responsibility of direct agents and the responsibility of indirect agents (accomplices). In the first case, the act is the direct causal result of A's movements, whereas in the second, A's act can be identified in the causal chain leading up to the act, meaning that A's behaviour is a contributing cause to X, but that other, intermediate agents were necessary for the effect to come about.[4] This distinction is indeed useful, but we should note that it is not clear-cut. Someone who acts alongside others, and who could not have brought something about him- or herself, but who nonetheless stands in a direct or immediate relation to the effect (say, one of ten people who push a car over a cliff) could reasonably be called a direct agent with direct responsibility, whereas someone who suggested that the car be driven that way and that the car *could* be pushed over the cliff, yet was not there and never actively pushed the car, or never actually insisted that it be done, would be an indirect agent. As we see from such examples, it is by no means clear where the line should be drawn. In attributing praise or blame (i.e., assigning liability), however, it certainly seems to make a difference how direct the relationship between one's action and the ensuing effect is, and we will therefore assume that there is a line to be drawn here, although it is not possible to be unequivocal about where to draw it. We will treat indirect causal responsibility under the term *complicity* below, although the term complicity can admittedly also be used when the causal connection is more direct.

In order actually to be held not only responsible but also liable (i.e., liable to be punished or rewarded, praised or blamed)[5] for causal contribution, there is a requirement of freedom, meaning that A was free to act otherwise than she in fact did. Freedom to act otherwise may be

---

[4] Certainly, *in*action may 'cause' serious harm under certain circumstances. Modern accounts of causality therefore do not consider causality only as an 'active push', but construe causality as a field of causal conditions which can be both positive and negative, and thus include omissions. Birnbacher, 'Philosophical Foundations of Responsibility', pp. 13–14.

[5] We distinguish between responsibility and liability, the latter being narrower in meaning than the former. To be responsible is to be answerable, whereas to be liable means to be an appropriate object of attitudes, judgments and actions, and in the case of culpability of resentment, blame and punishment. A responsible agent is a potential object of such reactions, but need not actually be held liable. Often, however, the two terms are used interchangeably.

restricted by mental or physical incapacity, as well as by lack of information, or by lack of acceptable alternatives.[6] Freedom is gradual, and only
in the complete absence of freedom to act otherwise is an agent totally
exempted from liability.[7] In addition, there is the requirement that the
agent acted with knowledge of the possible consequences (or, through
her own fault, lacked that knowledge). In the case of shareholders, as
long as the decision to invest and/or engage in certain companies is voluntary, and information about the companies is available, one may be
held liable in some fashion for the causal effects of one's investments.

But what, then, are these causal effects? In what ways does an institutional investor with broadly diversified investments, most often imply-
ing small holdings in each company, causally affect the companies
invested in and their activities? The answer can be divided into four.[8]

First, the investor contributes, obviously, through the capital invested.
While this is not dissimilar from what customers and lenders do – i.e.,
provide funds – stockowners do so by contributing a secure base capital
that is prioritized lower than the goods or funds owed customers and
lenders in cases of financial difficulty or bankruptcy. In other words, an
especially secure and predictable form of financing is secured by means
of shareowners' funds.

Second, the investor becomes a part-owner of the company, with
all the rights associated with that. This includes in many cases a voting right at general assemblies, but it also includes a right to receive
information about the company, and to ask questions about that information – or request more of it – when deemed necessary. One thus
has, even if only in a limited fashion, a say over the actions, direction
and future of the company. An important example of the way in which
investors influence the direction of a company can be found in jurisdictions where shareowners have a right to suggest board directors for the
ballot, and/or vote directly for or against board directors.

Third, an investor – and especially a large institutional investor –
gives the companies in which it invests a certain financial and/or
moral legitimacy by placing its funds there. This point must not be
overemphasized, since many institutional portfolios, especially among
pension-fund managers, are invested broadly according to bench-
marks or indexes, the choice over exactly which stocks to choose thus
being limited. However, in most cases either the fund's principals or its

---

[6] Birnbacher, 'Philosophical Foundations of Responsibility', p. 12.   [7] Ibid.
[8] We should note that we primarily have *equity* holders (i.e., share-/stockholders) in
mind, although the third and fourth categories are also relevant for fixed-income
(bond) investments.

managers will have some say over what kinds of investments to avoid for moral or political reasons, and thus over what to include in the index. And either way, the flow of money from large, respected institutional investors will inevitably be seen as a sign that there is at least a minimum of trust in the company and market invested in.

Finally, making an investment creates a precedent (although the same allowance for the lack of actual choice in investment objects in indexed funds has to be made for this point). Thus, one's investment in a certain kind of product, company, sector or market may create a greater likelihood that similar investments will be admitted into the fund.

All of these are tangible and predictable consequences of stock investments by institutional investors.

By emphasizing responsibility for such consequences, we are using a mainly consequentialist moral approach. Rather than looking at which duties are obeyed or what intentions are displayed, we are analysing the sorts of consequences produced by one's actions. Such an approach, however, while obviously important, can be both insufficient and excessively demanding when determining moral responsibility – and we should reflect on this before proceeding.

First, a purely consequentialist approach is often insufficient because there are other types of responsibility that may give rise to liability. For example, common-sense morality suggests that I may be responsible in some way (even if in a weaker way) for something I knowingly take part in, even if I were not a necessary or sufficient cause of the crime in question – for instance, if I assist in or encourage something that would have happened even if I had not assisted in or encouraged the action, or I truly wanted something to happen, but for some reason I never made it to the actual event. In order to make sense of complicity, which we will turn to next, as well as omissions, we seem to need an account of individual duties and obligations, and even intentions, in addition to an account of pure causality.

Second, the consequentialist perspective easily becomes too demanding – and possibly incoherent – because it seems to stipulate, at least *prima facie* (until a further differentiation has been done), that I am equally responsible for all the effects I bring into the world, and so it does not as such provide any definite demarcation of my responsibility. The class of possible actions open to me is endless, so whatever I do, there is an indefinite number of other things I could do. This objection harmonizes with the intuition that *we are not equally responsible for everyone and everything.* We must start with considering our various social and moral relations to one another, and then move from there to what we ought to do. This is what Richard Norman calls 'a social model of moral responsibility'.[9] Only in the light of a proper understanding of our responsibilities can we consider what consequences are relevant, and how they are relevant. In order to delimit responsibility for the causal effects we bring into the world, general duties and special obligations are needed. In other words, a proper understanding of what an agent has done is itself partly determined by social and moral relations, and by the legitimate expectations and rules that govern each societal activity.

Nonetheless, a causal/consequentialist approach is often the starting point for any delineation of responsibility. Causing something to come about through one's actions and then asking counterfactually what would have happened if I had chosen to act otherwise, together constitute the most basic building blocks of moral responsibility. At the same time, it all too easily ignores the social and shared character of many actions, and the part individuals and individual entities play in collective agency. This we now turn to.

2.1   Complicity

While responsibility commonly is ascribed to agents on the basis of actions they have intentionally brought about and have a direct and decisive causal relation to, agents are sometimes also held responsible for things brought about indirectly through their associations with other people or with the social, economic and political institutions in which they live their lives and make their living.[10] This is often called complicity, and it takes into account that actions are often *shared* and thus the outcome of the contributions of many persons or entities.

We divide complicity – which we treat as a subset of causal responsibility – in two: there may be participation in intention or participation in action. Intentional participation frequently lacks the clear causal connection, for instance (which we have touched on above), when A gives B advice, directives or encouragement and thus becomes an accomplice before the fact, although taking no part in the physical execution of the act itself. In participation in action, on the other hand, agents take part in the unethical acts by making these acts possible by their own acts, physically speaking, or because of their obvious power to prevent them. (When the latter should be subsumed under direct causal responsibility, and when it is more aptly termed complicity, depends on the extent

[9] Richard Norman, *Ethics, Killing and War* (Cambridge University Press, 1995), p. 104.
[10] Christopher Kutz, *Complicity: Ethics and Law for a Collective Age* (New York: Cambridge University Press, 2000), p. 1.

of the connection between one's actions and the results – there is, as also noted above, certainly not a clear dividing line between the two.)

Thus, even in the absence of a direct causal link between owning shares in a company and the unethical acts or crimes carried out by that company, it seems that shareholders may rightly be considered as responsible and liable for these crimes as *accomplices*, especially to the extent that the actions of the company can be seen to be flowing from the underlying 'order' or 'directive' of the investors to earn money, or through their enabling the acts by supplying the financial means to do them. Indeed, this is what we enumerated above: investment decisions *do* have consequences, since by placing one's money in a company, expecting that company to maximize (or at least secure) returns on one's investment (albeit within implicit and explicit parameters, such as the law), one also helps direct what the company actually does.

Our point here, however, is that these consequences are often quite remote, in the sense that the investor does not actually make concrete decisions related to the acts of the portfolio companies. Therefore, indirect responsibility or complicity is often a more apt term than direct causal responsibility, since it better encapsulates the fact that one plays a role, often along with many others, in actions over which one has little or no direct say.

The collective character of many acts may lead us to conclude either that everyone (i.e., every relevant, contributing party) is guilty of harm, or no one is: everyone, because everyone participates at some stage, and no one, because no one's individual contribution was large enough to imply full-fledged responsibility for that particular contributor. The latter view follows from a strictly individualistic conception of moral agency.[11] According to this conception, individuals are only liable for local effects, and thus responses to collective harm find no proper target. However, this perspective is surely too narrow as it excludes the point of view of those affected by our harm. In contrast, Kutz suggests that we regard collective actions as cooperative behaviour. This means emphasizing *shared intentions*. Kutz proposes a concept of collective

[11] Christopher Kutz formulates the following three principles of accountability: the Individual Difference, Control and Autonomy Principles, which he believes define an individualistic conception of moral agency: ibid., pp. 3–4. The Individual Difference Principle holds that I am only accountable for some harm if something I did made a difference to its occurrence. The Control Principle holds that I am only accountable for events over which I have control, and whose occurrence I could have prevented. Finally, the Autonomy Principle holds that I am not accountable for the harm another agent causes unless I have induced or coerced that person into performing that act (p. 3). As Kutz points out, the main problem with an individualistic conception of moral agency is that it fails to account for the individual's role in collective agency.

action, according to which responsibility is ascribed when the members of a group *share the conception of the collective end to which they intentionally contribute,* and thus that they have overlapping 'participatory intentions'.[12]

Against this background we argue, with Kutz, that the fact that harm occurred without direct causal and substantial contribution, or outside one's control, does not exclude the possibility of being held responsible.

In the case of shareholders, it will often be difficult to show any direct causal link between participation or assistance in the financial sense and the *concrete actions* (including, of course, crimes) of a company, in spite of the fact that investors clearly create company-specific effects through their investment activity (see our four-point list above). In the absence of direct causal links between agents and harms, what is the basis for complicity as a form of responsibility? We believe that the notion of participatory intention is useful in order to assess individual (and institutional) responsibility for joint action, and more specifically as the basis for legitimate claims of complicity. It indicates that one is responsible for what others do when one *intentionally participates* in the wrong they do or harm they cause.[13] This idea also seems well grounded in common-sense morality, where participation in intention is arguably considered a requirement for assigning (at least some degree of) blame, sometimes in addition to and sometimes even in lieu of participation in the actual, physical action.[14]

However, the idea of intentional participation as the basis of complicity conflicts with another common-sense principle, namely, 'the individual difference principle'.[15] The underlying idea of this principle is that one cannot be held responsible for an action unless one's causal contribution is significant, meaning that the action would not have occurred – at least not in the exact same way – if one did not contribute. Thus, agent A is responsible for action X only if something A did made a difference to the occurrence of X. This principle, as Kutz notes, reveals itself most often in our pleas for excuse. In the case of many institutional shareholders, it may be argued that, since their share in a given company is so small, they do not make any difference to the activity of the company, and so shareholders cannot be held liable for this activity.

---

[12] Ibid., pp. 90 and 144.   [13] Ibid., p. 122.

[14] This is, of course, a conjectural assumption about something very loose: 'common-sense morality'. But we feel justified in putting this forward as a general claim about the way in which the concept of blame is understood in everyday language usage.

[15] Christopher Kutz, 'Acting Together', *Philosophy and Phenomenological Research*, 61:1 (2000), e.g., p. 3.

There seems to be several ways to respond to this plea for excuse. First, it may of course be contested in factual terms whether one's contribution makes any difference or not, since this may be difficult to determine in cases where many different actors contribute. For example, a group of shareholders may not have any substantial impact on the activities of a company if their share is relatively small, yet if one takes into account the *signalling effects* (or legitimating effects) of their actions, and their possible influence on other shareholders, their contribution may be significant nonetheless. We touched on this previously and will come back to it below, when we discuss what we call attitude responsibility.

Second, and most importantly in the current context, we argue (following Kutz) that *agents who contribute to crimes only indirectly and marginally may be culpable along with those who do so directly and substantially,* due to the fact that they share ends, and knowingly accept the means chosen. One reason for thinking that mere participation warrants a less harsh response than direct wrongdoing is that being a more distant participant means being less committed to bringing about the wrong than what is the case in being a direct actor, since agents often participate in wrongs they would not bring about themselves. But given the assumption that the agents have the same ultimate end, and actively pursue that end through their actions, responsibility and liability apply to both kinds of agents – main agent and participatory agent – in spite of their different degrees of participation. Certainly, causal connections are not irrelevant for determining the *degree* of responsibility in individual cases. But having a clear wish to see the action (including the harm) come about, and not doing anything to stop it, but rather taking part (albeit marginally) in its execution, certainly seems to make ascription of responsibility relevant.

The exact degree of responsibility for such intentional participation in wrongdoing (i.e., complicity) on the part of the investor should in our view hinge on three factors: (a) the extent to which the harm done is not only part of one's overall intention, but actually condoned and wished for; (b) the extent to which one actively benefits from the harm done; and (c) the extent to which one could have contributed to stopping or at least in some fashion changing the act by withdrawing one's contribution.

It has now been argued that moral responsibility does not hinge only on direct causal contribution, but rather also on participation in intention. This seems to imply that some kind of knowledge of the crimes carried out is a requirement for complicity.

But does this mean that the harms committed must be intended, either by the investor or the portfolio company? It seems not. Responsibility for unintended consequences (i.e., side effects) can also be made sense of in terms of participatory intentions.[16] Agents who know that their actions contribute to harm, although they do not intend that harm, may still be responsible (and morally or legally liable), as long as the unintended harm is knowable, and as long as it is not an unavoidable *and* proportionally allowable side effect of an otherwise legal action. (By proportionally allowable we mean that it is insignificant when weighed against the advantages of the main aim of one's actions.) In other words, significant yet unintended side effects about which one cannot reasonably claim to be ignorant do form part of the overall make-up of one's action and can thus be seen as part of the overall 'intention' that an actor participates in.[17]

It seems fair to say that the less reasonable it is that an agent was (or could claim to be) ignorant of the nature of the act(s) committed, the stronger we hold the causal connection between the agent and the harm to be.[18] If the agent *should have known*, in the sense that information was readily available (but not actively sought), or in the sense that the activity in question customarily involves the unwanted side effects – hence it is unreasonable to claim ignorance – then ignorance does not excuse.[19]

In the case of institutional shareholders, as long as they reasonably ought to know that their acts contribute to harm, it is also reasonable to say that they are in some sense accomplices, because of the ways in which investments do have company-specific effects (as we have argued above). Accordingly, the Graver Report presented to the Norwegian Parliament in 2003[20] as a basis for the ethical guidelines of the Norwegian Government Petroleum Fund,[21] defines unacceptable complicity to include the owning of shares in companies that one can reasonably expect will commit 'grossly unethical actions'.[22] In such severe cases, the guidelines recommend withdrawal from the companies in question.

However, understanding investors' complicity in the relatively wide sense here indicated does not necessarily mean that being an accomplice

---

[16] Ibid., p. 142.
[17] Likewise, in the legal sphere, complicity does not demand evil intentions, merely knowledge of the illicit purpose of the principal perpetrator. See Andrew Clapham, *Human Rights Obligations of Non-State Actors* (Oxford University Press, 2006), p. 250. Philosophically, this terrain is covered by the principle of double effect. See L. Bomann-Larsen and O. Wiggen (eds.), *Responsibility in World Business* (Tokyo: United Nations University Press, 2004) for the principle's use in business ethics.
[18] 'Knowledge can implicate a participant, but ignorance can never fully exculpate.' See Kutz, *Complicity*, p. 157.
[19] We leave aside here a discussion of cases of strict legal liability.
[20] Norwegian Government White Paper, NOU 2003:22, p. 22.
[21] The fund has been renamed as of 2006 the Norwegian Government Pension Fund – Global.
[22] Norwegian Government White Paper, NOU 2003:22, p. 51.

through one's investments should always lead to withdrawal as a share-holder (i.e., divestment). There are two reasons for this:

First, the entity actually committing the wrong (or allowing it to happen) can be so remote that there is no reasonable moral connection between the investor and the harm. If, for instance, one is invested in company A which has a subsidiary B that in turn buys some of its products from subcontractor C, which manufactures parts for an illegal weapons system (this, however, having nothing to do with the products that A manufactures), it seems that an investment in A cannot be called immoral *per se*, since it is hard to talk about a 'participatory intention' in this case – even though one should, as an investor, encourage transparency in such cases, and possibly encourage company A through its subsidiary to pressure the subcontractor into stopping production of the parts in question – or make the subsidiary use another subcontractor. This is, of course, only an example; and myriads of others can be constructed. No matter how many examples we construct or cases we cite, we would be hard pressed to say *exactly* where remote, insignificant participation ends and immoral complicity begins. Yet, the criteria of participatory intention and reasonable knowledge help us part of the way. And our criteria (a) to (c) above, namely, whether one condones, benefits from, or could have changed the course of events – will in turn be important for deciding the exact extent of one's responsibility (and subsequent liability).

Second, sometimes an investment is so crucial to one's overall task as an investor – to create and safeguard value for one's owners – that some immoral actions of the portfolio companies simply must be accepted. For a fund with a (partly or wholly) indexed portfolio, withdrawing from large investments that form a central part of the benchmark is rarely an option, even though such large companies, if nothing else because of their size, can reasonably be expected to contribute – somehow, somewhere – to human rights abuses or environmental degradation. In such cases, where the wrongdoing is not so large-scale and at the same time abhorrent or entrenched that divesting seems the only morally acceptable option, active engagement can reasonably be said to be the right strategy – morally and financially – for an institutional investor, since it makes it possible to remain an investor while addressing the issue at stake.[23] This leads us naturally to thinking through what it means to *be* a large institutional investor.

---

[23] For the Norwegian Government Pension Fund – Global, active ownership to safeguard the long-term returns of the Fund is an important part of the overall strategy. Since long-term returns for such a widely dispersed fund with a long time horizon

3.   Role responsibility

Representing a different viewpoint than direct and indirect causal responsibility, role responsibility is primarily forward-looking and concerns what is to be done, given one's position or role (although it also, of course, helps delineate responsibility for actions already carried out). It assigns responsibility to agents, not only for actions, but also for *objects* within their sphere of influence or authority. Related to a deontological perspective on moral agency, it is concerned with special obligations that follow from one's role and position. We do not claim that there is a clear and unequivocal dividing line between causal and role responsibility, but they do represent different angles from which to analyse the responsibility of the investor.

Role responsibility can also be understood as representing a *virtue-ethical* approach, which will become clearer below when we discuss responsibilities for attitudes, character and for the signals one sends through one's actions. We first, however, analyse role responsibility from the perspective of duties, and make an overall distinction between general duties and special obligations.

General duties – or, as we may also call them (using language from the natural-law tradition), *natural* duties[24] – are opposed to special obligations. General or natural duties are 'moral requirements which apply to all men [and women] irrespective of status or of acts performed [...] owed by all persons to all others'.[25] According to such a view, responsibility is something that belongs to human beings independently of any voluntary act.[26]

Whereas natural or general duties are directly based on the intrinsic nature and worth of persons, i.e., the intrinsic nature of those to whom the duties are owed, special obligations are acquired through some actions of one's own or through one's status. Hence, while general duties are in principle owed to all persons, special obligations, such as

will likely be affected by a host of questions normally termed ethical, social or environmental, this gives the Fund manager (Norges Bank Investment Management) a mandate to raise such issues with companies in the portfolio and with standard setters in the markets. This also means that moral concerns can be raised through one's ownership activities rather than only through divestment. See the World Wide Web for Norges Bank Investment Management's annual reporting on its corporate governance and active ownership activities.

[24] Although we should note that the natural law tradition also endorses the idea of natural special duties, for instance, towards family and local community.

[25] A. J. Simmons, *Moral Principles and Political Obligations* (Princeton University Press, 1979), p. 13.

[26] See, e.g., R. E. Goodin, *Protecting the Vulnerable: A Reanalysis of our Social Responsibilities* (University of Chicago Press, 1985).

ownership obligations, are owed not (necessarily) to all persons, but to some limited class of persons.

There are two ways of looking at special obligations. First, we have a kind of reductionism, which holds that *special obligations arise as a result of our voluntary acts only*; and second, a non-reductionist approach, which argues that individuals have *special obligations beyond those specified by promises or contracts*,[27] the latter category thus falling between natural or general duties on the one hand and special obligations on the other.

In making a promise or contract, the agent voluntarily agrees to carry a certain burden for the person to whom he makes the promise or with whom he agrees to the contract.[28] Contractual obligations are normally obligations to persons from whom one has received or will receive a benefit. If we hold to a reductionist approach, and concentrate on contractual relationships, responsibility is primarily a *reciprocal relation*, comprising one party with certain rights on the one hand, and another party with corresponding obligations on the other.

It may be worthwhile to consider in more detail the assumptions that such a contractual perspective builds on.[29] First, it rests on the idea of *desert*, and thus the issue is whether the other deserves my support, or alternatively, whether I deserve hers. Second, the idea of desert presumes that there is some kind of *reward* for taking responsibility for the other. Thereby, one arguably opens the door for calculating and bargaining with responsibility. Third, the model rests on the idea that the other is one who is capable of returning my favours, and thus she must co-exist with myself. And fourth, it is taken for granted that responsibility is an *option*, and thus something the individual may choose to take or not to take.

There is a danger that a purely contractual perspective leads to a too narrow understanding of obligations and responsibilities, and that it fails to account for our very real responsibility towards human beings

---

[27] We borrow this terminology from S. Scheffler, 'Relationships and Responsibilities', *Philosophy and Public Affairs*, 36 (1997), pp. 189–209. It is worth noting that this reductionism pertains to special obligations. Voluntarism with respect to all of our duties would seriously delimit our moral responsibilities, and for that reason is held by virtually no one.

[28] There are, of course, other ways than through mutually agreed contracts that an actor can enter into special obligations with others, say, if one knowingly subjects another party to harm, irrespective of consent. However, contractual obligations merit particular attention in the context of this chapter, since the relationships that investors have with other parties are most often of a contractual nature. We will come back to non-contractual special obligations below.

[29] See A. J. Vetlesen, *Menneskeverd og ondskap: Essays og artikler 1991–2002* (Oslo: Gyldendal Norsk Foralg, 2003), p. 88.

outside of explicitly contractual relationships. If duties and obligations are restricted to commitments entered into by a voluntary act (with a corresponding right on the part of the respondent), then we cannot say that we have an obligation to help someone in need or jeopardy if such a prior agreement is missing, or to future generations. A purely contractual model thereby fails to accommodate obligations often acknowledged by common-sense morality, especially the obligations we feel towards those we are in a position to help, outside of contractual relationships. Thus, at the very least, we need general or natural duties as a supplement to contractual obligations. Our claim here, however, is that special obligations often imply a number of accompanying duties of a more general or non-contractual kind that are easily obscured if we concentrate too one-sidedly on the contractual aspects of one's obligations. In other words, we need to take account of a category of responsibilities that lie between the general and the purely contractual ones.

Now, it may be useful to distinguish between two different types of non-contractual special responsibilities or obligations.

First, an obligation to help a person who walks by on the street may arise simply because one is in a causal and epistemic *position* to help, meaning that one can do so without excessive risk to oneself. More precisely, the capacity of individuals to 'produce consequences that matter to others', based simply on where they happen to be, makes them responsible.[30] This view holds that special obligations, such as the duty to help another when he is in need or jeopardy, are *derivative general duties*. As derivative general duties, such special obligations may be valid regardless of any explicit voluntary act, and they are owed to persons generally. This has the important implication that if one is in a *causal and epistemic position* to help, there is an obligation to do so, independently of individual choice. Responsibility for others on the basis of special capacity, even in the absence of special personal, communal or causal relationships, constitutes what may be called *capacity responsibility*, as a subset of role responsibility. We suggest that this includes non-voluntary aspects of positions which one has voluntarily sought and accepted.

Second, one may be an appropriate target of responsibility if one occupies a social position which one has not freely chosen, like that of being a son or daughter, or being a member of a culture or nation.[31] These can clearly be construed as special obligations, being based on

---

[30] Goodin, *Protecting the Vulnerable*, p. 110.
[31] Birnbacher, 'Philosophical Foundations of Responsibility', p. 19.

particular roles or relationships; yet they are not voluntary in the sense of having been consciously chosen.[32]

We should note, however, that the notion of non-contractual obligations is controversial. Here we will mention two arguments against the idea of non-contractual obligations on the grounds of special capacity.

First, it seems to conflict with the idea that the only way in which we can acquire special obligations is by giving our consent, an idea implicit in the liberal, social contract tradition, where societal obligations are ideally derived from the prior consent of each individual (although social contract theorists *in practice* would hardly deny that there are special obligations that do not correspond to any concrete, physical contract). This is what we may call 'the voluntarist objection'. It may thus be argued that because obligations are burdensome and thus may be costly and difficult to discharge, it would be unfair if people could be ascribed obligations against their will. Against this objection, we must hold the common-sense view that even voluntarily chosen positions or obligations will give birth to obligations that are *not* chosen, yet which one cannot shirk from. In many instances, these will be obligations that one would, morally speaking, expect *others* to perform if one were to find oneself in the position of being the beneficiary of such an obligation, rather than the executor. (If I find myself stuck on a highway, with my car broken down, and a repair truck passes by, I would expect the latter to stop and help me, even if there is no contractual obligation between the two of us, and even if, say, the driver of the repair truck has finished work for the day and is on her way home. The special obligation caused by having the competence of a repairman (or woman) in itself gives rise to a special, albeit on this case non-contractual obligation. It seems contrived to say that such obligations challenge the liberal principles of autonomy and free choice.)

A second objection takes a different form by arguing that special obligations to some may work to the disadvantage of others, as well as provide those who bear them with unfair advantages – this is what Scheffler calls 'the distribution objection'.[33] This may happen in several ways. For instance, if I consider A to be a friend, and B is a person with whom I have no special relationship, but one for whom I might perform favours, then most people will say that discharging my

---

[32] It is worth mentioning that, in order for such duties to be morally compelling, the social role must be legitimate. There are for example certain discriminatory social roles and traditions, such as apartheid, that do not form the basis of any legitimate duties or responsibilities. See L. May, *Sharing Responsibility* (University of Chicago Press, 1992).

[33] Scheffler, 'Relationships and Responsibilities', p. 192.

responsibilities to A must take priority over performing favours for B, at least if the two are in direct competition. In addition, my responsibilities to A will often confer advantages on me as well, insofar as prioritizing A will contribute to the flourishing of our friendship, which is not the case if I attend to the needs of B. But why should my friendship with A give rise to a distribution that is favourable to A and myself, and unfavourable to B?

Now this last point raises a question of priority. Considering our limited stock of time, attention and resources, there is a need to select some obligations over others. Indeed, possible conflicts between general duties and special obligations call for making priorities. Special obligations, as voluntary or self-imposed obligations, are often said to be special in the sense of being *especially binding*. Thus, if someone freely takes upon herself a certain responsibility (by promise or contract), it is generally honoured by giving it priority over responsibilities imposed by others.[34] However, it is not self-evident why special obligations should take priority over general duties, not least given 'the distribution objection' mentioned above. One way of solving this problem in the case of institutions is by reference to the quite necessary division of labour that must exist in any well-regulated society. Special institutions have special and well-defined tasks that enable them to do the work they are suited and equipped for. While there may be cases where these tasks should not be understood in too restricted a way, it is still reasonable, morally and politically, to assume that one's responsibility must be defined according to one's task and competence, and that this also excuses one from taking certain morally worthy considerations, since they are not within the purview of one's legitimate activity.

Nonetheless, the distribution objection should be noted and remembered, since it usefully challenges us to think through whether the discharging of special obligations sometimes works as a convenient, yet morally insufficient smoke-screen, which hides one's negligence when one avoids performing actions that actually are in one's power, and that could have highly beneficial results.

To sum up, we hold that there are non-contractual special obligations – these can be understood as derivative general duties that are instituted independently of prior assent or choice, whereas purely contractual or appointed obligations are instituted by assignment and acceptance of task and are thus dependent upon choice. Following from one's particular role in society, these non-contractual obligations

[34] Birnbacher, 'Philosophical Foundations of Responsibility', pp. 18–19.

do belong to the realm of special obligations rightly understood. They are not *simply* natural or general duties, but obligations given by one's role, position or status. They cover the kinds of obligations that arise for someone (be it a person or an institution) with a certain position in society, or for someone within a family, circle of friends or community – that is, for those who hold roles and positions which are part of social relationships that *ipso facto* create obligations that are not explicit or carved out through a contract, yet are tangible and real.

We can get an even better grasp of the perspective we are trying to develop by attending to the difference between negative and positive duties. Negative duties are duties not to harm, whereas positive duties are duties to help.[35] It is a commonplace in ethical theory to hold that, in general, a negative duty is stricter and thus more binding than positive duties. Whereas each of us has a moral duty to go to great lengths to avoid inflicting harm on another, or more generally to avoid doing wrongful acts, we do not feel (and it does not seem) that we have a parallel duty to go to almost any length actively to save others, or to perform worthy actions.[36]

One reason why negative duties are said to 'trump' positive ones, is that whereas it is possible to avoid doing negative acts, it is not always practically possible to do positive acts. This is partly because of the fact that whereas a negative duty can be discharged completely without the help of any others, some positive duties, such as the individual's duties of aid, cannot fully be carried out by the agent alone. Thus, *positive duties are often discharged by institutional mechanisms and special assignments.* For example, whereas each of us has a duty to call the police if we discover that someone is being robbed (and even more: a duty not to rob anyone ourselves!), we have no positive duty to fight the robber. That is the special responsibility of the skilled professional – those with role obligations. Thus, we must keep in mind the earlier distinction between general duties and special obligations. Whereas negative duties seem to outweigh positive ones where general duties are concerned, they do not appear to do so where special obligations are involved.[37] 'Both in law and morals, failing to discharge a positive duty, when you have some special responsibility for doing so, constitutes an "onerous offense" rather than a "mere omission".'[38] This indicates that the inaction or silence of persons with special obligations in virtue of role, such

---

[35] Goodin, *Protecting the Vulnerable*, p. 18.
[36] John Rawls, *A Theory of Justice* (Cambridge, MA: Harvard University Press, 1971), p. 114.
[37] Goodin, *Protecting the Vulnerable*, p. 21.   [38] Ibid.

as persons in positions of authority, can involve guilt as strong as the guilt of one who is carrying out the misdeed in question.[39]

Against this background, we can ask whether the special obligations of shareholders in a broad sense, including the obligations to victims of crimes carried out or harms done by companies, are primarily negative or positive – an obligation to abstain from doing something, or an obligation to do something. In practice, it seems reasonable that an investor should decide this on the basis of effectiveness – what actions can contribute to the necessary change in the companies, while also preserving one's fiduciary duty as an investor vis-à-vis one's end-owners. For an increasing amount of institutional investors, this seems to point in the direction of active ownership strategies, instead of more passive screening and divestment strategies (where certain investments are taken out of the portfolio, or others are prioritized), although the two can also be combined. The emphasis on active ownership strategies is especially pertinent for investors that are measured against a benchmark or an index, and for whom the choice over what to own is therefore limited. These investors can still fulfil their moral obligation to address the indirect effects of their investments, while keeping their financial focus as an investor, by interacting with companies in their portfolio, based on a premise that adherence to very basic moral norms as well as internationally recognized documents where such norms are formulated (such as the UN Global Compact) will in the long run be in the interest of one's portfolio and of the markets in which one is invested. We should add here that the presence of institutional (and other) investors with long-term value-securing agendas – which include social and environmental issues – can reasonably be claimed to constitute a more responsible market than an alternative market where such players simply protest by withdrawing their investments from companies that they, for some reason (financial, moral or both), disapprove of.

If it is true that investors can reasonably be said to have a responsibility to use their ownership rights to influence companies in which they are invested, it becomes a challenge to find the right issues to address as well as cost-efficient and realistic ways of communicating with and influencing the companies. It is the view of these authors that the right to nominate and elect board directors, and the ability to communicate meaningfully with boards that have the necessary independence from company management and include members with analytic abilities,

---

[39] See also H. Syse and H. Ingierd for a clearer delineation of the different aspects of being a legitimate authority with special responsibilities, in 'What Constitutes a Legitimate Authority?', *Journal of Social Alternatives*, 24 (2005), pp. 11–16.

diverse backgrounds and the ability to integrate relevant social and environmental perspectives into one's business perspective, are primary tools that fit well with the role of the investor. But this is not the place to go into detail on that point.

What we do wish to emphasize is that there are a number of non-contractual elements to the special obligations of large institutional investors, related to their role in society. Such investors often have – especially in the case of pension funds and natural-resource funds such as the Norwegian Petroleum Fund (or Government Pension Fund) – long-term agendas and broad, global portfolios which make them eminently suited for raising environmental, social and governance issues of significance to future generations. The largest funds also have a kind of position in their respective communities, and in the society of investors, that causes them to be listened to, and this gives them the opportunity to set an agenda – and change settled agendas. The kind of responsibility hereby delineated can hardly be called purely and simply contractual, yet it follows from the specific role, power and interest of the large institutional investor. To shirk from such a responsibility because it is not clearly defined or delineated, or because one can wait for others to take it and hope to be a free rider, is hardly morally feasible, given the challenges in terms of governance-related, environmental and social issues that the investment and business community faces today.

3.1   Principal/agent

Before we move on to attitudes and characters as part of role responsibility, we need to investigate an aspect of role responsibility that we have not touched on explicitly, and which is especially pertinent to contractual relationships in the investment community (which is why we need to spend time on it here), namely, the roles of principals and agents.

The relationship between principal and agent represents an important sub-group of contractual relationships, which, in spite of the importance just attached to non-contractual obligations, remain a crucial part of the framework surrounding institutional investors. It is a relationship where someone has voluntarily agreed to act on behalf of someone else. The distinction between principal and agent concerns delegation of authority and responsibility from one party to another. Put briefly, the responsibilities of the principal include the communication of the tasks delegated, the monitoring of the agent and also holding the agent liable. The responsibility of the agent, on the other hand, is better termed fiduciary responsibility. The fiduciary owes an obligation to the principal to carry out the responsibilities agreed upon.

For example, shareholders of a company (i.e., principals, through the board) elect management (i.e., agents) to act on their behalf, and end-owners of capital (i.e., principals) choose fund managers (i.e., agents) to manage their assets. Managers are thus employees of shareholders (or stockholders); they are entrusted with their money for the express purpose of earning a return on it.

There are two often-discussed problems for the principal, which may lead to the delivery of a product or a service in a manner or in an amount different from what is ordered by the principal(s): first, the problem of goal variance, where agents have goals independent of those of the principal, and second, the problem of information asymmetry, where agents have an information advantage over the principal.[40]

A pressing question is how responsibility is shared between principals and agents, and thus to what extent principals can be held responsible and indeed liable – that is, can be blamed or praised, punished or rewarded – for acts of the agents, and also to what extent agents are held liable for their acts when acting according to directions from principals.

There are two opposite perspectives here. One view emphasizes the responsibility of the principal, building on what we may call 'the agency principle', which stipulates that agent B is not responsible for action X if B does X in the service of principal A.[41] The opposite perspective requires a clear causal connection between agent and harm, and thus builds on the idea of causal responsibility, viewing the agent as the responsible actor, given the fact that she actually carries out the action. A more moderate version of this latter view may refer to 'the Autonomy Principle' (mentioned earlier), which says that principal A is not responsible for action X carried out by agent B unless A has induced or coerced B into performing X.

We hold that the control a principal has over an agent is one of the most important factors when distributing responsibility, and given the possibility to exercise control, the principal cannot escape responsibility for the acts of the agent completely. The agent must, however, accept her share of responsibility, given the fact that she actually carries out the action and that she has certain obligations in virtue of her role, and

---

[40] N. J. Mitchell, *Agents of Atrocity: Leaders, Followers, and the Violation of Human Rights in Civil War* (New York: Palgrave, 2004), p. 45.

[41] Thomas Hobbes' theory of the social contract between the sovereign and the subjects represents one extreme version in this respect, since he makes a complete separation of authority and responsibility. In his scheme, the principals (the subjects) delegate full and supreme authority to the agent (the sovereign), but the principals remain wholly responsible for the acts of the agent, who is not considered to be liable for his deeds (*Leviathan*, chapter 14).

a certain leeway to exercise her judgment. Thus a pure version of 'the agency principle' must be rejected.

Institutional investors find themselves in the position of being both principals and agents. Vis-à-vis their owners, often represented by a board of trustees (or in the case of state funds, a government ministry or agency), they are agents, acting on the wishes and directives of their principals. But as stockholders vis-à-vis the companies in their portfolio, they are principals, with duties and rights against their agents, i.e., the companies and their boards. This in-between position aptly illustrates the need to define and clarify the contractual relationship between principals and agents, and the need to distribute responsibility fairly between the two. But it also, we believe, shows that the self-understanding of each person and institution, whether principal or agent (or both), needs to encompass a non-contractual understanding of one's obligations, based on one's position in society and one's general duties towards it. Agents that ignore the long-term interest of their principals, or conversely follow the directions of their principals blindly without any regard for the social consequences of those directions and without informing (and actively discussing with) the principals what these consequences are, both fail to live up to the expectations we may rightly have of large institutions (be they investors or companies) that operate in the public sphere.

Let us note here that overall in this chapter we do not distinguish clearly between principals and agents in terms of distinguishing between end-owners or fiduciaries on the one hand and the investment manager on the other, although we have more explicitly focused on the latter. In general, when we talk about 'the responsibilities of large institutional investors', we are talking about a *shared* responsibility between the end-owners of the invested capital, their boards of trustees (or, in the case of the Norwegian Government Petroleum (Pension) Fund, the politicians) and the professional investment organization. While the responsibility in most cases must be shouldered and handled *in practice* by the investment manager – which is indeed why we said earlier that the investment institution has a responsibility *to its owners*, and which is why we make the institutional investor our main addressee and topic here – the principals clearly have an overall responsibility for integrating central moral constraints and goals into their guidelines for the fund manager. In turn, the investment professionals (i.e., the investment management) must keep an open dialogue with their trustees and fiduciaries about how to enact these, and how better to secure important values – financial and social – in cases where this may conflict with other duties of the professional investor (such as preserving the environment in the long term over securing relative returns important to the success of the fund in the short term). An investment management unit that takes on a wide range of social responsibilities to the detriment of the overall returns of their principals, without any order or understanding that they should do so, probably acts outside its mandate, by postulating needs, wishes and responsibilities of its fiduciaries that have been neither explicitly nor implicitly stated.

To sum up, clarity about the relationship between principals and agents constitutes a potentially decisive part of the delineation of the responsibilities and role of institutional investors. This is especially true when it comes to the actual fund managers, who in practice find themselves in a position of being both principals and agents vis-à-vis the end-owners and the corporations respectively.

3.2   Attitude responsibility

As another subset of role responsibility, we will conclude our analysis of institutional investor responsibility with what we have chosen to call 'attitude responsibility', which is essentially character-based. Such a perspective is important because it acknowledges a responsibility that is not (exclusively) based on duties or obligations.

The concept of *attitude responsibility*, as we use it here, attempts to make sense of the responsibility one has for the forming of attitudes, characters and cultures.[42] A pressing question, originally discussed by Aristotle, is whether, and to what extent, someone may be held to account for an act if he is not responsible for his character or for the traits of personality that cause him to deliberate and act as he does. In short, his answer is that even though we do not have full control over the development of our character (since we do not know what the cumulative effect of particular actions will be on our character), we may still be held responsible, since we often have control over the exercise of the capacities that lead to a settled character.[43]

---

[42] The notions of character and virtues are relevant when analysing moral responsibility in many respects. For example, there may be a question of whether a ruined character exempts one from moral responsibility in general. Or, one may claim that one acted 'out of character' in a particular situation due to some particular stress, and thus that one should be temporarily exempted. In these cases, then, consideration of character may reduce or altogether exempt from guilt and is thus used to deny liability. In other cases, however, reflections on character may rather seem to lead to stronger guilt for a particular harm. According to Socrates, an evil person is someone who deliberately and over a long time cultivates vices, aiming to become good at doing harm to others. For more on this point, see A. J. Vetlesen, *Evil and Human Agency: Understanding Collective Evildoing* (New York: Cambridge University Press, 2005), p. 258.

[43] Aristotle, *Nicomachean Ethics*, book III, chapter 5, 1115a.

We suggest that attitude responsibility assigns responsibility on the basis of *who one is* and *the attitudes one conveys to others*. Thus, we are here in fact concerned with two sub-groups of responsibility: first, *internal responsibility*, which denotes responsibility for one's own character and actions, and second, *external responsibility*, which concerns the responsibility one has for the character and actions of others.[44] Both are closely related to the signals we send or the 'atmosphere' we create, and the way in which these in turn create fertile ground for the development of a culture and habits conducive to moral behaviour.

Attitude responsibility overlaps with causal responsibility when there are close causal connections between the signals sent and the actions carried out. Concerning the internal type, this is the case when my action is closely linked to an enduring trait of my character. In such a case I am primarily assigned responsibility due to a causal connection, and this responsibility becomes stronger the clearer the connection between the act in question and my character. Our point in naming this 'attitude responsibility' is primarily that my attitudes and character are closely connected to my actions, and that I am judged on the basis of those attitudes. Also, they send signals about right and wrong behaviour, right and wrong cultures and habits to others; so that 'who I am' (or at least 'who I come across as') sets standards for others, especially if I find myself in a position of great strength, size or influence.

This latter point moves us into the territory of external responsibility. Here, the causal connections are arguably weaker and more difficult to determine. In such cases, I do not directly produce the actions of others, but I exert influence over them (to a smaller or greater extent) and can be held liable on that account. I may become responsible for the attitudes of other persons when I clearly contribute to the forming of these attitudes. This is especially the case for someone with role responsibility, and more particularly for leaders – and principals – who bear a responsibility for the formulation and communication of ends.

There is a question as to whether attitude responsibility implies responsibility even if there are no causal or intentional links between agents and harms. Kutz defends a certain degree of responsibility on the basis of character alone, primarily by invoking counterfactual considerations, and by pointing to the connection between purely vicarious guilt and shame.[45] Thus he argues that even if A neither caused X, nor intended X, some blame against A may be warranted nonetheless, if

---

[44] G. Moran, *A Grammar of Responsibility* (New York: The Crossroad Publishing Company, 1996), pp. 198–203.

[45] Kutz, *Complicity*, p. 44.

there is reason for thinking that A could clearly have caused or endorsed X in the right circumstances. An example would be holding A responsible for a racist attack carried out by B, when A did not cause the harm, consciously or otherwise, but in effect, on account of his racist attitudes, strongly supported the act happening.[46] However, this seems to leave us with a concept of vicarious liability that is deeply problematic from a legal point of view.[47] Feinberg rightly points out that 'we have no way of confirming statements about what a man with a given character structure would do if the circumstances were different; so if we are determined to avoid punishing the genuinely faultless, we had better wait until the circumstances *are* different'.[48]

In the moral sphere, however, as opposed to the legal, the case is somewhat different, and more specifically, causation as a necessary condition of liability is weakened, so that Kutz' intimations can be made more sense of. However, we believe that in order to be held morally liable for the acts of others on account of attitude responsibility, there must have been, as a minimum, an exercise of influence on the attitudes and acts of others which implies the increased likelihood of harm, and thus causal responsibility in a weak sense; hence, our emphasis on 'signals' and 'the creation of attitudes'.[49] Considerations of social role, degree of willingness to exercise influence in a certain direction, as well as degree of identification with the harm carried out, help determine the degree of responsibility further.

This is obviously relevant to large institutional investors who set examples in the community of investors – and in the business community more widely – through the way they communicate and the public profile they have. Both the way in which their internal organizations are built up, and the way in which they use their position of strength externally to communicate attitudes and ideals, can and should be analysed from this perspective. This does not mean that institutional investors should become something they are not: agents of charity or social development. The idea and meaning of an investment organization is to create and safeguard financial values. However, in doing so, one holds responsibility for how this is actually done, and one holds responsibility for the kind of society and ideals one helps create. Furthermore, if an institutional investor seriously believes that a future world not dominated by corruption, human rights abuse, violent conflict and

---

[46] This is related to the notion of 'participatory intention' discussed above (under complicity).
[47] J. Feinberg, 'Collective Responsibility', *The Journal of Philosophy*, 65 (1968), pp. 674–88.
[48] Ibid., p. 682.   [49] May, *Sharing Responsibility*, p. 36.

environmental degradation is more conducive to predictable and stable wealth creation for one's fiduciaries than its opposite, then the way in which one contributes to creating such a world and forms attitudes suited to fighting such evils, is surely relevant.

4.   Conclusion

We have tried above to make a conceptual map of perspectives on moral responsibility pertaining to a large institutional investor, in a world of widely spread investments and complex business relationships. Based on this, we have tried to indicate what follows from this in practice for an institutional investor.

In conclusion, we should remind ourselves that responsibility is *dynamic*, rather than static. Hence, the content of one's responsibility is not determined once and for all, nicely delineated according to a 'conceptual map', but may be changed by different circumstances. This is not least important as regards role responsibility: one's role in society changes as society changes, and this is indeed a crucial premise of our article, namely, that the role of large institutional investors must be thought through anew, so that we appreciate fully the kinds of responsibilities that such investors may come to have.

Furthermore – as regards the dynamic character of responsibility – we should keep in mind the distinction between the obligations we would have if everyone else discharged their responsibilities ('ideal theory'), and the obligations that arise because others do not do their part ('non-ideal theory'). This challenges us to clarify what happens to one's responsibility when others neglect theirs. Is it the case that such neglect on the part of others increases *my* responsibility?

From the point of view of what we above called non-reductionism, one may become responsible for something because one is (or happens to find oneself) in a *position* to carry out responsibilities, such as when one happens to pass a child in great need, and the parents and/or social institutions with the primary responsibility to help that child are not doing so. This perspective allows for the ascription of responsibility on the basis of the fact that others do not do their part, when one happens to be in a position to discharge that responsibility instead. A good example pertaining to investors may be furnished by environmental degradation generally and climate change in particular. Regulatory political agencies can reasonably be said, given the complexity of the issues and the many actors involved, to have the main obligation to define the limits within which businesses should move in terms of environmental standards. The companies, in turn, have a duty to follow up on these regulations, and to think creatively about how this can best be done in the individual case. But investors who understand the dangers posed by such environmental challenges, and who observe that efficient regulatory regimes are not yet put into place and/or companies do not do their part, can come to see their role as taking on tasks related to such concerns, even though such tasks *prima facie* belong to others. This applies to a range of issues that an institutional investor can very well address as part of its active ownership strategy, while retaining one's financial investor focus: inefficient governance systems, corruption, child and slave labour, severe environmental challenges, or contribution to armed conflict, to name but a few.

Large institutional investors can reasonably be said to have responsibilities associated with both the perspectives treated in this chapter – causal and role responsibility – and various subsets of these. By saying 'can reasonably be said to have' we hold, based on the arguments made throughout this chapter, that the burden of proof rests on those who deny that institutional investors have such responsibilities. Taking on these responsibilities is, we believe, compatible with the primary aim of the investor: to secure financial returns for one's fiduciaries. Indeed, living up to these responsibilities (albeit in close cooperation and understanding with one's fiduciaries[50]) is absolutely necessary, since *not* discharging them may seriously hurt the trust, reputation and position of the institutional investor in modern society, as well as the long-term value of the funds under management. This is especially true in a world where large institutional investors are becoming ever more crucial players in a global economy that is dependent for its progress and survival on responsible actors able and willing to see further than next month's balance sheet – yet their primary responsibility is clear: to produce returns for their owners, and to do so by investing in companies and markets capable of providing such returns.[51]

---

[50] See our remarks on this point under the discussion of principals and agents above.

[51] See O. P. K. Gjessing and H. Syse for an elaboration of this argument, often called the 'Universal Ownership' argument, in 'Norwegian Petroleum Wealth and Universal Ownership', *Corporate Governance*, 15 (2007), pp. 427–37.

9   Sovereign wealth funds and (un)ethical
     investment: using 'due diligence' to
     avoid contributing to human rights
     violations committed by companies
     in the investment portfolio

Bruno Demeyere

1.   Introduction: New kids in town

'Governments are very different from other economic actors. Their investments should be governed by rules designed with that reality very clearly in mind.'[1]

This introduction consists of two parts. The first part situates sovereign wealth funds within the international monetary and financial system. The second sets the stage for the specific angle from which this contribution has been written, and introduces the questions it seeks to address.

1.1   *Sovereign wealth funds as actors in the international*
          monetary and financial system

Over the last five to ten years, sovereign wealth funds (SWFs) have come to be perceived as the new giants of the international monetary and financial system. While the 2008 international financial crisis has left its impact felt upon the depth of their pockets,[2] they surely represent forces which need to be reckoned with for the decades to come. The mainstream assumption underlying any debate about SWFs, indeed,

---

[1] L. Summers, 'Funds that Shake Capitalist Logic', *Financial Times* (29 July 2007).

[2] For an actualized overview of the funds, ranked by assets managed, see www.swfinstitute.org/funds.php. For a historic overview, see Edwin M. Truman, 'Sovereign Wealth Funds: The Need for Greater Transparency and Accountability', Peterson Institute for International Economics, Policy Brief, No. PB07–6 (August 2007), p. 3. For a narrative overview, see Eric Langland, 'Misplaced Fears Put to Rest: Financial Crisis Reveals the True Motives of Sovereign Wealth Funds', *Financial Times* (7 January 2009), p. 263.

seems to be that SWFs are not only there to stay, but that they are also bound to grow.

As a consequence, international financial markets – along with those at the political level having the capacity to regulate these markets – are starting to realize that SWFs' growth may lead to a situation in which the world as they know it may possibly be a thing of the past.

Calls for international regulation,[3] including self-regulation,[4] are therefore increasingly expressed and implemented.[5] While some of

---

[3] See Ronald J. Gilson and Curtis J. Milhaupt, 'Sovereign-Wealth Funds and Corporate Governance: A Minimalist Response to the New Mercantilism', *Stanford Law and Economics Online*, Working Paper No. 355 (18 February 2008) (arguing that increasing the transparency of SWFs does not suffice, and proposing to suspend their voting rights of equity investments in US corporations as a way of curtailing the concern that SWFs would make their decisions based on motives of a domestic-strategic rather than a financial nature), as well as Edward F. Greene and Brian A. Yeager, 'Sovereign Wealth Funds – A Measured Assessment', *Capital Markets Law Journal*, 3 (2008), p. 247 (arguing that the policy debates must acknowledge the different types of investments and investment objectives pursued by SWFs, and that policy should focus its reaction on the types which raise concerns from the angle of market integrity or national security). Arguing against regulation, see Richard A. Epstein and Amanda M. Rose, 'The Regulation of Sovereign Wealth Funds: The Virtues of Going Slow', *University of Chicago Law Review*, forthcoming, p. 111.

[4] Since 2008, the cornerstone document in this field are the 'Santiago Principles', full title 'Sovereign Wealth Funds: Generally Accepted Principles and Practices', adopted by the International Working Group of Sovereign Wealth Funds; www.swfinstitute. org/research/santiagoprinciples.pdf. This voluntary set of standards will not be subject to any further analysis in this contribution. Suffice it to say, however, that the 'Santiago Principles' are agnostic/without prejudice to the applicability of notions of 'socially responsible' investment to the realm of SWFs, as results from a combined reading of Principles 15 and 19. The baseline obligation to comply with applicable legislation in any country in which one operates is affirmed in Principle 15: 'SWF operations and activities in host countries should be conducted in compliance with all applicable regulatory and disclosure requirements of the countries in which they operate.' Furthermore, Sub-principle 19.1 does say that 'If investment decisions are subject to other than economic and financial considerations, these should be clearly set out in the investment policy and be publicly disclosed.' The Principles' 'Explanation and Commentary' states as follows at p. 22: 'Some SWFs may exclude certain investments for various reasons, including legally binding international sanctions and social, ethical, or religious reasons (e.g., Kuwait, New Zealand and Norway). More broadly, some SWFs may address social, environmental, or other factors in their investment policy. If so, these reasons and factors should be publicly disclosed.' For an in-depth analysis of the Santiago Principles, see Anthony Wong, 'Sovereign Wealth Funds and the Problem of Asymmetric Information: The Santiago Principles and International Regulations', *Brooklyn Journal of International Law*, 34 (2009), p. 1081, with a discussion of the Santiago Priniciples at pp. 1103–9. See also Paul Rose, 'Sovereigns as Shareholders', *North Carolina Law Review*, 87 (2008), p. 83. For an argument to maintain the current approach to develop 'soft law' rather than 'hard law' regulation of SWFs, see Langland, 'Misplaced Fears Put to Rest', p. 263.

[5] From within the realm of multilateral institutions, see, e.g., (1) Mark Allen and Jaime Caruana, 'Sovereign Wealth Funds – A Work Agenda', *International Monetary Fund* (29 February 2008): www.imf.org/external/np/pp/eng/2008/022908.pdf; (2) OECD

these calls are inspired by concerns over the (perceived) shifting global wealth distribution, others raise profound questions about the role of the state and its entanglement in possibly conflicting values: maximization of financial value versus respect of human rights. Given the recent character of the debate, and contrary to what is the case for state-owned enterprises in general,[6] the regulation of SWFs through codes of conduct and other regulatory instruments is therefore a very new phenomenon.

Whether by amassing reserves thanks to the proceeds from the sale of natural resources, or through building up foreign exchange currency reserves based on other sources of income, an increasing number of states have indeed started to invest their wealth abroad. At the opposite end of the spectrum from states struggling with sovereign debt management and restructuring, SWFs are used as a tool by states having excess funds.

It largely remains an open question whether SWFs are a tool exclusively devoted towards wealth maximization, or whether some states see them equally as a tool to gain political influence abroad. The possibility that the latter may be the case haunts the political debates in states at the receiving end, e.g., when SWFs would seek to acquire voting rights in sectors of strategic domestic importance.[7] The debate, therefore, has

Report, 'Sovereign Wealth Funds and Recipient Country Policies' (OECD Investment Committee, 4 April 2008): www.oecd.org/dataoecd/34/9/40408735.pdf; and (3) Commission of the European Union, 'Communication from the Commission to the European Parliament, The Council, The European Economic and Social Committee and the Committee of the Regions' (27 February 2008): available via ec.europa.eu/ internal_market/finances/docs/sovereign_en.pdf.

[6] In order to complement its 'Corporate Governance Principles' for the private sector, the OECD Council adopted, in April 2005, 'Guidelines on the Corporate Governance of State-Owned Enterprises' which deal with themes such as 'Ensuring an Effective Legal and Regulatory Framework for State-Owned Enterprises'; 'The State Acting as an Owner'; 'Equitable Treatment of Shareholders'; 'Relations with Stakeholders'; 'Transparency and Disclosure'; and 'The Responsibilities of the Boards of State-Owned Enterprises'. On these Guidelines, see Organisation for Economic Co-Operation and Development, *Corporate Governance of State-Owned Enterprises: A Survey of OECD Countries* (Paris: OECD Publishing, 2005).

[7] See generally the OECD Report, released on 4 April 2008 and entitled 'Sovereign Wealth Funds and Recipient Country Policies': 'Investments by SWFs can raise concerns as to whether their objectives are commercial or driven by political, defence or foreign policy considerations', p. 7, available via www.oecd.org/dataoecd/34/9/40408735.pdf; and Allen and Caruana, 'Sovereign Wealth Funds – A Work Agenda', p. 10: 'There is no clear evidence that SWF investments have been motivated by narrow political objectives.' On this debate, see Jennifer Cooke, 'Finding the Right Balance for Sovereign Wealth Fund Regulation: Open Investment vs. National Security', *The Columbia Business Law Review*, 2 (2009), p. 728; Amy D. Keller, 'Sovereign Wealth Funds: Trustworthy Investors or Vehicles of Strategic Ambition – An Assessment of the Benefits, Risks and Possible Regulation of Sovereign Wealth Funds', *Georgetown*

as much to do with western fears of being in decline as it has to do with genuine arguments for regulating a hitherto unknown feature of global financial interconnectedness with multiple implications from the perspective of financial stability.

For better[8] or for worse, these SWFs – one of the possible[9] vehicles through which states can invest public funds and the definition of which has only been recently crystallized[10] – are pumping their capital into the international financial markets. By acquiring securities such as stocks and bonds that are issued by foreign corporations of the private sector, such cross-border investments engender a situation whereby sovereign states increasingly own part of publicly traded private sector companies abroad.

Observers are still grappling to come up with a term that manages to capture this new phenomenon, the prospects of which are daunting when one starts to think through its ramifications. Via a SWF as an intermediary acting on its behalf, a state is indeed involved in exactly the same type of economic activities as the ones that are deployed by innumerable institutional investment funds belonging to the private sector, such as pension funds, mutual funds, etc. The crucial difference, however, lies in the *nature* of the investor, which is a sovereign state. In parallel with the term 'nationalization', concepts such as cross-border nationalization[11]

Journal of Law & Public Policy, 7 (2008), p. 333; and Matthew Saxon, 'It's Just Business, Or Is It? How Business and Politics Collide With Sovereign Wealth Funds', *Hastings International and Comparative Law Review*, 32 (2009), p. 693.

[8] Arguing pro the positive effects which can result from investments by SWFs, see Patrick Keenan and Christiana Ochoa, 'The Human Rights Potential of Sovereign Wealth Funds', *Georgetown Journal of International Law*, 40 (2009), p. 1151.

[9] See generally Robert M. Kimmitt, 'Public Footprints in Private Markets: Sovereign Wealth Funds and the World Economy', *Foreign Affairs*, 87 (2008), p. 119 (dividing investments of public funds into four separate categories, of which SWFs are but one, next to international reserves, public pension funds and state-owned enterprises). See also Larry Catá Backer, 'The Norwegian Sovereign Wealth Fund: Between Private and Public', *Georgetown Journal of International Law*, 40 (2009), p. 1271.

[10] In 2007, the US Department of the Treasury stated as follows: 'There is no single, universally accepted definition of a SWF', in turn dividing them into 'commodity funds' versus 'non-commodity funds'; see www.treas.gov/offices/international-affairs/ economic-exchange-rates/pdf/2007_Appendix-3.pdf. As of 2008, the 'Santiago Principles' define SWFs as follows: 'SWFs are defined as special purpose investment funds or arrangements, owned by the general government. Created by the general government for macroeconomic purposes, SWFs hold, manage, or administer assets to achieve financial objectives, and employ a set of investment strategies which include investing in foreign financial assets. The SWFs are commonly established out of balance of payment surpluses, official foreign currency operations, the proceeds of privatization, fiscal surpluses, and/or receipts resulting from commodity exports.'

[11] Stephen R. Weisman, 'Sovereign Funds Stir Growing Unease: As Foreign State-Controlled Investors Gain Leverage, Washington Starts to Fret', *International Herald Tribune* (21 August 2007).

or internationalization[12] have been proposed to account for the situation whereby sovereign states own a share of foreign private corporations abroad.

1.2   Scope of this contribution

Against this broader background, the present contribution has a rather specific focus. The assumption is as follows: a foreign private corporation in which a SWF has invested is allegedly involved in violations of public international law standards,[13] especially human rights law and international criminal law standards.

This assumption will be assessed from the angle of the following question: is, in legal terms, the state to which the SWF belongs 'complicit' in these violations? If so, does this raise the latter state's international legal responsibility?

In order to elaborate upon the assumption, imagine a scenario in three chronological steps: (i) the SWF first does not know of these (alleged) violations when making the investment; (ii) the SWF subsequently receives information about these allegations at a later stage; and (iii) finally, the receipt of this information does not lead the SWF to divest from the corporation in question.

The questions that are focused on in this contribution are as follows: in step (iii), as described in the previous paragraph, is the SWF (and the state to which it belongs) in any way whatsoever in violation of international legal obligations binding upon it when choosing not to divest? Is there, in other words, an affirmative obligation for a SWF to divest from such a corporation, on the grounds that the SWF would have (un)knowingly contributed to the violations committed by the corporation in question?

The purpose of the present contribution is to look at these questions from the angle of public international law. Section 3.1.2 below will further complicate the scenario so as to take account of the specific circumstances that are present when SWFs embark upon investment in foreign private corporations.

As will be analysed in greater detail below (see section 3.1), as a matter of currently existing law, the answer to all these questions shall

---

[12] 'Sovereign-Wealth Funds: The World's Most Expensive Club', *The Economist* (26 May 2007).

[13] The present contribution is confined to public international law, and not to any other of the multiple legal frameworks regulating international capital markets. On the latter, see generally Herbert Kronke, 'Capital Markets and Conflict of Laws', *Recueil des Cours*, 286 (2000), p. 291.

be rather firmly in the negative. There is, indeed, no responsibility in legal terms for the SWF (and the state to which it belongs) in the scenario presented here. Legally speaking indeed, even under the most extensive forms of existing human rights protection standards – coming from a regional or potentially universal treaty – that may be binding upon it, such a state does nothing wrong vis-à-vis its obligations under public international law.

Yet, as ever, the law only proscribes minimal obligations that need not be the end of the debate. Thus, a shift of perspective is in order, away from the strictly legal(istic) perspective. As the example of the Norwegian Government Pension Fund – Global demonstrates, there is of course a solid policy argument to be made in favour of assessing the scenario described here from a different angle. It makes sense, indeed, and this for a wide variety of reasons, to be more flexible than what the law calls for, i.e., to seek to incorporate sensitivities of a human rights nature into one's portfolio management.

This chapter will argue that a 'due diligence' yardstick can play a compelling role in terms of structuring the SWF's behavioural pattern. 'Due diligence', indeed, is a concept which allows for a two-step approach: first, seek to actively engage the corporation's management; second, leave open the option of divesting as a matter of last resort.

Some further words about the angle from which the present contribution has been written are called for. This contribution's unit of analysis is SWFs as state-entities, thus excluding investment activities by non-state actors on the one hand, and the activities or responsibilities of multilateral intergovernmental organizations, on the other. *Substantively*, the focus is upon a state's responsibility under public international law. *Ratione materiae*, the scope is limited to portfolio investment with a transnational character. Thus, not dealt with are those instances in which a SWF invests in entities incorporated in its own jurisdiction. In such a case, legally speaking, a different picture may emerge (especially as per human rights law) which will not be dealt with here. For these scenarios of an exclusively domestic nature, the state's obligation to protect human rights[14] indeed applies

---

[14] John Ruggie, 'Promotion and Protection of all Human Rights, Civil, Political, Economic, Social and Cultural Rights including the Right to development. Protect, Respect and Remedy: A Framework for Business and Human Rights; Report of the Special Representative of the Secretary-General on the Issue of Human Rights and Transnational Corporations and Other Business Enterprises' (Report 2008), United Nations Human Rights Council, UN Doc. A/HRC/8/5 (7 April 2008), paras. 27–50.

unequivocally. Equally untouched is the legal configuration as it results from the acquisition of real estate abroad.

The structure of this contribution is as follows: section 2 analyses 'Socially Responsible Investment' from the conceptual angle, providing examples of various modalities that are possible as to the 'what, when, and how' of implementing such a policy. Against this background, section 3 dives into the heart of the matter, namely (section 3.1) an explanation as to why, in principle, existing international law does not consider SWFs to be responsible for the activities committed by the companies they have invested in abroad; and (section 3.2) how, as is argued here, the 'due diligence' construct could play a role in structuring SWF's portfolio management in a self-interested manner. In some states, the truth of the matter is indeed that, no matter what the law may or may not require, reputational damage suffered by the company in which the SWF has invested abroad, reflects poorly upon the SWF and, most important of all, the sovereign state behind it.

2.   On socially responsible investment

2.1   The concept

Broadly defined, 'socially responsible investment' (hereafter 'SRI'), also referred to as ethical investment, implies that a portfolio manager's investment strategy considers not only classic financial assessment tools, but also criteria of a social, environmental or human rights nature when making up his institutional mind as to which companies to invest in. All these non-financial criteria serve alongside the more classic ones about a company's predicted value trajectory. The financial and non-financial criteria may point in the same direction. Or they may not.

There has been much talk lately to underpin such an investment strategy from a purely economic angle. In other words: can a 'business case' be made to underpin SRI as a vehicle which, by taking on board non-financial criteria, actually serves an investor's purpose of enhancing the investment fund's value maximization? Is it more profitable – in the long if not necessarily in the short-run – to invest in companies the activities of which are more sustainable by their not impacting negatively upon social, environmental and human rights factors?[15]

---

[15] Arguing that SRI improves an investment fund's financial profitability, see Russell Sparkes and Christopher J. Cowton, 'The Maturing of Socially Responsible Investment: A Review of the Developing Link with Corporate Social Responsibility', *Journal of Business Ethics*, 52 (2004), p. 45, and S. Prakash Sethi, 'Investing in Socially Responsible Companies is a Must for Public Pension Funds – Because there

Leaving the larger debate aside, the purpose of the present section is much more limited. Its sole ambition is to conceptually structure the various types of SRI which have been resorted to in practice by the managers of private investment funds.[16] It is these dynamics, as they play out in practice, which will be mirrored below (see section 3.2) in the presentation of the various steps alongside which the 'due diligence' concept evolves.

Of course, SRI does not need to depend upon the private sector's sole initiative. In fact, a state can – as some have done[17] – play an encouraging role here by adopting legislation or recommendations applicable to the private investment funds that are operating in, or from within, its jurisdiction, or by providing in turn for a regulatory framework[18]

---

is No Better Alternative', *Journal of Business Ethics*, 56 (2005), p. 99; versus, arguing that it does not lead to such increased profitability, see Matthew Haight and James Hazelton, 'Financial Markets: A Tool for Social Responsibility?', *Journal of Business Ethics*, 52 (2004), p. 59.

[16] Hence, outside the scope of the present contribution are public procurement policies which seek to leverage their influence by requiring respect for certain criteria, or which disqualify a given category of companies from applying for public tenders. Among the most hotly debated examples in this respect was a statute that had been enacted in 1996 by Massachusetts, barring corporations that were doing business with Burma from bidding for contracts with that US state's public bodies. The statute was, eventually, declared unconstitutional by the US Supreme Court, the majority of which considered it to violate the foreign policy pursued by the US federal state, which had subsequently put sanctions in place against Burma. This litigation demonstrated that, while private sector funds can do whatever they please in this regard, public organs need to be more careful, as such a campaign may go against the country's foreign policy efforts. Hence, likewise, divestment which is purely based on the sole criterion – objective though it may be – that a corporation is 'doing business in' a particular country, will likely only be an option for a SWF in case such requirement be in line with the state's foreign policy point of view. For an historic overview of the Massachusetts campaign, and whether such campaigns could still take place while respecting the US Supreme Court's Judgment, see Robert Stumberg, 'Preemption & Human Rights: Local Options after Crosby v. NFTC', *Law and Policy in International Business*, 32 (2000–1), p. 109, and Wendy L. Wallace, 'Are States Denied A Voice? Citizen-Driven Foreign Policy After Crosby v. National Foreign Trade Council', *Case Western Reserve Journal of International Law*, 52 (2002), p. 793.

[17] See, e.g., the US 'Sudan Accountability and Divestment Act' of 2007 (S.2271), signed by the US President on 31 December 2007, at Section 3: '(a) Sense of Congress – It is the sense of Congress that the United States Government should support the decision of any State or local government to divest from, or to prohibit the investment of assets of the State or local government in, a person that the State or local government determines poses a financial or reputational risk; (b) Authority To Divest – Notwithstanding any other provision of law, a State or local government may adopt and enforce measures ... to divest the assets of the State or local government from, or prohibit investment of the assets of the State or local government in, persons that the State or local government determines [have certain well-defined business ties to Sudan].'

[18] The absence of such a framework leads to much legal uncertainty in practice, as demonstrated by Ronald B. Ravikoff and Myron P. Curzan, 'Social Responsibility

setting out the boundaries beyond which fund managers cannot go if they wish to avoid seeing their professional liability invoked.[19]

The wide variety of modalities according to which SRI-activities are deployed, can be assessed along two different axes of analysis. The first such axis concerns the moment in time when the non-financial criteria are taken into account by the investment fund. The second axis concerns the type of reaction which can possibly be resorted to by the fund once it finds out about the allegations/proof of a given corporation's activities which infringe upon certain standards of behaviour. Both will be dealt with in turn.

2.1.1   When are the non-financial criteria taken into account?   As to the moment in time when the non-financial criteria are looked at by the investment fund, the analysis is simply of a binary nature: either it is before, or it is after the decision to invest. Of course, having looked at those criteria prior to the investment does not preclude continuing to do so after this step has been taken.

If the non-financial criteria are looked at *prior* to reaching a decision as to whether or not to proceed with a given investment, one can do so by using either positive or negative 'screens'.

'Positive screens' means that the investment fund actively looks for corporations which themselves highly value non-financial criteria throughout their operations.

'Negative screens' imply that the investment fund avoids investing in corporations which are engaged in a given range of activities that are in breach of certain standards or values that are considered important by the investment fund. Examples of such negative screens are funds pledging not to invest in corporations engaged in the production or trade of certain goods such as, e.g., weapons, tobacco, alcohol or biofuels.[20] Another example relates to the policy of certain funds

in Investment Policy and the Prudent Man Rule', *California Law Review*, 68 (1980), p. 591.

[19] For an analysis of a court case that arose in the United Kingdom, in which it was held by the court that, at least as far as charities are concerned, some degree of ethical investment will be permitted, see Peter Luxton, 'Ethical Investment in Hard Times', *The Modern Law Review*, 55 (1992), p. 587.

[20] For example, the 2010 edition of the Norwegian Government Pension Fund – Global's 'Guidelines for Observation and Exclusion from the Goverment Pension Fund Global's Investment Universe', version adopted 1 March 2010, states in Section 2(1) as follows: 'The assets in the Fund shall not be invested in companies which themselves or through entities they control: a) produce weapons that violate fundamental humanitarian principles through their normal use; b) produce tobacco; c) sell weapons or military material to states mentioned in section 3.2 of the guidelines for the management of the Fund' (Ethical Guidelines 2010, see Appendix 1 below).

consisting of their imposing disclosure requirements upon a corporation it is considering investing in. If the data obtained during such a disclosure process reveal certain types of information that are considered to fall within the 'negative screen', the fund will decide not to invest in this corporation. For sure, imposing such disclosure requirements can be part of a larger 'due diligence' strategy, in line with the way in which this concept is used in the corporate realm and which recently received a boost forward in terms of its normative value for the broader field of the interrelationship between the realm of 'business', on the one hand, and the realm of 'human rights', on the other.[21]

In all these instances of 'negative screens', the investment fund is purely seeking to *avoid* investing in corporations which do not comply with certain standards of a non-financial nature. The decision not to invest in such a corporation will be implemented no matter how financially profitable it may appear to proceed with the investment. Hence, one simply wishes to *prevent contributing* to certain forms of corporate conduct considered undesirable, and this irrespective of their potential financial profitability. Obviously, such a policy pursued by an investment fund may lead to attracting a certain niche of customers which are sensitive to these considerations, e.g., not to invest in armaments production.

As indicated above, there is a second axis of analysis along which SRI activities can be ranged. These relate to the various reactions that can be taken by an investment fund when it finds out that a corporation in which it has invested, is (allegedly) involved in activities infringing upon certain non-financial criteria. This point is of crucial importance for understanding the nature and dynamic of the 'due diligence' construct proposed here. It will be dealt with next.

2.1.2   Which reactions can be resorted to?   When assessing the various reactions that can be resorted to by an investment fund when it finds out about certain activities of a corporation in which it has invested and which are considered undesirable, it is useful to situate the scenario against its broader background. Either the fund did not do any screening prior to investing, or it turns out that – despite a screening which has been carried out – the corporation is nevertheless (allegedly) engaged in conduct considered undesirable.

---

[21] Ruggie, Report 2008, paras. 56–64; and John Ruggie, 'Report of the Special Representative of the Secretary-General on the Issue of Human Rights and Transnational Corporations and Other Business Enterprises: Further Steps toward the Operationalization of the "Protect, Respect and Remedy"-Framework' (Report 2010), UN Doc. A/HRC/14/27 (April 2010), paras. 79–86.

Two strategies that can be resorted to will be presented here. Both have in common that they seek to influence the company's behaviour.[22] The first such strategy consists of actively engaging with the corporation's management. The second such strategy consists of divestment. While divestment necessarily precludes further engagement, the reverse is not the case and is arguably to be preferred as the order in which to sequence the respective mechanisms. This is exactly the whole point of 'due diligence' as applied to a SWF's strategizing over its own conduct, and which will be dealt with in section 3.2.

Active engagement will be dealt with first, to be followed by an analysis of divestment.

2.2   Active engagement

Actively engaging with a corporation's management is quite often preferred by many SRI-policies as the strategy which ought to come before anything else.[23] Through such a policy, one seeks to enter into a dialogue with the corporation so as to share the concerns over the corporate behaviour's (alleged) non-compliance with certain criteria of a non-financial nature. Since the investors maintain the powers of the purse, it is hoped that such a dialogue can lead to pressure being exercised upon the management, and that the latter will agree to modify the corporation's behaviour.

Three arguments can be advanced in favour of embarking upon this road before even considering divestment.

First, active engagement is a much less drastic course of action than divestment. Once the decision to divest has been implemented,

---

[22] There is no shortage of studies which have been undertaken to assess whether SRI yields any impact in terms of actually modifying the behaviour of the company in which the investment has been made. For a cautious assessment that SRI can manage to affect corporate behaviour, but only to some extent, see Michael S. Knoll, 'Ethical Screening in Modern Financial Markets: The Conflicting Claims Underlying Socially Responsible Investment', *The Business Lawyer*, 57 (2001–2), p. 681. Arguing that the effectiveness of environmental regulation can be enhanced when it encourages institutional investors to take environmental criteria into account, thus making the investor community an integral component of an environmental regulatory scheme, see Benjamin J. Richardson, 'Enlisting Institutional Investors in Environmental Regulation: Some Comparative and Theoretical Perspectives', *North Carolina Journal of International Law and Commercial Regulation*, 28 (2002–3), p. 247.

[23] On such engagement process, see Wim Vandekerckhove, Jos Leys and Dirk Van Braeckel, 'That's Not What Happened and It's Not my Fault Anyway! An Exploration of Management Attitudes Towards SRI-Shareholder Engagement', *Business Ethics: A European Review*, 16 (2007), p. 403. For an example in Belgium of such a screening mechanism which seeks to engage 'in a dialogue process that has the objective to obtain information and to improve [the company's] practices', see www.portfolio21.be.

indeed, the end of the road has been reached. No more direct leverage can be exercised at all over the corporation.[24] The newsflash of the divestment may capture headlines, though if the corporation is non-responsive all leverage has been lost. This is not to deny the fact that there may be situations in which the only sensible option left is to divest.

Second, engagement can be done discreetly or more publicly. Of course, both approaches can be sequenced: one can choose to first discreetly approach the management with one's concerns, while keeping open the option of publicly disclosing these concerns later on, if no perceived improvement takes place.

Finally, engagement can be informal or formal. Belonging to the latter category are the wide variety of initiatives known under the banner of 'shareholder activism',[25] whereby shareholders use their entitlements – as owners – to raise their concerns. The range of these entitlements will, evidently, entirely be determined by the national legal framework governing the corporation's corporate life.[26] By using domestic corporate law mechanisms available to them as shareholders, investors formally attempt to modify the corporation's behaviour in a visible way. Though definitely not always impactful, and requiring significant resources if done vis-à-vis a series of companies which the fund is invested in, the investor community acknowledges the potential role of such engagement practices.[27]

---

[24] Along the same lines, see UN Human Rights Council, 'Report of the United Nations High Commissioner on Human Rights on the Sectoral Consultation Entitled "Human Rights and the Financial Sector"', UN Doc. A/HRC/4/99 (March 2007), para. 17: 'Some participants suggested that when financial institutions become aware of human rights violations in their investments, they should withdraw their support from those investments. A number of participants pointed out that if [financial institutions] withdraw, they have no leverage at all to improve the human rights impact of the project. Withdrawal should be a last resort and it may lead to negative consequences ...'

[25] See generally Aaron A. Dihr, 'Realigning the Corporate Building Blocks: Shareholder Proposals as a Vehicle for Achieving Corporate Social and Human Rights Accountability', *American Business Law Journal*, 43 (2006), p. 365 (analysing the shareholder proposal mechanism in North America, through which shareholders may be able to compel a company's management to hold a shareholder vote on a particular issue).

[26] See generally Mark Mansley, 'Private Financial Actors and Corporate Responsibility in Conflict Zones', in Karen Ballentine and Heiko Nitzschke (eds.), *Profiting from Peace: Managing the Resource Dimensions of Civil War* (Boulder, CO: Lynne Rienner, 2005), p. 205.

[27] See UN Global Compact Office, 'Report of the Informal Consultation with the Institutional Investor and Business Communities: Responsible Investment in Weak or Conflict-Prone States' (New York, 17 January 2007), p. 5; www.unglobalcompact. org/docs/news_events/meeting_reports/Meeting_Report_Final.pdf.

As previously indicated, active engagement may end up yielding little to no results. Either the corporation is simply not interested in pursuing such a dialogue with its investors, or it refuses to modify its behaviour in line with, and as far as, what investors would have wished. In those cases, 'divestment' ought to be brought on the table as an option.

2.3   Divestment

Divestment can be resorted to for a wide variety of reasons, financial and non-financial alike. In the SRI realm, where non-financial criteria are often at stake which appeal to certain segments of public opinion, a decision to (consider to) divest often goes hand in hand with a targeted media campaign. Steered by activist groups or not, such process at the investors' level may end up being paralleled by a consumer boycott at the street level.

Divestment, in essence, is the privilege of the investor: the link between the corporation's activities and the alleged violations of certain standards of behaviour neither need to necessarily be real nor serious. In practice, perception of such a link may result in an investor's decision to divest for fear of being perceived to be associated with certain corporate conduct.

Neither does divestment need to be based on actual 'faults' being attributable to the corporation in question. Divestment, indeed, can be solely politically motivated (or not motivated at all). An investor may define his own divestment criteria in such a loose fashion that divestment is being resorted to irrespective of actual, individualized culpability. An example thereof may be to announce divestment from *any* corporation 'doing business in or with' a particular country. Some of the corporations which will be divested from on this basis, may in fact not be engaged in any harmful conduct at all. This will not preclude the divestment. Other divestment policies are possible. For example, one divests not because of a nexus with a given country, but because of a nexus with a given activity in which the company in question is involved. Examples of such activities are a corporation's resort to slave and/or child labour.[28] In these cases, clearly, liability may be at stake, at least in terms of the conduct in question being criminally sanctionable as per the domestic legislation of the country in which the investment fund is incorporated. While, as a matter of strict law, the investment fund may not necessarily be liable itself for the mere fact of having

---

[28] Naomi Roht-Arriaza, 'From Country-Based to Corporate Campaigns', *Berkeley Journal of International Law*, 21 (2003), p. 185.

invested in such a corporation, it wishes to avoid to be associated with such behaviour.

While minor exceptions sometimes exist to avoid absurdities or for other reasons, investment funds with country-based campaigns voluntarily[29] divest across the board from any company which is present in, or has economic ties to, a particular country (or region of the latter, depending on the circumstances). Among the most well-known historic examples of such a campaign, in the 1980s, was the divestment campaign that was directed against any corporation which was 'doing business' in or with apartheid-era South Africa. A more recent example can be found in the campaign embarked upon by certain funds, especially US public pension funds, to divest from any corporation which is doing business in or with Sudan.[30] These initiatives, undertaken by investment funds, often run in parallel with so-called investor liability litigation initiated by private plaintiffs.[31]

Just as divestment policies may be pursued for a wide variety of reasons – or for no reason at all – the objective(s) they intend to achieve by those pursuing them, may be equally wide-ranging. These objectives may be of a political and/or of an economic nature. Clearly, some of the divestment policies exclusively aim to make a political statement for the audience in the home state. They may also attempt to economically hurt the targeted country's regime by isolating it from foreign investment. The signal given to companies around the world, indeed, is that if they continue to be economically active in that targeted country, the investment fund will divest. For some (though definitely not all!) companies, concerned about reputational damage in certain corners of the world, such divestment policy leads them to suspend activities in, or with, the targeted company altogether. Whether or not such a divestment policy ends up being effective, will therefore depend on the

---

[29] Hence, this is a different situation as compared to when the UN Security Council, acting pursuant to Chapter VII of the UN Charter, requests its member states to enact legislation prohibiting any investment in certain industries of a given country. For an example thereof, see Resolution 1747 on Iran, UN Doc. S/RES/1747 (2007), para. 6. Similarly, for reasons of domestic foreign policy, a state can resort to measures prohibiting anyone within its jurisdiction from investing in corporations listed in a particular jurisdiction. This decision may then be materialized in a domestic piece of legislation.

[30] Lucien J. Dhooge, 'Condemning Khartoum: The Illinois Divestment Act and Foreign Relations', *American Business Law Journal*, 43 (2006), p. 245; and Dhooge, 'Darfur, State Divestment and the Commerce Clause', *North Carolina Journal of International Law and Commercial Regulation*, 32 (2007), p. 391.

[31] For an overview of cases brought in US courts, see Michael D. Ramsey, 'International Law Limits on Investor Liability in Human Rights Litigation', *Harvard International Law Journal*, 50 (2009), p. 2, especially section 2 ('An Overview of Investor Liability Litigation').

degree to which corporations which are economically active in the targeted country, depend on investment flows coming from the type of countries in which these policies emerge.

By divesting, one wishes to make a statement, possibly but not necessarily[32] in the hope of influencing the corporation's[33] behaviour. Whether or not the company in question will feel the urge to modify its behaviour, may depend on factors such as the investment fund's perceived authority, on the one hand, and the corporation's chances to obtain funding sources elsewhere, on the other. Divestment by some small-scale entity no one has ever heard of, is likely to be perceived as much less authoritative as compared to the scenario in which divestment is done by a large, established institution.[34] Definitely, divestment by a SWF carries an even greater signal. No matter all rhetorical attempts to the contrary, a divestment decision implemented by a state-owned SWF will be perceived to carry a political connotation.

Effective or not in terms of its ability to modify corporate behaviour, divestment is the end of the road. If the corporation from which one has divested turns out not to be receptive to the outcry, or if other investors happily take the seat, this is as far as one can go as a foreign investment fund. Regulatory and disciplinary authority over the company divested from is – indeed – likely to belong exclusively to the state in the jurisdiction of which the company in question is incorporated.

Both active engagement with a corporation's management, on the one hand, and divestment, on the other, are among the options available to an investment fund wishing to pursue a SRI policy. While neither of both

---

[32] See, e.g., the approach taken by the Norwegian Graver Report preceding the creation of the Council on Ethics, Norwegian Government White Paper, NOU 2003:22, para. 5.1 (not recommending the use of divestment as a means of influencing corporate behaviour, and arguing that the use of ownership rights may be more effective to achieve such objective).

[33] Still a different debate from the issue of whether, and how, to use corporate presence abroad as a tool of engaging a repressive regime, e.g., for the purpose of inducing it to adopt views that are much conducive to greater human rights compliance. On this issue, see generally Craig Forcese, 'Globalizing Decency: Responsible Engagement in an Era of Economic Integration', *Yale Human Rights & Development Law Journal*, 5 (2002), p. 1.

[34] University funds in the US played a very active role in the South Africa divestment campaigns. See Martha J. Olson, 'University Investments with a South Africa Connection: Is Prudent Divestiture Possible?', *New York University Journal of International Law and Politics*, 11 (1978–9), p. 543. For the literature from the time, see Patricia M. C. Carroll, 'Socially Responsible Investment of Public Pension Funds: The South Africa Issue and State Law', *New York University Review of Law & Social Change*, 10 (1980–1), p. 407; and Grayling M. Williams, 'In Support of Azania: Divestiture of Public Pension Funds As One Answer to United States Private Investment in South Africa', *Black Law Journal*, 9 (1984), p. 167.

options are mandatory as a matter of public international law (a point which will be elaborated upon in greater detail below), states remain at liberty to render them compulsory as a matter of domestic law.

Leaving the legislative (non)-requirements for what they are, the actual practice of investment funds has not hesitated to structure its work along the lines of both active engagement and divestment. For many large institutional investors, indeed, it has become mainstream to assert that they subscribe to policies along those lines. The most high profile and standard-setting endeavour in this regard are the *Principles for Responsible Investment*, a UN-backed private sector initiative pursuant to which institutional investors voluntarily commit themselves to take into account certain criteria, both for their investment decision-making and for the exercise of their ownership rights. These 'UNPRI', as they have come to be known, clearly emphasize a preference for engaging the companies' management over the divestment option. While these *Principles* acknowledge that divestment may be a sound practice for certain types of investors, a clear policy choice has been made to the effect that engagement is to be preferred over divestment, as well as over the use of certain screening criteria which avoid initiating the investment in the first place.[35]

The attitude that is prescribed, therefore, is to proceed on the basis of a two-step approach. While one will first seek to prevent the company from continuing its harmful behaviour by actively engaging with its management, one keeps the option to divest if no improvement is perceived. Such a binary logic mirrors the 'due diligence' construct. The next section explains why this construct is well suited to carry the weight of shaping SWFs' investment policy.

3.   On sovereign wealth funds, international legal state responsibility and 'due diligence'

3.1   *Sovereign wealth funds and human rights violations committed by the foreign companies in which they invest: the classic view of international law*

Other contributions in this book deal with the question whether, as a matter of law or ethics, investment funds can be considered 'complicit'

---

[35] UN Principles for Responsible Investment; www.unpri.org. Principle 2 reads: 'We will be active owners and incorporate Environmental, Social and Corporate Governance issues into our ownership policies and practices', followed by a list of 'possible actions', which include 'develop an engagement capability (either directly or through outsourcing)'.

in the environmental, social or human rights violations committed by the companies in which they invest. The present subsection 3.1 looks at this very question from a different angle: does the fact that a SWF made an investment in a foreign private corporation which is allegedly involved in human rights violations, lead to the international legal responsibility of the state to which the SWF belongs?

The analysis pursued in this subsection is limited by the following four parameters: (a) the assessment is made solely from the angle of public international law; (b) it is limited to state responsibility as per the latter legal framework; (c) the question of state responsibility remains assessed solely at the conceptual level, i.e., irrespective of the possibility to (judicially or otherwise) enforce it;[36] and (d) only violations of human rights standards will be included in the analysis. The latter, therefore, is confined to human rights law, without prejudice to the picture that may emerge when standards of an environmental or a social norm have been violated.

One point about vocabulary: throughout the analysis, it will be assumed that SWFs qualify as 'state organs'[37] for the purposes of the law of state responsibility. The importance of this qualification

---

[36] Such enforcement is a different and possibly much harder matter altogether. As to when and where matters of sovereign immunity may be invoked as a defence by the state or its state-owned SWF, see generally Bart De Meester, 'International Legal Aspects of Sovereign Wealth Funds: Reconciling International Economic Law and the Law of State Immunities with a New Role of the State', *European Business Law Review* (2009), p. 779, and William C. Hoffman, 'The Separate Entity Rule in International Perspective: Should State Ownership of Corporate Shares Confer Sovereign Status for Immunity Purposes?', *Tulane Law Review*, 65 (1990–1), p. 535.

[37] International Law Commission, 'Draft Articles on the Responsibility of States for Internationally Wrongful Acts ("DASR")' (New York: UN International Law Commission, 2001), Article 5: '(1) The conduct of any State organ shall be considered an act of that State under international law, whether the organ exercises legislative, executive, judicial or any other functions, whatever position it holds in the organization of the State, and whatever its character as an organ of the central government or of a territorial unit of the State; (2) An organ includes any person or entity which has that status in accordance with the internal law of the State.' See also ICSID Case No. ARB/97/7, Decision of the Tribunal on Objections to Jurisdiction, para. 76: 'the test that has been developed looks to various factors, such as ownership, control, the nature, *purposes and objectives* of the entity ... and to the character of the actions taken' (emphasis added), as well as (from the same case) para. 77: 'must be examined first from a structural point of view. Here, a finding that the entity is owned, directly or indirectly, gives rise to a rebuttable presumption that it is a state entity'. In addition to this structural test, there also is a functional test, which is not relevant here, as SWFs do not embark upon (language of para. 77) 'functions which by their nature are not usually carried out by private businesses or individuals', in 40, *International Legal Materials*, 1141 (2001). Arguably, as per the structural test, the 'purposes and objectives' of a SWF, in combination with its feature of being owned by a state, are of such a nature as to qualify SWFs as state organs.

resides in the fact that the acts of 'state organs' have at the very least the potential to trigger the international legal responsibility of the state to which they belong. In this respect, it is acknowledged that the question as to whether a particular entity qualifies as a 'state organ' in fields such as the present one, is a highly uncertain field of international law.

While the theoretical debate is still open as to whether international law directly binds not only states, as the majority thinks, but also its organs,[38] it is ultimately – in practical terms – up to the state to make sure that its organs act in compliance with international law.

As a starting point, the scenario under analysis is the same as the one described above. As an additional element to be included in the scenario, it is assumed that a SWF has invested in a foreign private corporation which is allegedly involved in human rights violations which, if they were to have been committed on the territory of the state to which the SWF belongs, may qualify as a violation of the international legal obligations applicable to that state.

The key question to which the present subsection looks, is as follows: does the mere fact that a SWF has invested in such a corporation, lead to state responsibility under international law?

As a matter of currently existing international law (*'lex lata'*), the answer shall be in the negative, no matter how appealing (*'de lege feranda'*) it may appear to be at first sight to impose affirmative obligations on states vis-à-vis the conduct of non-state actors abroad.[39] A very limited range of exceptions can arguably be derived from certain treaties, mostly related to the law of weaponry, and even there only for very specific weapons (activity-specific prohibitions). These arguable exceptions will be dealt with separately below.

The next few paragraphs explain the background to this answer, it being acknowledged that – due to space constraints – the analysis is not able to represent all facets of this complex debate. The implications of this answer in the negative are without prejudice to the SWF's potential liability under other legal frameworks, e.g., under domestic law. The latter is not part of the analysis pursued here.

Given the constellation of facts described in the scenario under consideration here, two factors are crucial from the perspective of

---

[38] See Ward Ferdinandusse, 'Out of the Black Box? The International Obligations of State Organs', *Brooklyn Journal of International Law*, 29 (2003–4), p. 45.

[39] For an example of an article arguing in this direction, particularly in the realm of human rights law, see Danwood Mzikenge Chirwa, 'The Doctrine of State Responsibility as a Potential Means of Holding Private Actors Accountable for Human Rights', *Melbourne Journal of International Law*, 5 (2004), p. 1.

public international law. The first factor is the issue of attributability of the corporation's conduct to the SWF; the second factor is the matter of extraterritoriality. Both will be dealt with separately below. Finally, as previously indicated, separate analysis will be devoted towards the issue of activity-specific prohibitions which, for a (very) limited number of fields, impose obligations on states which, arguably, equally prohibit their SWFs from initiating or maintaining certain forms of investment.

3.1.1   Attributability   The first crucial factor which needs to be looked at, concerns the following question: is the conduct of the foreign private corporation (i.e., a non-state actor)[40] in which the SWF has invested, attributable to the state to which the SWF belongs?

The discipline's holy bible on the matter – Articles 4 to 11 of the Draft Articles on Responsibility of States for Internationally Wrongful Acts[41] – sets exacting thresholds before one can provide an affirmative answer to the question whether the corporation's conduct is attributable to the SWF. The default rule, indeed, is that such conduct is not attributable.[42] Exceptions do exist, however, and it is to a presentation of these exceptions that this paragraph turns now.

From among the exceptions enshrined in the said Draft Articles, only those mentioned in, respectively, Article 5, Article 8 and Article 11 are potentially applicable.[43] All three will be dealt with in turn. As a preliminary matter, it needs to be underlined that the factor of 'control'

---

[40] Having argued that the SWF qualifies as a 'state organ' for the purposes of the law of state responsibility it can be uncontroversially stated that the foreign private corporation in which the SWF has invested will qualify as a non-state actor. For a general discussion of the broader theoretical discussion under analysis here, see Jan Arno Hessbrügge, 'Human Rights Violations Arising from Conduct of Non-State Actors', *Buffalo Human Rights Law Review*, 11 (2005), pp. 46–64.

[41] International Law Commission, 'Report of the International Law Commission on the Work of its Fifty-Third Session', UN GAOR, 56th Session, Supp. No. 10, UN Doc. A/56/10 (2001), pp. 43–59.

[42] DASR, chapter 2 determines under which conditions there can be 'Attribution of conduct to a State'. For an article-by-article discussion, see James Crawford, *The International Law Commission's Article on State Responsibility: Introduction, Texts and Commentary* (Cambridge University Press, 2005). See generally Hessbruegge, 'The Historical Development of the Doctrines of Attribution and Due Diligence in International Law', *New York University Journal of International Law and Politics*, 36 (2003–4), p. 265.

[43] Not referred to here, in view of their manifest irrelevance for the present purposes, are Article 6 ('Conduct of organs placed at the disposal of a State by another State'); Article 7 ('Excess of authority or contravention of instruction'); Article 9 ('Conduct carried out in the absence or default of the official authorities'); and Article 10 ('Conduct of an insurrectional or other movement') of the 'Draft Articles on Responsibility of States for Internationally Wrongful Acts'.

does not matter all that much for the purposes of international law in this area.[44]

The first possible exception (Art. 5 of the Draft Articles)[45] to the default rule of non-attributability applies in case the foreign private corporation in which the SWF has invested, has been 'empowered by the law of that State to exercise elements of ... governmental authority' so as to have become a *de facto* organ of the state.[46] Clearly, this exception is not applicable in the case of an investment.

Similarly, the second possible exception (Art. 8 of the Draft Articles)[47] can be relatively easily dealt with: in principle, indeed, the foreign private corporation does not act 'on the instructions of, or under the direction or control of' the SWF.

---

[44] The issue as to how one should assess the 'control' criterion (i.e., how much capability does the SWF shareholder dispose of to influence the behaviour of the company invested in) constitutes an interesting opportunity to compare the standards used by the international legal framework on state responsibility – where 'control' is legally speaking not the determining factor – as opposed to the standards and discourse used by the Ethical Guidelines from the Norwegian Council on Ethics, which do not purport to be an expression of international law standards of the matter. For the Ethical Guidelines 2004 (para. 4.4), indeed, the relevant yardstick is whether the investment can constitute, because of the acts or omissions of the company invested in, *'an unacceptable risk that the Fund contributes to'* (see Appendix 2 below). Indeed, even minor contributions are contributions, hence obviating the importance which other normative frameworks may attach to the said contribution's quantitative significance, or to its potential impact. The issue has been applied by the Council on Ethics on p. 5 of its 'Recommendation of 11 April 2005 on Exclusion from the Government Petroleum Fund's Investment Universe of the Company Kerr-McGee Corporation': 'The Council on Ethics must determine whether investments in Kerr-McGee can constitute an unacceptable risk for contributing to possible violations of the Guidelines. The point of departure for the Ethical Guidelines is that *even modest investments can constitute such a contribution*. It is not necessarily only the size of the investment, but also the character of the alleged violation of the guidelines that must be taken into account. The share of the Petroleum Fund's ownership in Kerr-McGee is in any case considerable, and it seems unproblematic, in this case, to determine that such ownership can constitute a contribution within the meaning of the guidelines' (emphasis added).

[45] Full text of Article 5: 'The conduct of a person or entity which is not an organ of the State under article 4 but which is empowered by the law of that State to exercise elements of the governmental authority shall be considered an act of the State under international law, provided the person or entity is acting in that capacity in the particular instance.'

[46] Robert McCorquodale, 'Spreading Weeds Beyond Their Garden: Extraterritorial Responsibility of States for Violations of Human Rights by Corporate Nationals', *The American Society of International Law Proceedings*, 100 (2006), p. 85, especially pp. 95–102; Eduardo Savarese, 'Issues of Attribution to States of Private Acts: Between the Concept of De Facto Organs and Complicity', in *Italian Yearbook of International Law*, vol. XV (University of Siena, 2005), p. 111.

[47] Full text of Article 8: 'The conduct of a person or group of persons shall be considered an act of a State under international law if the person or group of persons is in fact acting on the instructions of, or under the direction or control of, that State in carrying out the conduct.'

The third exception (Art. 11 of the Draft Articles)[48] is possibly more relevant. This exception is, indeed, applicable when, and to the extent that, the state has 'acknowledge[d] and adopt[ed] the conduct in question as its own'. For this condition to be applicable, however, the legal yardstick is an exacting one. Much more is required, indeed, than mere knowledge of the non-state actor's conduct. Furthermore, time and again, the law on this subject posits that not only mere knowledge does not suffice, but that also mere endorsement of the non-state actor's action or omission cannot be considered sufficient for the exception to apply.[49] Thus, the mere fact that a SWF maintains its investment in a foreign private corporation which is allegedly involved in human rights violations does not suffice at all, even if the SWF knows of the allegations. Absent the absurd hypothesis of an explicit declaration by the SWF that it would embrace the corporation's conduct in this matter, the state to which the SWF belongs will not be responsible as a matter of public international law.

By way of conclusion, therefore, it can be summarily stated that the foreign private corporation's conduct is not attributable to the state to which the SWF belongs. To remain fair to international law on this topic, it must be acknowledged that the law's conceptual tools on the subject of state responsibility have been developed for scenarios which are radically different from the one under assessment here. These conceptual tools are, therefore, ill-fitted to deal with the 'SWF [that] has invested in a foreign private corporation involved in human rights violations' paradigm. Be that as it may, for the time being no attributability exists for the purpose of triggering state responsibility under international law.

So far we have considered the first important factor which needs to be taken into account. Attention shall turn now to the second such factor.

---

[48] Full text of Article 11: 'Conduct which is not attributable to a State under the preceding articles shall nevertheless be considered an act of that State under international law if and to the extent that the State acknowledges and adopts the conduct in question as its own.'

[49] International Law Commission, 'Report of the International Law Commission on the Work of its Fifty-Third Session', p. 121, where it is stated in the Commentary to Article 11 of the Draft Articles on State Responsibility that 'as a general matter, conduct will not be attributable to a State under article 11 where a State merely acknowledges the factual existence of conduct or expresses its verbal approval of it. In international controversies, States often take positions which amount to "approval" or "endorsement" of conduct in some general sense but do not involve any assumption of responsibility. The language of "adoption", on the other hand, carries with it the idea that the conduct is acknowledged by the State as, in effect, its own conduct.'

3.1.2   Extraterritoriality   In addition to the issue of attributability, the scenario under analysis here triggers the applicability of a second factor, the presence of which carries far-reaching implications as a matter of public international law: 'extraterritoriality'.

The basic idea of the underlying factual scenario – triggering the applicability of the legal notion of 'extraterritoriality' – is easy to convey: the SWF has made an investment in a private corporation which is incorporated abroad. The latter, in turn, may be economically active on the territory of its own state, or on the territory of a third state, which is where the human rights violations are alleged to take place (referred to as the 'territorial state' for the purposes of international law). Excluded from the analysis here is any combination of circumstances leading to the corporation's being economically active, and the violations alleged to occur, on the territory of the state to which the SWF belongs.

Thus, three different states are in the picture: (i) the state to which the SWF belongs; (ii) the state in which the corporation is incorporated; and (iii) the territorial state. While (ii) and (iii) may be identical, (i) needs in any event to be separate from either of both for there to be extraterritoriality (and for the analysis pursued in this chapter to be applicable).

In terms of currently existing international law, out of these three states, the state to which the SWF belongs bears the least responsibility of all in the case of the corporation in which the investment has been made being allegedly involved in violations of human rights standards. All the SWF has done, indeed, is to carry out an investment in this foreign private corporation. As per the currently existing rules of public international law, this corporation's conduct is not attributable to the SWF. The foreign corporation in which the investment has been made, indeed, is operating outside that state's territory and jurisdiction. This state is, in short, too far removed from the alleged harmful conduct to bear any responsibility for it.

Under currently existing international law, the territorial state (whether or not it is the same state as the corporation's home state), and possibly also the corporation's home state, may arguably carry responsibility if it does not intervene in a qualified manner, which is not the topic of the present contribution and will hence not further be dealt with. It needs to be emphasized, indeed, that the scenario under assessment here pertains to a SWF investing in a foreign private corporation. Thus, the assessment undertaken here is without prejudice to the situation which arises in the case where a state (the 'home state') invests, or otherwise supports, a corporation bearing *its own* nationality which is economically active abroad. In the latter scenario, equally as a matter of currently existing international law, much more persuasive arguments exist for retaining the home state's international legal responsibility.[50]

Actually, in the scenario under assessment here, it ought not to come as a surprise that no international legal responsibility arises for the state to which the SWF belongs: international human rights law remains firmly anchored in a vision of a world divided into sovereign states, each with, and within, their own respective spheres of territoriality and responsibility. A state carries human rights obligations for acts on its own territory (and sometimes for acts committed within its jurisdictional reach yet outside its own territory), not for what occurs beyond its borders. As a matter of currently existing human rights law, the state's duty to protect has an uncertain extraterritorial reach at best.[51]

In principle, indeed, a state does not have any responsibility as a matter of human rights law for acts committed on the territory of another state. Exceptions have gradually come to be recognized to this principle, such as when a state's organs are acting abroad and exercise a given form of effective control over territory or persons, which may be the case when military forces are deployed abroad.[52] In case of a relationship between the SWF, on the one hand, and a foreign private corporation in which an investment has been made, on the other, no such effective control over territory or persons exists at all.

---

[50] For a good overview of that scenario and the assessment of so-called 'home state responsibility', see Robert McCorquodale and Penelope C. Simons, 'Responsibility Beyond Borders: Extraterritorial Violations by Corporations of Human Rights Law', *Modern Law Review*, 70 (2007), p. 598. On the same topic, see also Surıya Deva, 'Acting Extraterritorially to Tame Multinational Corporations for Human Rights Violations: Who Should "Bell the Cat"?', *Melbourne Journal of International Law*, 5 (2004), p. 37.

[51] See John Ruggie, 'Promotion of all Human Rights, Civil, Political, Economic, Social and Cultural Rights, including the Right to Development. Business and Human Rights: Towards Operationalizing the "Protect, Respect and Remedy" Framework. Report of the Special Representative of the Secretary-General on the Issue of Human Rights and Transnational Corporations and Other Business Enterprises', UN Doc. A/HRC/11/13 (22 April 2009), available at www2.ohchr.org/english/bodies/hrcouncil/docs/11session/A.HRC.11.13.pdf, at para. 15: 'The extraterritorial dimension of the duty to protect remains unsettled in international law. Current guidance from international human rights bodies suggests that States are not required to regulate the extraterritorial activities of businesses incorporated in their jurisdiction, nor are they generally prohibited from doing so provided there is a recognized jurisdictional basis, and that an overall test of reasonableness is met. Within those parameters, some treaty bodies *encourage* home States to take steps to prevent abuse abroad by corporations within their jurisdiction' (emphasis added).

[52] The threshold for assessing such effective control over territory or persons ought not to be confused with the criteria used for attributability of non-state actors' conduct to a state under international law applicable to state responsibility.

The only field of international law where transnational state responsibility has been seriously contemplated – transnational environmental harm – remains unsettled. None of the other areas that are regularly cited as other possible applications of any such transnational responsibility, bears any relevance for the issue at hand, as all of them have originated in the context of completely different subject-matters, notably in the sphere of military and security operations (especially multinational operations) abroad.[53]

Therefore, under current international law and a limited number of recognized exceptions notwithstanding, no firm arguments can be withheld for the subject-matter under assessment here to conclude that states have consented to be bound by an obligation that they would need to control – through legislative or other regulatory means – 'their' corporations when the latter are acting abroad.[54] *A fortiori*, it can be concluded that states have not accepted that they would have any *legal* obligations vis-à-vis corporations which are neither their nationals, nor acting on their territory.

Both the classic theories of attributability and extraterritoriality lead, in sum as well as independently, to the same result: international law does not consider the SWF to be responsible for whatever actions or omissions that are (not) undertaken by the corporation in which the SWF has invested. The link between both entities is too weak, too

---

[53] For a general treatment, see the essays contained in Fons Coomans and Menno T. Kamminga, *Extraterritorial Application of Human Rights Treaties* (Antwerp: Intersentia, 2004). See also Damira Kamchibekova, 'State Responsibility for Extraterritorial Human Rights Violations', *Buffalo Human Rights Law Review*, 87 (2007), p. 87; Mark Gibney et al., 'Transnational State Responsibility for Violations of Human Rights', *Harvard Human Rights Journal*, 12 (1999), p. 267; Sigrun Skogley and Mark Gibney, 'Transnational Human Rights Obligations', *Human Rights Quarterly*, 24 (2002), p. 781; as well as McCorquodale, 'Spreading Weeds Beyond Their Garden', pp. 95–102.

[54] See the Ruggie 2007 Report on 'State Responsibilities to Regulate and Adjudicate Corporate Activities under the United Nations' Core Human Rights Treaties', prepared for the mandate of Professor John Ruggie, in relation to the UN core human rights treaties (February 2007), available via www.reports-and-materials.org/State-Responsibilities-to-Regulate-Corporate-Activities-under-UN-Core-Treaties-12-Feb-2007.pdf, at para. 84: 'What is difficult to derive from the treaties or the treaty bodies is any general obligation on States to exercise extraterritorial jurisdiction over violations by business enterprises abroad'; Similarly, see a June 2007 report dealing exclusively with the situation of the International Covenant on Civil and Political Rights, available via www.reports-and-materials.org/Ruggie-ICCPR-Jun-2007.pdf, para. 183: [there is] 'very little guidance on whether the [Human Rights Committee] supports or is likely to support an interpretation of the Covenant which would require States to regulate the activities of their nationals abroad, including corporations, in situations where the State does not have power or effective control over the relevant individuals affected by such activities.'

tenuous and too far removed so as to give rise to responsibility under the realm of public international law.

The treatment granted to, respectively, the generally applicable doctrines of attributability and extraterritoriality, is not the end of the story. Irrespective of the corporation's conduct being attributable or otherwise leading to any form of responsibility, some international legal norms apply and may bear relevance for the subject discussed here. What follows introduces the debate, thus paving the way to the presentation of the 'due diligence' notion.

3.1.3   Activity-specific prohibitions   In international law, treaties exist in specific domains which have – or may arguably have – the effect of rendering illegal an investment in a company the activities of which conflict with the treaty's provisions. Within the parameters of the respective treaties' own scope of application, such prohibition applies irrespective of any consideration pertaining to the attributability of the non-state actor's conduct to the SWF.

Three categories of examples of treaty provisions can be identified.

The first category remains, so far, a hypothetical one, for no such treaty provisions have been found: a treaty provision explicitly and literally prohibiting contracting states that have ratified[55] the treaty in question from 'investing in' certain activities covered by the text. One could even contemplate that such a treaty requires Contracting Parties, in turn, to enact domestic legislation prohibiting private investment funds under its jurisdiction from 'investing in' certain activities.

As to the second category of activity-specific prohibitions, these pertain to treaty provisions which, while not explicitly referring to invest(ment) as being a prohibited activity, nevertheless have such an effect. Examples can be found in weapons-related treaties, some of which contain a provision along the following lines: 'Each State Party to this Convention undertakes never under any circumstances ... to assist, encourage or induce, in any way, anyone to engage in any activity prohibited to a State Party under this Convention.'[56] As 'development'

---

[55] Reference must be made to the non-consensual mechanism through which the UN Security Council can impose sanctions upon Member States, based upon Chapter VII of the UN Charter, requiring them to adopt domestic legislation prohibiting 'investments' in particular industry sectors of a given country. An example thereof can be found in Resolution 1747 (2007) on Iran (UN Doc. S/RES/1747 (2007), paragraph 6).

[56] This phrase is used, for example, in the following four instances: (1) Art. I(1)(d) of the 'Convention on the Prohibition of the Development, Production, Stockpiling and Use of Chemical Weapons and on their Destruction', in 32, *International Legal Materials*, 800 (1993); (2) Art. 1(1)(c) of the 'Convention on Cluster Munitions', as adopted

and 'production' are often among the list of explicitly prohibited activities, a strong case exists for arguing that 'investment' by a SWF of a state who has become a Contracting Party to the text in question[57] contravenes that state's obligations and is therefore prohibited. Given the fact that such prohibitions of being involved in specific weapons-related activities have been rather thoroughly codified, it is unsurprising that a great number of the recommendations that have been taken by the Norwegian Council on Ethics are to be found in the realm of weapons production, a sector which has also been separately singled out by the Ethical Guidelines governing that Council's activities.[58] Thus, there have been recommendations[59] to divest from companies involved in the production of (key components for) nuclear weapons,[60] on the one hand, or to divest from companies involved in the production of anti-personnel mines and cluster munitions, on the other.[61]

Finally, the (arguable) third category pertains to so-called 'activity obligations' enshrined in certain treaties. As a subset of the second category, these are provisions requiring Contracting Parties to embark upon international cooperation so as to achieve the purposes of the treaty in question. While acknowledging that it may be too far-fetched

---

by the May 2008 Diplomatic Conference in Dublin, and opened for signature as of December 2008, in 48, *International Legal Materials*, 357 (2009); (3) Art. 1(1)(c) of the 1997 'Convention on the Prohibition of the Use, Stockpiling, Production and Transfer of Anti-Personnel Mines and on Their Destruction', in 36, *International Legal Materials*, 1507 (1997); and (4) slightly differently worded though substantively identical is Art. 3 of the 1972 'Convention on the Prohibition of the Development, Production and Stockpiling of Bacteriological (Biological) and Toxin Weapons and on Their Destruction', in 1015, *United Nations Treaty Series*, 164.

[57] As to the situation of other states, one will need to assess whether the same norm has crystallized to the point of being of a customary international legal nature.

[58] Ethical Guidelines 2004, para. 4.4: 'The Council shall issue recommendations on negative screening of one or several companies on the basis of production of weapons that through normal use may violate fundamental humanitarian principles.'

[59] See Council on Ethics, 'Recommendation of 19 September 2005, on the Exclusion of Companies that are Involved in Production of Nuclear Weapons.'

[60] In its Recommendation of 19 September 2005 – in which divestment from a number of companies was recommended – the Council on Ethics elaborated upon its understanding as to what qualifies as such. On (key components of) nuclear weapons, see also 'Recommendation of 15 November 2007 on Exclusion of the Company GenCorp Inc.'; as well as 'Recommendation of 15 November 2007 on Exclusion of the Company Serco Group Plc.'

[61] In its Recommendation of 16 June 2005 – in which divestment from a number of companies was recommended – the Council on Ethics elaborated upon its understanding as to what qualifies as such. On cluster munitions, see also Council on Ethics, 'Recommendation of 6 September 2006, on the Exclusion of Poongsan Corp.'; as well as 'Recommendation of 15 May 2007 on the Exclusion of the Companies Rheinmetall AG and Hanwha Corp.' (followed, on 5 September 2007, by a new recommendation stating that the grounds for excluding Rheinmetall AG were no longer valid).

in particular instances to develop such an argument, a provision to that effect could be argued to imply, by spirit if not by letter of the provision, that Contracting Parties ought to consider themselves precluded from investing in the activities covered.[62] Allowing them to invest, it could be argued, would otherwise defeat the provision's purpose.

Other than this handful of ad hoc exceptions, currently existing international law does not hold (the state of) the SWF responsible for the mere fact of having invested in a company the activities of which are, or turn out to be, in violation of the international legal obligations of that state.

Yet, this does not mean that the state needs to consider itself bound to remain silent when confronted with such activities. The 'due diligence' doctrine, as a matter of policy if not as a matter of law, allows to conceptually underpin SWF managers' behaviour when they are seeking to operationalize SRI.

3.2   Introducing 'due diligence' as a policy tool to shape sovereign wealth funds' investment policy

As demonstrated in section 3.1 – some limited arguable exceptions notwithstanding – current international law does not hold SWFs responsible for the actions or omissions of the foreign private corporations in which they have invested. The law in general and in international law in particular, however, are but one part of the regulatory structure underpinning the much more complex dynamics of social interaction. In the world of certain investors' reality, non-tangible notions like 'perception'[63] and 'reputation' may carry greater significance than abstract legal norms declaring there not to be any responsibility.

---

[62] Norwegian Petroleum Fund Advisory Commission on International Law, 'Memorandum to the Ministry of Finance: Question of Whether an Investment through the Petroleum Fund Can Constitute a Human Rights Violation' (2002), pp. 5–11; www.regjeringen.no/mobil/se/dep/fin/tema/statens_pensjonsfond/ansvarlige-investeringer/Advisory-Commission-Documents/advisory-commission-220302.html?id=105699.

[63] One of the image problems SWFs have been struggling with relates to their alleged lack of transparency: by withholding information about the identity of the companies in which they have invested, many SWFs did attract suspicion and nourish rumours as to their state's underlying motives. For some of the responses adopted so far, see the G8 Summit in Heiligendamm (8 June 2007), 'Chair's Summary', 'I. Growth and Responsibility in the World Economy', with paragraphs on 'Systemic Stability and Transparency of Financial Markets/Hedge Funds' and on 'Freedom of Investment, Investment Environment, and Social Responsibility', via www.g-8.de/Webs/G8/EN/G8Summit/SummitDocuments/summit-documents.html. In the 'Santiago Principles' that have been adopted thereafter (see note 4 above), transparency in several aspects has become a cornerstone notion.

While – in the scenario under consideration in this contribution – investment by a SWF does not trigger responsibility from the conceptual–legal point of view, it nevertheless risks creating significant reputational risks.

As forcefully noted in an official report by the most authoritative policy maker on the subject of the burgeoning 'business and human rights' field, it is indeed beyond the level of a strictly legal logic that states shall be concerned: if the company invested in violates certain norms – or at least that impression is created through, e.g., certain reports in the media or statements issued by activist pressure groups – such investment choices reflect poorly on the reputation of the state to which that SWF belongs. This means there is an 'incentive in the national interest' for a state to exercise greater regulatory oversight as to the type of corporations which attract investment by a nation's SWF.[64]

Against this background, none of what follows in the present section shall be considered to be required by international law. The present assessment is equally without prejudice to a scenario in which a SWF, as the home state, would invest in its own corporate nationals.[65]

As far as the scenario under consideration in this contribution is concerned, however, SWFs have no general[66] obligation under international law to manage their investment portfolio with 'due diligence' along the lines suggested by John Ruggie for private companies. Thus, matters such as actively pursuing a policy of monitoring human rights compliance of the companies in which one has invested, are by no means legally required for SWFs as far as public international law is concerned. Failure to have such a policy in place does not trigger state responsibility in international law. Again,[67] it needs to be acknowledged that the conceptual tools constituting the law of state responsibility are not particularly attuned to the specific environment in which SWFs operate.

Yet, as a policy matter of 'good practices' – the Norwegian example being a unique one – it is argued that compelling policy reasons exist

---

64 Ruggie, Report 2008, para. 32: 'Beyond any legal obligations, human rights harm caused by [State Owned Enterprises] reflects directly on the State's reputation, providing it with an incentive in the national interest to exercise greater oversight. Much the same is true of sovereign wealth funds and the human rights impacts of their investments.'

65 For that scenario, see McCorquodale and Simons, 'Responsibility Beyond Borders', p. 598. On the same topic, see also Deva, 'Acting Extraterritorially', p. 37.

66 Exception needs indeed to be made for the limited number of treaties the provisions of which result in a prohibition to invest in certain weapons-related activities.

67 This assertion is not unique to the subject-matter dealt with here. For a detailed overview of these issues, see Paul Schiff Berman, 'From International Law to Law and Globalization', *Columbia Journal of Transnational Law*, 43 (2004–5), p. 485.

to pay attention to arguments calling for the incorporation of non-financial criteria in the decision-making process of those managing such funds. The concept of 'due diligence' can offer guidance in this respect. Such a concept allows a policy to be structured so as to avoid that the SWF becomes – or remains – invested in companies with a doubtful record when it comes to human rights.

Whether or not this call will be heeded, depends on political considerations which go much beyond the scope of the present contribution: are states receptive to the argument that it is in their own interest to create an investment climate which encourages corporations to be in compliance with certain standards of behaviour?

The remainder of this subsection is divided into three parts. First, Part 3.2.1 situates 'due diligence' as it exists, and flourishes, within the investment realm yet outside international law. Second, Part 3.2.2 explains how public international law understands 'due diligence'. Finally, Part 3.2.3 applies 'due diligence' as a policy proposal to the realm of SWFs.

3.2.1   'Due diligence' outside the realm of international law   It is important not to confuse 'due diligence' as this concept is used in international law (and dealt with *infra*), with the same words used, *inter alia*, in the realm of financial services performed by certain non-state actors. While these sectors can most certainly inspire[68] the assessment for the present purposes, they are not to be confused.

Both in the bank sector and in the project finance-sector, 'due diligence' has become a widely accepted, sometimes even mandatory, business practice. In order to better appreciate and contradistinguish the precise dynamics of the 'due diligence' concept as applicable under international law, both the bank sector and the project finance sector are briefly touched upon in turn.

In the *bank sector*, 'know your customer' has become the keyword when carrying out procedures of so-called 'customer due diligence'. Rendered mandatory through domestic regulation as a business practice in many jurisdictions,[69] it is often inspired by the fight against terrorism. Thus, banks need to obtain certain data[70] about their prospective

---

[68] Andrew Clapham, 'Remarks at the 2006 American Society of International Law, Annual Meeting', *American Society of International Law Proceedings*, 100 (2006), p. 129.

[69] The Basel Committee on Banking Supervision plays a prominent role in this area; see its report 'Customer Due Diligence for Banks' (2002), available at www.bis.org/publ/bcbs85.pdf.

[70] Though the precise details obviously differ, such customer identification processes seek not only to identify a prospective customer's identity, but also to check whether

customers before being allowed to do business with them. Similar requirements have been introduced in certain jurisdictions in order to avoid that charities inadvertently serve to facilitate terrorism.[71] Here, 'due diligence' is a concept which seeks to *avoid* that the bank sector would inadvertently facilitate the commission of terrorist-related acts.

In the *project finance sector*, 'due diligence' is among the key terms explicitly used for operationalizing the Equator Principles. The latter are a voluntary[72] framework – based upon standards from the World Bank's International Finance Corporation – that can be used by the private sector's banks for projects with a total capital cost of US$10 million or more.[73]

Two out of the nine Equator Principles[74] explicitly use 'due diligence' as being required when assessing the social and environmental risks

there are certain risks that the bank system is being abused by such a customer for the purpose of committing (international) financial crimes such as money laundering, or facilitating terrorist activities. Unsurprisingly, in recent years following the 9/11 terrorist attacks, this topic has become quite prominent. See, among others, Ilias Bantekas, 'The International Law of Terrorist Financing', *The American Journal of International Law*, 97 (2003), p. 315, especially at pp. 325 and 332; Joseph M. Myers, 'The Silent Struggle against Terrorist Financing', *Georgetown Journal of International Law*, 6 (2005), p. 33; Charles Freeland, 'How Can Sound Customer Due Diligence Rules Help Prevent the Misuse of Financial Institutions in the Financing of Terrorism?', *European Journal of Law Reform*, 4 (2002), p. 201; Joe Kendall et al., 'The Diligence Due in the Era of Globalized Terrorism', *International Lawyer*, 36 (2002), p. 49; Anita Ramasastry, 'Secrets and Lies? Swiss Banks and International Human Rights', *Vanderbilt Journal of Transnational Law*, 31 (1998), p. 325, especially at pp. 342–6. See also Mark Pieth, 'Customer Due Diligence for Banks', in Mark Pieth (ed.), *Financing Terrorism* (Dordrecht, Boston, London: Kluwer Academic Publishers, 2002), pp. 189–210.

[71] Nina J. Crimm, 'Post-September 11 Fortified Anti-Terrorism Measures Compel Heightened Due Diligence', *Pace Law Review*, 25 (2004–5), p. 203.

[72] For an analysis as to why entities decide to adopt such a voluntary code of conduct and arguing that a strategic desire to maintain or enhance corporate reputation constitutes the key explanation, see Christopher Wright and Alexis Rwabizambuga, 'Institutional Pressures, Corporate Reputation, and Voluntary Codes of Conduct: An Examination of the Equator Principles', *Business and Society Review*, 111 (2006), p. 89.

[73] See www.equator-principles.com. Surveying the impact of the Equator Principles, see Paul Q. Watchman, 'Banking on Responsibility', *Frechfields Bruckhaus Deringer* (July 2005). See generally Miki Kamijyo, 'The "Equator Principles": Improved Social Responsibility in the Private Finance Sector', *Sustainable Development Law & Policy*, 4 (2004), p. 35; Robert F. Lawrence and William L. Thomas, 'The Equator Principles and Project Finance: Sustainability in Practice?', *Natural Resources & Environment*, 19 (2004–5), p. 20.

[74] These are Principles 1 and 7. Principle 1, 'Review and Categorisation' reads as follows: 'When a project is proposed for financing the [Equator Principles Financial Institution] will, as part of its internal social and environmental review and due diligence, categorise such project based on the magnitude of its potential impacts and risks in accordance with the environmental and social screening criteria of the

potentially associated with a given project for which a loan is solicited. In this framework, which has truly become a standard for most of this industry's actors, borrowers commit themselves to address and foresee the impact of the projects they are asked to finance in terms of social and environmental considerations. The Equator Principles are deliberately vague at the very moment a lawyer starts to search for definitions or for familiar conceptual boundaries.[75] Thus, the expression 'social and environmental considerations' has not been defined. There is, furthermore, not a single reference to 'human rights'.

This is not to imply that the Equator Principles are meaningless. In case of a lawsuit indeed, an actor from the project finance industry can seek to defend itself against allegations of misconduct by pointing towards 'due diligence' assessments that have been pursued as inspired by the Equator Principles. Such assertions may be a factor a judge may be willing to take into account in order to determine how the alleged fault may have been mitigated by such attempts at risk mitigation, as carried out under the 'due diligence' assessment.[76]

Thus, both in the bank and the project finance sectors, 'due diligence' constitutes a regular, often daily, business practice. The concept was recently boosted beyond that sector by John Ruggie in his 2008 report to the Human Rights Council as far as 'human rights' are concerned. As part of an entire section (paras. 56–64 of the report) entitled 'due diligence', it was recommended more generally that companies should, as a way of discharging their 'responsibility to respect' human rights law, carry out steps 'to become aware of, prevent and address adverse human rights impacts'.[77] It was suggested in the report referred to that this could be achieved, e.g., through the adoption and integration of a human rights policy, as well as through conducting human rights impact assessments and monitoring human rights performance and impact.

International Finance Corporation'; Principle 7, 'Independent Review' reads as follows: 'For all Category A projects and, as appropriate, for Category B projects, an independent social or environmental expert not directly associated with the borrower will review the Assessment, AP and consultation process documentation in order to assist the [Equator Principles Financial Institution]'s due diligence and assess Equator Principle compliance.'

[75] For a criticism of such features of the Equator Principles see Sheldon Leader, 'Human Rights, Risks, and New Strategies for Global Investment', *Journal of International Economic Law*, 9 (2006), p. 659.

[76] For an analysis from the legal angle, and about the potential risks for actors in the project finance industry to be held judicially accountable, see Eric Marcks, 'Avoiding Liability for Human Rights Violations in Project Finance', *Energy Law Journal*, 22 (2001), p. 301, discussing at pp. 315–18 the role of due diligence in this area.

[77] Ruggie, Report 2008, para. 56.

Therefore, the 'due diligence' notion stands good chances of becoming, over time, part of the private sector's mainstream discourse. By and large, the construct manages to carry the weight entrusted to it: preventing (becoming involved in) human rights violations in the first place, yet allowing a more forceful reaction should undesirable conduct occur after all.

3.2.2   'Due diligence' in international law   'Due diligence' and international law have a long history together. In international law, indeed, some obligations applicable to states are framed along the lines of a 'due diligence' modality.[78] In these sectors, 'due diligence' structures the relationship between a state, on the one hand, and a non-state actor, on the other. The crucial, defining feature of 'due diligence' is that it does not require any attributability of the non-state actor's conduct to the state.

Thus, as a substantive norm of conduct, 'due diligence' provides, in certain fields, an answer to the question as to how a state needs to behave vis-à-vis harmful conduct carried out by non-state actors, and this irrespective of any attributability. Clearly, in the abstract, this is an appealing notion for those wishing to insert the SRI-logic into the SWF realm.

The logic of 'due diligence' in international law is to proceed in two chronological steps: first, a state needs to take reasonable steps to prevent the harmful conduct from occurring in the first place; second, when the harmful conduct does occur, the state needs to take reasonable steps to react to it. The three keywords, thus, are 'prevent', 'react' and 'reasonable steps'.[79] If and when international law contains an actual, substantive obligation for a state to act vis-à-vis the conduct of non-state actors,[80] it bases the state's legal responsibility on its failure to

---

[78] For a general treatment of the matter in public international law, see Horst Blomeyer-Bartenstein, 'Due Diligence', in *Encyclopaedia of Public International Law*, Vol. I (Amsterdam: Elsevier Science Publishers, 1987), p. 1110.

[79] Though not new, the wording was authoritatively crystallized by the Inter-American Court of Human Rights in *Velasquez Rodriguez* v. *Honduras*, Inter-Am. Ct. H.R. (ser. C) No. 4 (29 July 1988), para. 174: a state 'has to take reasonable steps to prevent human rights violations and to use the means at its disposal to carry out a serious investigation of violations *committed within its jurisdiction*, to identify those responsible, to impose the appropriate punishment and to ensure the victim adequate compensation' (emphasis added). For a reference article on the subject, with multiple references to case law where it was applied, see Robert B. Barnidge, Jr., 'The Due Diligence Principle Under International Law', *International Community Law Review*, 81 (2006), p. 81.

[80] This is not only the case in certain circumstances involving the violation of civil and political rights, but also in respect of economic, social and cultural rights, as stated by the informal, non-binding restatement called 'The Maastricht Guidelines

act,[81] whereby 'act' can either be in the sense of 'preventing', or in the sense of 'reacting'.

As the word 'reasonable'[82] indicates, even where an obligation of a 'due diligence' nature applies, this is not an obligation that would be intolerant of some degree of failure, i.e., it is not an obligation of result.[83] This means, for example and as acknowledged by the Norwegian Council on Ethics,[84] that an investor cannot be held accountable for acts committed by the foreign private corporation that could not reasonably be expected. If violations do occur unexpectedly, however, the

---

on Violations of Economic, Social and Cultural Rights', which can be found in Victor Dankwa, Cees Flinterman and Scott Leckie, 'Commentary to the Maastricht Guidelines on Violations of Economic, Social and Cultural Rights', *Human Rights Quarterly*, 20 (1998), p. 691. In the latter document, Guideline 18, on 'Acts by Non-State Entities' states: 'The obligation to protect includes the State's responsibility to ensure that private entities or individuals, including transnational corporations over which they *exercise jurisdiction*, do not deprive individuals of their economic, social and cultural rights. States are responsible for violations of economic, social and cultural rights that result from their failure to exercise due diligence in controlling the behaviour of such non-state actors' (emphasis added). In Dankwa, Flinterman and Leckie, 'Commentary to the Maastricht Guidelines', p. 724, the following commentary is added thereto: 'Inaction by a state in controlling the conduct of these individuals or private entities will result in the state being assigned responsibility for the violations of the former.'

[81] See generally Gordon A. Christenson, 'Attributing Acts of Omission to the State', *Michigan Journal of International Law*, 12 (1990–1), pp. 323–4.

[82] On this concept in international law and the functions it fulfils, see generally Olivier Corten, 'The Notion of "Reasonable" in International Law: Legal Discourse, Reason and Contradictions', *International and Comparative Law Quarterly*, 48 (1999), p. 613; as well as, more extensively, Corten, *L'Utilisation du 'Raisonnable' par le Juge International: Discours Juridique, Raison et Contradictions* (Brussels: Bruylant, 1997).

[83] For an extensive treatment of the nature of 'due diligence' obligations, see Ricardo Pisillo-Mazzeschi, 'The Due Diligence Rule and the Nature of the International Responsibility of States', *German Yearbook of International Law*, 35 (1992), p. 9.

[84] Council on Ethics, 'Recommendation of 14 November 2005, Concerning whether Investments in Total, Due to the Company's Operations in Burma, are Contrary to the Petroleum Fund's Ethical Guidelines (Total Recommendation)', p. 10, under the heading 'Complicity and delimitation of companies' liability': 'In order (for an investor) to be complicit in an action, the action must be possible to anticipate for the investor. There must be some form of systematic or causal relationship between the company's operations and the actions in which the investor does not wish to be complicit. Investments in the company cannot be regarded as complicity in actions which one could not possibly expect or be aware of or circumstances over which the company has no significant control. ... The company's unethical conduct must be expected by the investor. Moreover, there must be a link between the company's operations and the unethical actions. It is explicitly stated that circumstances beyond the company's control cannot entail complicity on the part of the investor. This must indirectly also be taken to mean that the company itself cannot be considered to be complicit in ethical norm breaches that are beyond the company's control or which the company could not possibly expect or be aware of.'

interrelationship between active engagement and divestment captures the idea of how to operationalize an investment policy based upon 'due diligence'.

And a policy suggestion it is bound to remain. As a matter of existing international law, indeed, the scope of application of a state's 'due diligence' obligation is and remains strictly territorial.[85] Historically, indeed, the 'due diligence' doctrine under international law arose in the context of a state's obligations to protect aliens on its *own* territory. Extraterritoriality is simply not envisaged here. Therefore, in none of the scenarios under consideration in this contribution is 'due diligence' required under international law.

3.2.3   'Due diligence' and sovereign wealth funds' investment policy   As indicated in the previous paragraph, tying 'due diligence' and 'SWFs' together is not required as a matter of international law. In view of the territorial limitations inherent in the 'due diligence' notion as it exists in international law, the scenario under analysis in the present contribution simply transcends the reality that is grasped by the reach of the 'due diligence' notion.

Yet, this does not detract from the fact that 'due diligence' constitutes an appealing notion for the purposes of structuring a SWF's investment policy, and that SWFs are advised to consider adopting it out of self-interest: prevention comes first; reaction comes thereafter if prevention failed (or never took place). Both prevention and reaction can mirror the internal dynamics between active engagement with a corporation's management, on the one hand, and divestment, on the other. Given the very tight nexus between a state and its SWF, a compelling policy argument exists indeed to make sure that the SWF's investment

---

[85] Arguments have been made in the opposite direction. Most prominently, see M. Sornarajah, 'Linking State Responsibility for Certain Harms Caused by Corporate Nationals Abroad to Civil Recourse in the Legal System of Home States', in Scott Craig (ed.), *Torture as Tort* (Oxford University Press, 2001), p. 507, referring to a state's general responsibility not to knowingly cause harm in another state, and arguing that the following argument can be constructed: 'Where a state knows that its national's activities will cause, or are causing, harm to other states or peoples, it is consistent with this duty that it should prevent harm. As a matter of general principle, if the state has the right to have its nationals protected abroad, a concomitant duty to ensure that the nationals act in a manner consistent with international norms should be recognised.' The case of a SWF investing in a company incorporated in another state's jurisdiction, is even further removed from Sornarajah's argument, which only applies to that 'home state': 'Since a capacity to control exists in *the home state* with respect to a multinational which operates abroad, the same rules can therefore be extended to render home states liable when they are aware of the conduct of their multinational corporate nationals and do not curb such conduct through the means available to them' (ibid., emphasis added).

practices promote behaviour which is in compliance with human rights standards.[86]

Active engagement ought to be prioritized, ahead of the much more radical – though sometimes inevitable – option of divestment. Through such active engagement, one provides the corporation's management with an opportunity to remedy the alleged misconduct. Divestment ought to remain an option which is on the table, though only as a matter of last resort. For the purpose of assisting those making such a call, the Norwegian Ethical Guidelines propose various criteria.[87]

Prevention is and remains both the key term and the policy's ultimate objective. 'Due diligence' is particularly well-suited when it comes to prevention, for it requires a consideration of what is foreseeable or, in the words and yardsticks employed by the Norwegian Ethical Guidelines, that there is 'an unacceptable risk that the company [in which the investment has been made] contributes to or is responsible for'.[88] This term implies, as stated in the Recommendation concerning the corporation Total, that it should be 'associated with the degree of probability that unethical actions will take place in the future'. Of course, in order to assess such probability as to what may occur in the future, the company's past activities can tilt the balance.[89]

---

[86] John Ruggie, 'Putting the "Protect, Respect and Remedy Framework" Into Practice' (29 April 2010); www.institutehrb.org/blogs/guest/putting_the_protect_respect_remedy_framework_into_practice.html: 'One principle seems clear: the closer an entity is to the State, or the more it relies on statutory authority or taxpayer support, the stronger is the State's policy rationale for ensuring that the entity promotes respect for human rights.'

[87] Ethical Guidelines 2010, Section 2(4): 'In assessing whether a company shall be excluded in accordance with paragraph 3, the Ministry may among other things consider the probability of future norm violations; the severity and extent of the violations; the connection between the norm violations and the company in which the Fund is invested; whether the company is doing what can reasonably be expected to reduce the risk of future norm violations within a reasonable time frame; the company's guidelines for, and work on, safeguarding good corporate governance, the environment and social conditions; and whether the company is making a positive contribution for those affected, presently or in the past, by the company's behaviour' (see Appendix 1 below).

[88] Ibid., Section 2(3).

[89] Council on Ethics, 'Recommendation of 15 May 2007 on Exclusion of Vedanta Resources Plc.', p. 6: 'The Council would like to stress that existing and future violations are the ones covered by the Guidelines, both with regard to environmental damage and human rights abuses. This implies that one must assess whether there is a risk that the company's unacceptable practice will continue in the future. The company's previous actions may give an indication as to how it will behave in the future, and thus form a basis for the assessment of whether there is an unacceptable risk that unethical actions will occur henceforth. This also means that proof of future unethical actions is not required – it is sufficient to establish the existence of an unacceptable risk.'

'Due diligence' asks one to be forward-looking and to assess whether certain behaviour by the company in which the investment has been – or is about to be – made, may foreseeably take place, in which case one has to prevent such behaviour from occurring, or from being repeated. In order to calibrate its approach, the Norwegian Ethical Guidelines have introduced an intermediate step: rather than being subject to divestment right away, a company can be put under observation.[90] If such a policy were to be implemented by other SWFs, the implications could be far-reaching for the financial system both at the level of individual professionals; at the institutional level of the SWFs; as well as at the level of the global system of financial markets.[91]

'Due diligence' exercises such appeal because it does not originate at all from within the subject-matter where its operationalization is being proposed. Indeed: 'due diligence' is a true legal transplant,[92] which is able to migrate in between, and be downloaded from[93] the private to the public realm, on the one hand, and in between various entities of the public realm, on the other. For the foreseeable future at least, SWFs will continue to interact with the international financial markets, in which they find themselves side-by-side with private investment funds and corporations. Thus, business practices or legal concepts which have originated in the private realm, can easily be internalized into the public realm. Substantive change to such practices or concepts should not be a reason to worry, to the contrary even: a voluntary reception of such a transplant virtually always leads to some degree of modification.

Such migration of concepts from one realm to the other is exactly how transnational legal processes take shape.[94] In Rome, do as the Romans do: by venturing into the financial capital markets alongside innumerable private investment funds – some of which openly commit themselves to certain principles for responsible investment – gravitational

---

[90] Ethical Guidelines 2010, Section 3.

[91] All three of which are different fields of research, see Luc Van Liedekerke, Jef Van Gerwen and Danny Cassimon, *Exploration in Financial Ethics*, Ethical Perspectives Monograph Series (Leuven: Peeters Publishers, 2000), pp. 3–4.

[92] Alan Watson, *Legal Transplants: An Approach to Comparative Law* (Edinburgh: Scottish Academic Press, 1974), at p. 21, as 'the moving of a rule or a system of law from one country to another, or from one people to another'.

[93] The expression is from Harold Hongju Koh, 'Why Transnational Law Matters', *Penn State International Law Review*, 24 (2005–6), p. 753. Neither purely international nor purely national, the framework of analysis labelled 'transnational law', is defined here as being 'a kind of hybrid between domestic and international law that can be downloaded, uploaded, or transplanted from one system to another'.

[94] Harold Hongju Koh, 'Transnational Legal Process', *Nevada Law Review*, 75 (1996), at p. 204: 'As transnational actors interact, they create patterns of behaviour and generate norms of external conduct which they in turn internalize.'

pull exists for SWFs to allow themselves to be inspired by these private funds' practices.

By arguing in favour of having SWFs embrace 'due diligence' – a concept having its roots both inside and outside public international law – international law's foundational logic is turned upside down, both at the descriptive and at the argumentative level. As a discipline founded upon 'states' as its primary 'subjects', international law's disciplinary worry – engendered by its binary logic[95] – has always been whether it should, and how it could, give non-state actors, as newcomers, their place within its realm.[96] Thus, international law takes states' predominance as its point of departure. The situation is quite different as far as international financial markets are concerned: states are the newcomers here amidst innumerable non-state actors. These markets are challenged by the newcomers' sovereign status, with their concomitant bundle of sovereign rights and obligations. Hence the argument for SWFs to morph their modalities of operation along the lines of those already adopted by some of the private sector's actors.

In turn, in the realm of international financial markets, SWFs are confronted with the regulatory challenge created by the existence of private governance mechanisms. In this realm indeed, innumerable codes of conduct challenge states' normative supremacy.[97] Such mechanisms may, on the other hand, also turn out to have positive effects for the enhancement of the regulatory framework's overall efficiency.[98]

Finally, some words about possible[99] blind spots one needs to be acutely aware of before shifting from rhetoric to practice: if a multitude of SWFs start to issue their value judgments on foreign corporations' conduct, the result (a cacophony of voices?) may be less rosy than one would picture it to be.

---

[95] See generally Philip Alston, 'The "Not-a-Cat" Syndrome: Can the International Human Rights Regime Accommodate Non-State Actors?', in Philip Alston (ed.), *Non-State Actors and Human Rights* (Oxford University Press, 2005).

[96] See generally, Peter J. Spiro, 'New Players on the International Stage', *Hofstra Law & Policy Symposium*, 2 (1997), p. 19.

[97] Saskia Sasson, 'The State and Economic Globalization: Any Implications for International Law?', *Chicago Journal of International Law*, 109 (2000), p. 116.

[98] For an argument along those lines, applied to the case of 'sharing' environmental regulation between the State and institutional investors, see Benjamin J. Richardson, 'Enlisting Institutional Investors in Environmental Regulation: Some Comparative and Theoretical Perspectives', *North Carolina Journal of International Law and Commercial Regulation*, 28 (2002–3), p. 247.

[99] For a more detailed assessment from this angle, see Simon Chesterman, 'The Turn to Ethics: Disinvestment from Multinational Corporations for Human Rights Violations – The Case of Norway's Sovereign Wealth Fund', *American University International Law Review*, 23 (2008), pp. 610–14.

One crucial factor, outside the scope of the present contribution, ought not to be discounted either: who guards the guardians? In other words: what is the integrity of those making the divestment decision on the basis of these non-financial criteria? In a world where perception is key, this aspect may turn out to be the Achilles' heel of the entire construct.

Furthermore, at the level of principle, a SWF's divestment mechanism based on value judgments is not there to further foreign policy objectives.[100] At the level of reality, no matter all rhetoric surrounding the divestment decision, perception may very well be that there is a foreign policy component to it, hence undermining the decision's perceived legitimacy.

4.   Conclusion

The present contribution has assessed, from the perspective of Sovereign Wealth Funds (SWFs), the interrelationship between the world of 'socially responsible investment', on the one hand, and the world of international legal obligations, on the other.

As a matter of currently existing law – with a limited exception which is arguably applicable to specific weapons-related activities – there is no such relationship at all: in principle, an investment made by a SWF in a foreign private corporation which is – or turns out to be – involved in human rights violations does not trigger the international legal responsibility of the state to which the SWF belongs.

International law's classic machinery, no matter from which angle it is put in motion, always comes to a standstill in the 'no responsibility' square. Legal reasons cited (either individually or combined) in support of this conclusion, include the following: (i) that the company in question has not been empowered to exercise any public function; (ii) that its actions or omissions cannot be attributed to the state to which the SWF belongs; and (iii) that the latter does not have to be concerned about conduct from a foreign private corporation which is acting outside of that state's territory (the issue of extraterritoriality). The relationship between the SWF and the company in which it has invested is, in short, too weak for there to be any scope for legal responsibility.

---

[100] The issue arose during the Total Recommendation, para. 3 of which stated: 'Assessing whether exclusion of one or more companies might contribute to a better political development in Burma would go beyond the Council's mandate. This is clear from the preparatory work which contains the following statement: "The committee presumes that the majority of our foreign policy objectives will be better achieved with existing policy instruments than by imposing guiding principles on the Petroleum Fund's investment strategy."'

Framing the issue as one of 'legal obligations' leads onto a road to nowhere else but one where some will argue that international law suffers from a conceptual mismatch between concepts on paper, on the one hand, and facts on the ground, on the other.

Though as such not a new phenomenon, SWFs have increased over the course of the decade from 2000 to 2010, both in terms of the number of countries establishing such a fund, and in terms of the financial value these funds represent. The fact that a SWF has no legal obligation to take an interest in the conduct of the companies in which it has invested abroad, however, does not mean there would be no policy reasons for doing so. Many institutional investors of a private nature have – alongside other actors of the financial services industry – already signalled their interest by subscribing to one or more of the voluntary codes of conduct that contain principles for SRI. The present contribution presented a call to SWFs to follow that example, and to download the notion from the realm of financial services into the private sector, to the realm of SWFs.

'Due diligence' is, for private investors, a common business practice through which they seek to avoid becoming involved in investments supportive of harmful corporate conduct. 'Due diligence' is, likewise, a doctrine familiar to international law. SWFs ought to consider embracing it in view of the appeal exercised by this flexible doctrine's two-track approach: (i) reasonable measures need to be taken so as to *prevent* certain harm by non-state actors from occurring (or from repeating itself) in the first place; while (ii) having to adopt reasonable measures to *react* to such harm in case it occurred nevertheless, or regardless. Active engagement with the corporation's management remains to be preferred as long as possible. Divestment remains the option of last resort.

The question remains whether the upsides of implementing this call outweigh its possibly unanticipated downsides. The debate about the respective merits and demerits of doing so needs to take place both in the domestic arena of each SWF, on the one hand, and in the multilateral-international arena, on the other. Only such a debate will tell how receptive to reputational concerns SWFs are, and how legitimate will be the processes eventually put in place by SWFs to operationalize SRI. Which role are SWFs able and willing to take at the juncture where financial and non-financial considerations meet?

10   Corporations and criminal complicity

Andrew Clapham

1.   International law is perhaps a starting point but not the be all and end all

This chapter looks at corporate complicity in international crimes such as war crimes and genocide. It is not suggested that the legal framework is the exclusive framework in this field. In many situations the ethical or moral arguments will be more persuasive for corporate actors. Furthermore an ethical framework may be more beneficial for the victims of abuse; this is due to the fact that the international criminal law framework often builds in important guarantees for defendants in order to ensure that individuals are not deprived of their liberty in unfair or unjust ways. Criminal law, and international criminal law in particular, may not therefore provide the best framework for determining blameworthiness in the context of corporate conduct. On the one hand corporations may wish to prevent and compensate acts which are not strictly speaking illegal under criminal law, on the other hand those strict penal rules are designed to safeguard the liberty of the individual defendant rather than apportion blame to different legal entities. International criminal law should perhaps be seen as part of the story of corporate complicity, rather than the last word.

Despite these obvious differences between the criminal law framework and alternative ethically based approaches there has been, in recent times, a drift, or even a shift, towards framing the corporate responsibility debate in terms of legal liability, corporate accountability and even corporate criminality. This can be detected in the developing focus of attention in the legal scholarship,[1] but also in the wider context of the

---

[1] Maurice Punch, 'Why Corporations Kill and Get Away with It: The Failure of Law to Cope with Crime in Organizations', in André Nollkaemper and Harmen van der Wilt (eds.), *System Criminality in International Law* (Cambridge University Press, 2009), pp. 42–68; Andrew Clapham, 'Extending International Criminal Law beyond the Individual to Corporations and Armed Opposition Groups', *Journal of International Criminal Justice*, 6 (2008), pp. 899–926; O. De Schutter (ed.), *Transnational Corporations and Human Rights* (Oxford: Hart Publishing, 2006); De Schutter, 'The

reports produced by, *inter alios*, the United Nations' Special Representative of the Secretary-General on the issue of human rights and transnational corporations and other business enterprises, Professor John Ruggie.[2] This trend is not, however, universal. There are situations where careful boundaries are being drawn between what could be considered a violation of international law and what might be described as unethical corporate behaviour. In particular we can note the dualist approach taken by the Norwegian Council on Ethics for the Government Pension Fund – Global. Under the Council's Ethical Guidelines 'Upon request of the Ministry of Finance, the Council issues recommendations on whether an investment may constitute a violation of Norway's obligations under international law.'[3] But the Guidelines also explain:

The ethical basis for the Government Pension Fund – Global shall be promoted through the following three measures:

- Exercise of ownership rights in order to promote long-term financial returns, based on the UN Global Compact and the OECD Guidelines for Corporate Governance and for Multinational Enterprises.
- Negative screening of companies from the investment universe that either themselves, or through entities they control, produce weapons that through normal use may violate fundamental humanitarian principles.
- Exclusion of companies from the investment universe where there is considered to be an unacceptable risk of contributing to:
  - Serious or systematic human rights violations, such as murder, torture, deprivation of liberty, forced labour, the worst forms of child labour and other child exploitation

---

Accountability of Multinationals for Human Rights Violations in European Law', in P. Alston (ed.), *Non-State Actors and Human Rights* (Oxford University Press, 2005), pp. 227–314; S. Joseph, *Corporations and Transnational Human Rights Litigation* (Oxford: Hart Publishing, 2004); C. Wells, *Corporations and Criminal Responsibility*, 2nd edn (Oxford University Press, 2001); M. Kamminga and S. Zia-Zarifi (eds.), *Liability of Multinational Corporations Under International Law* (The Hague: Kluwer, 2000).

[2] John Ruggie, 'Interim Report of the Special Representative of the Secretary-General on the Issue of Human Rights and Transnational Corporations and Other Business Enterprises', UN Human Rights Council, UN Doc. E/CN.4/2006/97 (22 February 2006), and subsequent reports: A/HRC/4/035; A/HRC/8/5 and A/HRC/8/16 (Clarifying the Concepts of 'Sphere of influence' and 'Complicity'); A/HRC/11/13; A/HRC/14/27; all available at www.business-humanrights.org/SpecialRepPortal/Home; International Council on Human Rights Policy, *Beyond Voluntarism: Human Rights and the Developing International Legal Obligations of Companies* (Versoix: ICHRP, 2002); M. Monshipouri, C. E. Welsh and E. T. Kennedy, 'Multinational Corporations and the Ethics of Global Responsibility: Problems and Possibilities', *Human Rights Quarterly*, 25 (2003), pp. 965–89; and R. Shamir, 'Between Self-Regulation and the Alien Tort Claims Act: On the Contested Concept of Corporate Social Responsibility', *Law & Society Review*, 38 (2004), pp. 635–63.

[3] Ethical Guidelines of the Norwegian Government Pension Fund – Global (Ethical Guidelines 2004), para. 4.3 (see Appendix 2 below).

- Grave breaches of individuals' rights in situations of war or conflict
- Severe environmental damages
- Gross corruption
- Other particularly serious violations of fundamental ethical norms (Ethical Guidelines 2004, para. 2).

The language here is clearly intended to allow for an evaluation of behaviour which, while not necessarily in violation of a particular rule of international law, is seen as undermining the rule of international law in its spirit and purpose. The references to the Global Compact and the OECD Guidelines reinforce the idea that the applicable standards are not legally binding; referring to 'fundamental humanitarian principles' and 'particularly serious violations of fundamental ethical norms', without further explanation, makes it clear that the examination will move beyond rights and rules, and include principles and norms. These might be considered as semantic differences, but the message is clear. Should there be any doubt, the Advisory Council is careful to reinforce the distinction between violations of international law and violations of the Ethical Guidelines. Responding to a request from the Ministry with regard to whether two particular weapons systems might be contrary to international law the Council stated:

A given weapons system could be inconsistent with the Ethical Guidelines, even if it does not conflict with international law. The Advisory Council is already in the process of assessing whether the above mentioned weapons systems could be in violation of the Ethical Guidelines. The Council might therefore issue recommendations on the relationship between these weapons systems and the Ethical Guidelines at a later time, irrespective of this recommendation which pertains to the international law issues.[4]

In this situation the issue is not whether the use of the actual weapon may violate international law (let us assume for the sake of argument that it does), the issue is whether investment by the Petroleum Fund renders a state party complicit in a violation of the Ottawa Convention on the Prohibition of the Use, Stockpiling, Production and Transfer of Anti-Personnel Mines and on Their Destruction (1997). In the words of the Recommendation: 'Investments that might be seen as undermining international law standards would normally not constitute violations of international law. Certain treaties, however, contain provisions on complicity that are so far reaching that this might be the

---

[4] Council on Ethics, 'Recommendation of 20 September 2006 Concerning whether the Weapons Systems Spider and Intelligent Munition System (IMS) might be Contrary to International Law – Letter to Ministry of Finance from Advisory Council on Ethics.'

case.'[5] We should pause here to notice that the concern here is that the investment might be *contributing* to the violation of international law, and that in some circumstances this could be considered *complicity* giving rise to international responsibility for the investor. This contribution/complicity through investment is explained in the introductory chapter to the present book. The focus of my chapter is, however, on another type of complicity: the complicity between a company and another actor (it could be a state, a rebel group, another company or even an individual). The company is a secondary actor assisting the primary perpetrator. There have been multiple allegations of this kind of corporate complicity and our focus will be on: what constitutes corporate complicity in violations of international criminal law?

2.   The emergence of complicity studies

Before looking at the scope of complicity under international law, let us first ask ourselves how this concept came to play such a prominent role in the discourse around corporate social responsibility. I would suggest that there are a few developments which stand out.

First, as human rights organizations became more interested in reporting on the behaviour of multinational corporations they found themselves confronted with a legal conundrum. Unlike ethical investors, or those in the corporate social responsibility movement, international human rights organizations prided themselves on their legal methodology. Moreover they based all human rights reporting on violations of applicable international law. These violations were usually expressed in terms of violations of human rights treaties which the relevant state had ratified. The legal methodology did not seem suited to complaining about the behaviour of corporations. The Amnesty International 'Human Rights Principles for Companies' (1998) included a policy recommendation that 'Companies should establish procedures to ensure that all operations are examined for their potential impact on human rights, and safeguards to ensure that company staff are never complicit in human rights abuses.' Similarly, without radically altering the traditional understanding of human rights law, groups such as Human Rights Watch argued that, although the corporations did not have obligations as parties to the human rights treaties, the states they were operating in did have such obligations, and the behaviour of the corporations could be seen as contributing to violations by those states. It therefore made sense to talk about the corporations being complicit

---

[5] Ibid.

in such violations.[6] The Human Rights Watch 1999 Enron report in particular highlighted the fact that corporations were benefiting from human rights violations and that investors would be facilitating such violations.

> In addition to the state, Human Rights Watch believes that the Dabhol Power Corporation and its parent company Enron are complicit in these human rights violations. Enron's local entity, the Dabhol Power Corporation, benefited directly from an official policy of suppressing dissent through misuse of the law, harassment of anti-Enron protest leaders and prominent environmental activists, and police practices ranging from arbitrary to brutal. The company did not speak out about human rights violations and, when questioned about them, chose to dismiss them altogether.
>
> But the Dabhol Power Corporation's responsibility, and by extension that of the consortium and principally Enron, goes beyond a failure to speak out about human rights violations by the state police. The company, under provisions of law, paid the abusive state forces for the security they provided to the company. These forces, located adjacent to the project site, were only stationed there to deal with protests. In addition, contractors (for DPC) engaged in a pattern of harassment, intimidation, and attacks on individuals opposed to the Dabhol Power project. When the victims of these acts attempted to file complaints with the police, they were met with official silence. Police refused to investigate complaints, and in several cases, arrested the victims for acts they did not commit. When these activities were brought to the company's attention, the Dabhol Power Corporation refused to acknowledge that its contractors were responsible for criminal acts and did not adequately investigate, condemn, or cease relationships with these individuals.
>
> Other institutions bear responsibility for human rights violations as well. Human Rights Watch considers that the financiers of Phase I of the project's construction (1992–99) and U.S. government agencies that financed and lobbied for the project are complicit in the human rights violations.[7]

We see here very clearly the two types of complicity addressed in the same report. First, the complicity of the company with the host government, and second the complicity of the investor in the project. The notion that investors should avoid being tainted with complicity was at that time seen as a vehicle for campaigning against companies. In a separate campaign Amnesty International quoted Alan G. Hevesi, Comptroller of the City of New York Pension Funds, and a shareholder in Talisman Energy, as stating in the same year:

---

[6] See e.g., Human Rights Watch, 'Oil Companies Complicit in Nigerian Abuses' (New York: Human Rights Watch, 1999), and 'The Enron Corporation: Corporate Complicity in Human Rights Violations' (New York: Human Rights Watch, 1999).

[7] Human Rights Watch, 'The Enron Corporation', pp. 3–4.

I believe a company that is doing business in a country under a repressive regime must not provide financing or other resources for the perpetuation of wrongdoing or atrocities. As long-term investors, we believe a company that is cavalier about its moral and social responsibility presents an unacceptable investment risk. The expanding divestment campaign against Talisman Energy for alleged complicity in the horrors in Sudan is just one indication of that risk.[8]

The use of the complicity concept in this context was not, however, simply generated by activists as a campaigning tool.[9] In the specific case of Talisman it formed part of the corporation's commitment to human rights. The Human Rights Watch report on the complicity of oil companies in Sudan stated:

In late 1999, after months of pressure from the Canadian government, Talisman finally signed the International Code of Ethics for Canadian Business; this committed the company to the 'value' of 'human rights and social justice' and to 'support and respect the protection of international human rights' within its 'sphere of influence' (undefined), and 'not be complicit in human rights abuses'.[10]

Second, in 1999 the UN Secretary-General Kofi Annan launched the Global Compact with a speech in Davos. He addressed business leaders in the following terms:

You can uphold human rights and decent labour and environmental standards directly, by your own conduct of your own business. Indeed, you can use these universal values as the cement binding together your global corporations, since they are values people all over the world will recognize as their own. You can make sure that in your own corporate practices you uphold and respect human rights; and that you are not yourselves complicit in human rights abuses.[11]

The Global Compact was developed the following year and its first two principles were announced as follows: Principle 1: Businesses should support and respect the protection of internationally proclaimed human rights; and Principle 2: make sure that they are not complicit in human

---

[8] Amnesty International, 'Sudan: The Human Price of Oil' (3 May 2000). The reference for the quote is 'Letter, written by Alan G. Hevesi to Mr James Buckee, president and chief executive officer of Talisman Energy, September 27, 1999.'

[9] See also the connection with the campaign over arms transfers: Alexandra Boivin, 'Complicity and Beyond: International Law and the Transfer of Small Arms and Light Weapons', *International Review of the Red Cross*, 87 (September 2005), pp. 467–96.

[10] Human Rights Watch, 'Sudan, Oil, and Human Rights' (New York: Human Rights Watch, 2003), p. 34.

[11] UN Press Release, 'Secretary-General Proposes Global Compact on Human Rights, Labour, Environment, in address to World Economic Forum in Davos.'

rights abuses. In the 'learning forum' that grew up around the Compact considerable time and energy was then spent on considering what was meant by complicity in this context.[12] Needless to say the emphasis was not on international law but rather on what might be expected in the context of the Global Compact (the Compact's reference to complicity here had in turn been inspired by the International Code of Ethics for Canadian Business).

Third, the growing number of cases being litigated under the Alien Tort Statute (also known as the Alien Tort Claims Act) in the United States Federal Courts has focused attention on the scope of complicity in this context. The Alien Tort Statute confers upon the federal district courts original jurisdiction over 'any civil action by an alien for a tort only, committed in violation of the law of nations' (28 U.S.C. § 1350). It is perfectly possible to bring a suit against a corporation for violating international law as the principal perpetrator and not raise complicity at all,[13] and suits have indeed been brought, for example with regard to allegations of violations of international law, including torture and inhuman or degrading treatment, by contractors providing interpretation and interrogation services to the United States at Abu Ghraib prison in Iraq;[14] and against Blackwater alleging war crimes under the Alien Tort Statute in connection with the killing of civilians on 16 September 2007.[15]

We will concentrate, however, on some recent rulings concerning the scope of 'complicity' in violations of international criminal law in general, and complicity in war crimes and genocide in particular. This is particularly relevant with regard to the Ethical Guidelines quoted above which refers to 'an unacceptable risk of contributing to … Grave breaches of individuals' rights in situations of war or conflict.' To be clear we might repeat that we will be looking at the complicity of the corporation and not the complicity of the investor.

---

[12] For one set of documents see UN Global Compact Office and OHCHR, 'Embedding Human Rights in Business Practice' (New York: UN Global Compact Office, 2004); www.unglobalcompact.org/docs/issues_doc/human_rights/embedding.pdf.

[13] Here we differ from the authors of the introduction to this book in that we would assert that corporations in this circumstance are being sued for violations of international law, and are not merely being accused of having contributed to a state's violation of international law.

[14] For the background see the Order of 6 November 2007 *Ibrahim et al.* v. *Titan et al.* and *Saleh et al.* v. *Titan et al.*, United States District Court for the District of Columbia, James Robertson US District Judge, Case 1:05-cv-01165-JR.

[15] See *Abtan et al.* v. *Blackwater Worldwide et al.*, Case 1:07-cv-01831 (RBW), filed 26 November 2007. The case was settled, see Associated Press: 'Blackwater settles series of civil lawsuits' (7 January 2010).

3.   Corporate complicity and the Alien Tort Statute

In the simple situation where a corporation's activities actually constitute genocide, slavery or war crimes the issue is clear. The corporation will have violated international criminal law and can be held accountable in the US courts under the Alien Tort Statute. The US courts have been gradually refining the list of violations of the 'law of nations' which attach to non-state actors as such. Accordingly, recent rulings have determined that genocide, slave trading, slavery, forced labour and war crimes are actionable even in the absence of any connection to state action.[16] In addition, according to the *Kadic* v. *Karadzic* judgment in the US courts, where rape, torture and summary execution are committed in isolation these crimes 'are actionable under the Alien Tort Act, without regard to state action, to the extent they were committed in pursuit of genocide or war crimes'.[17] An alien can sue in tort before the US Federal Courts under the Alien Tort Statute Act with regard to any of these international crimes. In fact the list is not exclusive as international criminal law continues to evolve. The Appeals Chamber of the International Criminal Tribunal for the former Yugoslavia confirmed that there is no need for a public official to be involved for a private individual to be responsible under international law for the international crime of torture.[18] In the context of violations of the law of nations outside the context of war crimes, the US courts have, however, started to circumscribe the scope of what should be considered an actionable violation of the law of nations. In the case of the *Bridgestone Corporation* the court did not consider the workers in Liberia to be 'forced' to work in the sense of forced labour:

there is a broad international consensus that at least some extreme practices called 'forced labor' violate universal and binding international norms. But the adult plaintiffs in this case allege labor practices that lie somewhere on a continuum that ranges from those clear violations of international law (slavery or labor forced at the point of soldiers' bayonets) to more ambiguous situations involving poor working conditions and meager or exploitative wages. The *Sosa*

---

[16] *Wiwa* v. *Royal Dutch Shell Petroleum (Shell)*, 28 February 2002, p. 39. US District Court for the Southern District of New York. See also *Doe I* v. *Unocal Corporation* 18 September 2002 at para. 3ff.

[17] *Kadic* v. *Karadzic* 70 F. 3d 232 at 243–244 (2d Cir. 1995) cited with approval in *Doe* v. *Unocal* 2002 (supra), para. 3.

[18] 'The Trial Chamber in the present case was therefore right in taking the position that the public official requirement is not a requirement under customary international law in relation to the criminal responsibility of an individual for torture outside of the framework of the Torture Convention.' *Kunarac et al.*, ICTY (IT-96-23 and IT-96-23/1 A), Appeal Judgment, 12 June 2002, para. 148.

Court ultimately concluded that the plaintiff's claim based on arrest and detention depended on an aspiration in 'the present, imperfect world' that exceeded any binding customary rule that was sufficiently specific to reach his case, and so ordered dismissal.[19]

In the *Sosa* case the Supreme Court had rejected a claim that arbitrary detention short of 'prolonged' arbitrary fell short of what could be considered a violation of the law of nations for the purposes of the Statute, and determined that violations of the 'law of nations' under this statute must be those that are 'specific, universal and obligatory', suggesting that the drafters of the Alien Tort Statute probably had in mind a narrow set of violations such as piracy or an assault on an ambassador. The list is nevertheless not exhaustive, as international law continues to evolve.[20]

A corporation being sued in the US Courts under the Statute as the primary perpetrator of an international crime is relatively rare, and most of the cases which have recently been brought under this Statute concern situations where corporations are alleged to have aided and abetted a state or a rebel group in violations of international criminal law. The question of what obligations a corporation has under international law is shifted as the relevant primary obligations are those borne by the principal perpetrator. Judge Katzmann's words remind us why complicity is so crucial in this context: it allows a claim to be made against a corporation for a violation of the law of nations that would often normally require state action. In his words: 'International law, too, recognizes that criminality is assessed by reference to the actions of the principal, not the aider and abettor.'[21] These cases then turn on accomplice liability, or, complicity. Although the Supreme Court has offered the guidance that the violations of the law of nations must be 'specific, universal and obligatory' at the time of writing the Supreme Court has yet to rule on the component of complicity. There is, however, a petition before the Court on exactly this point and we will therefore examine some of the arguments in the *Talisman* litigation in some detail.

The Court of Appeals for the Second Circuit handed down its decision in the *Talisman* case on 7 October 2009. Its description of the facts helps to set the scene:

Because GNPOC's [Greater Nile Petroleum Operating Company Limited, in which Talisman acquired twenty-five per cent stake in October 1998] operations took place amidst civil war, security arrangements were made for Consortium

---

[19] *Roe v. Bridgestone Corporation*, Case No. 1:06–cv–0627–DFH–JMS (27 June 2007), pp. 44–5.

[20] *Sosa v. Alvarez-Machain et al.*, 542 US 692 (2004), pp. 732 and 734–7.

[21] *Khulumani v. Barclay National Bank, Ltd; Ntsebeza v. Daimler Chysler Corp.*, 12 October 2007, 05–2141-cv, 05–2326-cv. US Court of Appeals for the Second Circuit, pp. 46–7.

personnel in coordination with the Government and military forces. Plaintiffs contend that these arrangements resulted in the persecution of civilians living in or near the oil concession areas.

In May 1999, GNPOC and the Government built all-weather roads traversing the oil concession areas and linking the concessions to military bases. To protect GNPOC's employees and equipment, these roads served the dual purposes of moving personnel for oil operations and facilitating military activities ....

Talisman employees saw outgoing flights by helicopter gunships and Antonov bombers. One Talisman security advisor observed 500-pound bombs being loaded on Government-owned Antonov bombers at Heglig and regular bombing runs from the airstrip. At both Heglig and Unity, GNPOC personnel refueled military aircraft, sometimes with GNPOC's own fuel.[22]

The crucial issue for the court can be summed up as a choice between demanding that the company assisted with 'purpose' or 'knowledge'. The court relies in particular on the analysis undertaken by Judge Katzmann in the *Khulumani* case and his use of the Rome Statute for the International Criminal Court and its Article 25(3) which reads in part:

(c) For the purpose of facilitating the commission of such a crime, aids, abets or otherwise assists in its commission or its attempted commission, including providing the means for its commission; [or]
(d) In any other way contributes to the commission or attempted commission of such a crime by a group of persons acting with a common purpose.
Such contribution shall be intentional and shall either:

(i) Be made with the aim of furthering the criminal activity or criminal purpose of the group, where such activity or purpose involves the commission of a crime within the jurisdiction of the Court; or
(ii) Be made in the knowledge of the intention of the group to commit the crime[.]

In both cases the Court only looked at Article 25(3)(c) but it is worth briefly considering the scope of 25(3)(d) before turning to the debate over the significance of Article 25(3)(c).

3.1   Contribution to a Group Crime under Article 25(3)(d)

The reference in the ICC Statute to a group of persons acting with a common purpose is similar to the joint criminal enterprise doctrine developed by the ICTY and this form of conspiracy liability was rejected in the *Talisman* appeal. But the International Criminal Court has now

---

[22] *Presbyterian Church of Sudan* v. *Talisman Energy, Inc.*, Decision on summary judgment dated 12 September 2006 453 F. Supp. 2d 633 (S.D.N.Y. 2006), Docket No. 07–0016-cv, at pp. 12–14.

addressed the scope of this provision and their approach merits our attention. This type of participation in the crime requires one to identify two different intentions. According to the words of the ICC Statute we need: first an intentional contribution, and second, knowledge of the intention of the group. The secondary participant, or in our case, the complicit corporation, can either intend to further the crime, or simply intentionally contribute with knowledge of the others' intention to commit the crime. The Statute is complex in this regard but it does admit that one can be criminally liable even where one only has knowledge of the crime rather than a shared purpose to commit that crime.

The Pre-Trial Chamber of the International Criminal Court has explained that this residual form of liability presents a threshold for a different, seemingly less engaged state of mind, and can be likened to joint criminal enterprise:

In this regard, the Chamber notes that, by moving away from the concept of co-perpetration embodied in Article 25(3)(a), Article 25(3)(d) defines the concept of (i) contribution to the commission or attempted commission of a crime by a group of persons acting with a common purpose, (ii) with the aim of furthering the criminal activity of the group or in the knowledge of the criminal activity of the group or in the knowledge of the criminal purpose.

335. The Chamber considers that this latter concept – which is closely akin to the concept of joint criminal enterprise or the common purpose doctrine adopted by the jurisprudence of the ICTY – would have been the basis of the concept of co-perpetration within the meaning of Article 25(3)(a), had the drafters of the Statute opted for a subjective approach for distinguishing between principals and accessories.

336. Moreover, the Chamber observes that the wording of Article 25(3)(d) of the Statute begins with the words '[i]n any other way contributes to the commission or attempted commission of such crime.'

337. Hence, in the view of the Chamber, Article 25(3)(d) of the Statute provides for a residual form of accessory liability which makes it possible to criminalise those contributions to a crime which cannot be characterized as ordering, soliciting, inducing, aiding, abetting or assisting within the meaning of Article 25(3)(b) or Article 25(3)(c) of the Statute by reason of the state of mind in which the contributions were made.[23]

The Chamber's more general comments on knowledge and intention are also worth mentioning here as they represent an authoritative reading of the ICC Statute. The Chamber is clear that Article 30's references to intent and knowledge cover three types of *dolus*: first *dolus directus* of the first degree – the suspect knows that his or her actions will bring

---

[23] Decision of the Pre-Trial Chamber of the ICC *Lumbanga* (ICC-01/04–01/06), 29 January 2007.

about the objective elements of the crime and undertakes such actions aware that their actions will bring about such elements as a necessary outcome. Second, *dolus directus* of the second degree, the suspect, without the concrete intent to bring about the objective elements of the crime, is aware that such elements will be the necessary outcome of their actions. Third, *dolus eventualis* – the suspect is aware of the risk of objective elements resulting from their actions and accepts such an outcome by reconciling themselves to it. The ICC Trial Chamber then adds a further layer of clarification:

353. The Chamber considers that in the latter type of situation, two kinds of scenarios are distinguishable. Firstly, if the risk of bringing about the objective elements of the crime is substantial (that is, there is a likelihood that it 'will occur in the ordinary course of events'), the fact that the suspect accepts the idea of bringing about the objective elements of the crime can be inferred from:

i.   the awareness by the suspect of the substantial likelihood that his or her actions or omissions would result in the realization of the objective elements of the crime; and
ii. the decision by the suspect to carry out his or her actions or omissions despite such awareness.

354. Secondly, if the risk of bringing about the objective elements of the crime is low, the suspect must have clearly or expressly accepted the idea that such objective elements may result from his or her actions or omissions.

355. Where the state of mind of the suspect falls short of accepting that the objective elements of the crime may result from his or her actions or omissions, such a state of mind cannot qualify as a truly intentional realization of the objective elements, and hence would not meet the 'intent and knowledge' requirement embodied in Article 30 of the Statute.

We can distil all this down to the idea that, once a corporation is made aware of a likelihood of contributing to a crime committed by a group, then, once it accepts that its actions may lead to elements of the crime occurring and it continues to act, it has the requisite mental involvement to give rise to a residual form of corporate complicity in international crimes.

3.2   *The* actus reus *component necessary for corporate complicity under Article 25(3)(c)*

As stated above the US courts made no reference at all to Article 25(3)(d) choosing instead to focus on 25(3)(c) and a reading of the international case law. Judge Katzmann summarized his approach as follows:

With respect to the *actus reus* component of the aiding and abetting liability, the international legislation is less helpful in identifying a specific standard.

However, in the course of its analysis of customary international law, the ICTY concluded that 'the *actus reus* of aiding and abetting in international criminal law requires practical assistance, encouragement, or moral support which has a *substantial effect* on the perpetration of the crime.' *Furundzija*, Trial Chamber Judgment, ¶ 235 (second emphasis added). My research has uncovered nothing to indicate that a standard other than 'substantial assistance' should apply. Accordingly, I conclude that a defendant may be held liable under international law for aiding and abetting the violation of that law by another when the defendant (1) provides practical assistance to the principal which has a substantial effect on the perpetration of the crime, and (2) does so with the purpose of facilitating the commission of that crime.[24]

The first question that arises is what does 'substantial' mean in this context? The corporate complicity context is often concerned with issues of presence in war zones. The case law from the *ad hoc* Tribunals has dealt with the issue of contribution through presence but these cases are really about encouragement through presence rather than the economic dimension of presence. Nevertheless it may be helpful to consider the summary of cases concerning complicity through presence. The ICTY summarized the issues by reference to three separate cases in the *Kvočka* judgment:

257. Presence alone at the scene of the crime is not conclusive of aiding or abetting, unless it is shown to have a significant legitimizing or encouraging effect on the principal. Presence, particularly when coupled with a position of authority, is therefore a probative, but not determinative, indication that an accused encouraged or supported the perpetrators of the crime.

258. For example, in the *Aleksovski* case, the Trial Chamber found that, in the absence of any objection by the accused, his presence during the systematic mistreatment of detainees created a necessary inference that the accused was aware that such tacit approval would be construed as a sign of his support and encouragement. Under the circumstances, the Trial Chamber found that Aleksovski contributed substantially to the mistreatment of detainees. Furthermore, the Trial Chamber concluded that he aided and abetted the repetitious brutality suffered by two detainees even when he was absent. The Trial Chamber found that abuse of this kind was committed near the accused's office so often that he must have been aware of it. Yet he did not oppose or stop the crimes, as his superior position demanded, and his silence could only be interpreted as a sign of approval. This silence was held to evince a culpable intent of aiding and abetting such acts as contemplated under Article 7(1) of the Statute.

259. The *Tadić* Trial Chamber considered that the presence of the accused when crimes were committed by a group was sufficient to entail his responsibility if he had previously played an active role in similar acts committed by the same group and had not expressly spoken against the conduct of the

---

[24] *Khulumani* v. *Barclay National Bank, Ltd*, pp. 38–9.

group. This holding is particularly notable because the defendant was a low level actor, a person without any official authority who entered camps, including Omarska, to beat and otherwise abuse detainees.

260. In the *Akayesu* case, an ICTR Trial Chamber held that the defendant had previously provided verbal encouragement for the commission of crimes, and that his status as 'bourgemeister' conferred upon him a position of authority. His subsequent silence was a signal in the face of crimes of violence committed nearby of official tolerance for the crimes.[25]

The point in these cases is that, although presence was a factor in finding moral encouragement, they all concerned people who were in a superior or official position, or in the case of Tadić, someone who was actually present or in the vicinity of the torture and abuse. It would be misleading simply to infer that corporate presence in a country can be assimilated to the presence of a superior in the vicinity of the torture scene. On the other hand, one could imagine a situation where corporate knowledge coupled with silence could be seen as encouragement akin to the sort of moral support which the individuals offered in the cases referred to above. This would certainly fit with the spirit of the Tribunal's approach to aiders and abettors. It is suggested that the case for corporate complicity would be particularly strong where the corporation was seen to benefit from the violations[26] (for example, the government or the rebel group clears land of inhabitants through illegal forced evictions, forced labour is involved in the production of goods supplied to the company, demonstrations are suppressed in violation of the right to life and the right to freedom of assembly).

3.3   The mens rea *component for complicity*

The *Talisman* Court of Appeals held as follows:

Thus, applying international law, we hold that the *mens rea* standard for aiding and abetting liability in ATS actions is purpose rather than knowledge alone. Even if there is a sufficient international consensus for imposing liability on individuals who *purposefully* aid and abet a violation of international law ... no such consensus exists for imposing liability on individuals who *knowingly* (but not purposefully) aid and abet a violation of international law.[27]

---

[25] ICTY *Kvočka* (IT-98–30/1-T), Trial Chamber Judgment 2 November 2001 (footnotes omitted).

[26] See e.g., Anita Ramasastry, 'Corporate Complicity: From Nuremberg to Rangoon. An Examination of Forced Labor Cases and Their Impact on the Liability of Multinational Corporations', *Berkeley Journal of International Law*, 20 (2002), pp. 91–159.

[27] *Presbyterian Church of Sudan v. Talisman Energy, Inc.*, pp. 41–2.

As stated above the plaintiffs are asking the Supreme Court to take the case and are arguing that the correct standard in this context is knowledge rather than purpose. Without rehearsing all the arguments,[28] we might refer to two expert *amici* briefs that have been filed with the Supreme Court and which are very pertinent for our discussion of corporate complicity more generally.[29] First, the brief filed on behalf of the International Commission of Jurists makes the point that the ICC Statute does not represent customary international law on this point and points to the relevant case law of the International Tribunals for the former Yugoslavia and Rwanda,[30] and concludes that the Tribunals: 'have uniformly upheld a *mens rea* requirement of knowledge for aiding and abetting liability.'[31] The International Commission of Jurists then set out relevant national practice:

Countries from civil law tradition such as Germany, Switzerland, and the Netherlands, require that the accused be aware of the possibility that his act will assist the main perpetrator and accept this circumstance. Others such as Croatia, Montenegro and Macedonia require intent (including *dolus eventualis*) which is a lower standard than purpose. African jurisdictions influenced by this tradition such as Rwanda, Burrundi and the Democratic Republic of the Congo also require knowledge. Most countries in the former Soviet Union (e.g., Kazakhstan, Azerbaijan, and the Russian Federation) require indirect intent, which relies partly on awareness of a possibility. Latin American countries generally require *dolus*, including *dolus eventualis*, where knowledge of the possibility that a crime will be committed is part of it. *Prosecution Response to General Ojdanic's amended Appeal Brief (public redacted), The Prosecutor v. Sainovic, et al.*, Case No. IT-05–87-A, p. 87–88.

---

28 The US case law is analysed in some detail in Doug Cassel, 'Corporate Aiding and Abetting of Human Rights Violations: Confusion in the Courts', *Northwestern University Journal of International Human Rights*, 6 (2008).

29 The present author was a member of the ICJ's Expert Legal Panel Report 'Corporate Complicity & Legal Accountability' (Geneva: ICJ, 2008) which comes to similar conclusions; www.icj.org/IMG/Volume_3.pdf.

30 'Both the ICTY and ICTR, in construing CIL [customary international law], have uniformly required a *mens rea* of knowledge for aiding and abetting liability. The tribunals have unvaryingly applied the knowledge standard in aiding and abetting cases since initially confronting the question in 1997. *Prosecutor v. Tadic*, Case No. IT-94–1-T, Opinion and Judgment, ¶ 692 (May 7, 1997). *See also Prosecutor v. Akayesu*, Case No. ICTR-96–4-T, Judgment, ¶ 545 (Sept. 2, 1998); *Prosecutor v. Furundzija*, Case No. IT-95–17/1-T, Judgment, ¶ 249 (Dec. 10, 1998); *Prosecutor v. Musema*, ICTR-96–13-T, Judgment and Sentence, ¶ 180 (Jan. 27, 2000); *Muvunyi v. Prosecutor*, Case No. ICTR-2000–55A-A, Judgment (Aug. 29, 2008), ¶ 79; *Prosecutor v. Milutinovic et al.*, Case No. IT-05–87-T, Judgment, vol. III, ¶ 281 (Feb. 26, 2009)', *The Presbyterian Church of Sudan* v. *Talisman Energy, Inc.*, On Petition for Writ of Certiorari to the United States Court of Appeals for the Second Circuit: 'Brief of the International Commission of Jurists and the American Association for the International Commission of Jurists, *Amici Curiae*, Supporting Petitioners', pp. 5–6.

31 Ibid., p. 8.

Countries whose legal system is influenced by the common law tradition generally require knowledge for the *mens rea* of aiding and abetting. Such is the case of English law, Australian and South African law. *Ibid.* pp. 88–89.[32]

In a similar, supporting brief Professor David Scheffer draws on his experience as the head of the US delegation to the negotiations on the ICC Statute to argue that Article 25(3)(c) cannot be seen as reflecting customary international law and that it has to be read in connection with Article 30.

Negotiators struggled to find compromise wording and ultimately settled on using neither 'intent' nor 'knowledge' but 'purpose.' Reaching this compromise was made easier, in the end, by the prior resolution of the final language of Article 30, an article that deals expressly with the issue of the mental element of crimes. Finalizing the language of Article 30 helped enormously, as it enabled negotiators to look to Article 30 for intent and knowledge standards while seeking an accommodation for Article 25(3)(c). However, if anyone had claimed we were writing customary international law on aiding and abetting liability in Article 25(3)(c), they would have been laughed out of the room.[33]

Article 25(3)(c)'s opening phrase, 'For the purpose of facilitating the commission of such a crime,' was agreed to in Rome during the final negotiations as an acceptable compromise phrase to resolve the inconclusive talks over whether to use the word 'intent' or the word 'knowledge' for this particular mode of participation. The 'purpose' language stated the de minimus and obvious point, namely, that an aider or abettor purposely acts in a manner that has the consequence of facilitating the commission of a crime, but one must look to Article 30(2)(b) for guidance on how to frame the intent of the aider or abettor with respect to that consequence.[34]

Whether or not the US Supreme Court rules on this issue, and whether or not it plumps for a knowledge test or a purpose test, the knowledge test has become particularly influential even outside the context of the Alien Tort Statute litigation. One recent report of John Ruggie states:

79. Legal interpretations of 'having knowledge' vary. When applied to companies, it might require that there be actual knowledge, or that the company 'should have known', that its actions or omissions would contribute to a human rights abuse. Knowledge may be inferred from both direct and circumstantial facts. The 'should have known' standard is what a company could reasonably be expected to know under the circumstances.

---

[32] Ibid., pp. 13–14.

[33] *Presbyterian Church of Sudan v. Talisman Energy, Inc.*, On Petition for Writ of Certiorari to the United States Court of Appeals for the Second Circuit: 'Brief of David J. Scheffer, Director of the Center for International Human Rights, as Amicus Curiae in Support of the Issuance of a Writ of Certiorari' (19 May 2010), pp. 12–13.

[34] Ibid., p. 19.

80. In international criminal law, complicity does not require knowledge of the specific abuse or a desire for it to have occurred, as long as there was knowledge of the contribution. Therefore, it may not matter that the company was merely carrying out normal business activities if those activities contributed to the abuse and the company was aware or should have been aware of its contribution. The fact that a company was following orders, fulfilling contractual obligations, or even complying with national law will not, alone, guarantee it legal protection.[35]

In turn this approach has been relied on by NGOs' reports on corporate complicity in international crimes. Such reports may trigger national prosecutions for corporate complicity; and this seems to be the case in at least one situation where Swedish prosecutors have reacted to the report by the European Coalition on Oil in Sudan.[36]

4.   Concluding summary

The emergence of concern over corporate complicity can be traced to a combination of factors: the focus by human rights organizations on corporate complicity as a way of bringing corporations within the state-centric legal framework for the protection of international human rights; the inclusion of the injunction to avoid complicity in ethical codes such as the Global Compact; the facts of the early cases under the Alien Tort Statute which focused on the nexus between certain corporations and repressive regimes. At the same time, the term complicity became associated with moral blameworthiness and the need to avoid benefiting from investments that appear to contribute to serious violations of international law in general and the international law of war crimes and crimes against humanity in particular.

The focus is currently on the meaning of complicity under international criminal law. While debate rages over the meaning of the Rome Statute, key scholars have argued that the customary international standard for complicity is to be found in the case law of the international tribunals and not in the text of Article 25(3)(c), and that 'the universally accepted *mens rea* requirement for aiding and abetting liability under customary international law is knowledge, not purpose'.[37]

---

[35] John Ruggie, 'Promotion and Protection of all Human Rights, Civil, Political, Economic, Social and Cultural Rights including the Right to Development. Protect, Respect and Remedy: A Framework for Business and Human Rights – Report of the Special Representative of the Secretary-General on the Issue of Human Rights and Transnational Corporations and Other Business Enterprises', United Nations Human Rights Council, UN Doc. A/HRC/8/5 (7 April 2008).

[36] European Coalition on Oil in Sudan, 'Unpaid Debt: The Legacy of Lundin, Petronas and OMV in Block 5A, Sudan 1997–2003' (Utrecht: ECOS, 2010).

[37] 'Brief of the International Commission of Jurists', p. 8.

Although presence has been interpreted as moral support for international crimes, and thus a material element in complicity, these cases relate to those in a position of authority and to those who were physically present in the vicinity of the abuses. Courts will be careful to limit individual convictions which represent 'guilt by association'. Mere presence would not normally translate into corporate complicity. Presence may, however, be very relevant to finding, both, knowledge of the crimes, and knowledge of the contribution which the company is making to the crimes. There is little legal practice concerning how the international complicity cases concerning the presence of individuals might be translated into a set of parameters which would tell us when corporate presence might lead to legal liability for complicity in violations of international law.

While the focus may remain on corporate complicity in international crimes due to the corporate and plaintiff interest in the Alien Tort Statute, other jurisdictions will eventually address this issue. Moreover the injunction in the Norwegian Ethical Guidelines is to avoid contributing to serious human rights violations and violations of individual's rights in conflict situations. Not every human rights violation represents an international crime. The criminal standards for complicity therefore represent a starting point but not the whole story. The complexity of the criminal law tests need not blind us to the ordinary meaning of the term complicity: knowing assistance to another's wrongdoing.

Appendices

Appendix 1: Norwegian Government Pension Fund – Global: Ethical Guidelines 2010

Ethical Guidelines of the Norwegian Government Pension Fund – Global ('Ethical Guidelines'), Guidelines for observation and exclusion from the Government Pension Fund – Global's Investment Universe (as amended 1 March 2010)

Adopted by the Ministry of Finance on 1 March 2010 pursuant to Act no. 123 of 21 December 2005 relating to the Government Pension Fund, section 7.

Section 1. Scope

(1) These guidelines apply to the work of the Ministry of Finance, the Council on Ethics and Norges Bank concerning the exclusion and observation of companies.

(2) The guidelines cover investments in the Fund's equity and fixed income portfolio, as well as instruments in the Fund's real-estate portfolio issued by companies that are listed in a regulated market.

Section 2. Exclusion of companies from the Fund's investment universe

(1) The assets in the Fund shall not be invested in companies which themselves or through entities they control:

a) produce weapons that violate fundamental humanitarian principles through their normal use;
b) produce tobacco;
c) sell weapons or military material to states mentioned in section 3.2 of the guidelines for the management of the Fund.

(2) The Ministry makes decisions on the exclusion of companies from the investment universe of the Fund as mentioned in paragraph 1 on the advice of the Council on Ethics.

243

(3) The Ministry of Finance may, on the advice of the Council on Ethics, exclude companies from the investment universe of the Fund if there is an unacceptable risk that the company contributes to or is responsible for:

a) serious or systematic human rights violations, such as murder, torture, deprivation of liberty, forced labour, the worst forms of child labour and other child exploitation;
b) serious violations of the rights of individuals in situations of war or conflict;
c) severe environmental damage;
d) gross corruption;
e) other particularly serious violations of fundamental ethical norms.

(4) In assessing whether a company shall be excluded in accordance with paragraph 3, the Ministry may among other things consider the probability of future norm violations; the severity and extent of the violations; the connection between the norm violations and the company in which the Fund is invested; whether the company is doing what can reasonably be expected to reduce the risk of future norm violations within a reasonable time frame; the company's guidelines for, and work on, safeguarding good corporate governance, the environment and social conditions; and whether the company is making a positive contribution for those affected, presently or in the past, by the company's behaviour.

(5) The Ministry shall ensure that sufficient information about the case has been obtained before making any decision on exclusion. Before deciding on exclusion in accordance with paragraph 3, the Ministry shall consider whether other measures may be more suitable for reducing the risk of continued norm violations or may be more appropriate for other reasons. The Ministry may ask for an assessment by Norges Bank on the case, including whether active ownership might reduce the risk of future norm violations.

Section 3. Observation of companies

(1) The Ministry may, on the basis of advice from the Council on Ethics in accordance with section 4, paragraphs 4 or 5, decide to put a company under observation. Observation may be chosen if there is doubt as to whether the conditions for exclusion have been fulfilled, uncertainty about how the situation will develop, or if it is deemed appropriate for other reasons. Regular assessments shall be made as to whether the company should remain under observation.

(2) The decision to put a company under observation shall be made public, unless special circumstances warrant that the decision be known only to Norges Bank and the Council on Ethics.

Section 4. The Council on Ethics for the Government Pension Fund – Global – appointment and mandate

(1) The Ministry of Finance appoints the Council on Ethics for the Government Pension Fund Global. The Council shall consist of five members. The Council shall have its own secretariat.

(2) The Council shall monitor the Fund's portfolio with the aim of identifying companies that are contributing to or responsible for unethical behaviour or production as mentioned in section 2, paragraphs 1 and 3.

(3) At the request of the Ministry of Finance, the Council gives advice on the extent to which an investment may be in violation of Norway's obligations under international law.

(4) The Council gives advice on exclusion in accordance with the criteria stipulated in section 2, paragraphs 1 and 3.

(5) The Council may give advice on whether a company should be put under observation, cf. section 3.

Section 5. The work of the Council on Ethics

(1) The Council deliberates matters in accordance with section 4, paragraphs 4 and 5 on its own initiative or at the behest of the Ministry of Finance. The Council on Ethics shall develop principles that form the basis for the Council's selection of companies for closer investigation. The principles shall be made public.

(2) The Council shall obtain the information it deems necessary and ensure that the case has been properly investigated before giving advice on exclusion from the investment universe.

(3) A company that is being considered for exclusion shall be given the opportunity to present information and viewpoints to the Council on Ethics at an early stage of the process. In this context, the Council shall clarify to the company which circumstances may form the basis for exclusion. If the Council decides to recommend exclusion, its draft recommendation shall be presented to the company for comment.

(4) The Council shall describe the grounds for its recommendations. These grounds shall include a presentation of the case, the Council's assessment of the specific basis for exclusion and any comments on the case from the company. The description of the actual circumstances of the case shall, insofar as possible, be based on material that can be verified, and the sources shall be stated in the recommendation unless special circumstances indicate otherwise. The assessment of the specific basis for exclusion shall state relevant factual and legal sources and the aspects that the Council believes ought to be accorded weight. In cases concerning exclusion pursuant to section 2, paragraph 3, the recommendation shall, as far as is appropriate, also give an assessment of the circumstances mentioned in section 2, paragraph 4.

(5) The Council shall routinely assess whether the basis for exclusion still exists and may, in light of new information, recommend that the Ministry of Finance reverse a ruling on exclusion.

(6) The Council's routines for processing cases concerning the possible reversal of previous rulings on exclusion shall be publicly available. Companies that have been excluded shall be specifically informed of the routines.

(7) The Ministry of Finance publishes the recommendations of the Council on Ethics after the securities have been sold, or after the Ministry has made a final decision not to follow the Council on Ethics' recommendation.

(8) The Council shall submit an annual report on its activities to the Ministry of Finance.

Section 6. Exchange of information and coordination between Norges Bank and the Council on Ethics

(1) The Ministry of Finance, the Council on Ethics and Norges Bank shall meet regularly to exchange information about work linked to active ownership and the Council on Ethics' monitoring of the portfolio.

(2) The Council on Ethics and Norges Bank shall have routines to ensure coordination if they both contact the same company.

(3) The Council on Ethics may ask Norges Bank for information about how specific companies are dealt with through active ownership. The Council on Ethics may ask Norges Bank to comment on other circumstances concerning these companies. Norges Bank may ask the Council on Ethics to make its assessments of individual companies available.

Section 7. Notification of exclusion

(1) The Ministry of Finance shall notify Norges Bank that a company has been excluded from the investment universe. Norges Bank shall be given a deadline of two calendar months to complete the sale of all securities. Norges Bank shall notify the Ministry as soon as the sale has been completed.

(2) At the Ministry's request, Norges Bank shall notify the company concerned of the Ministry's decision to exclude the company and the grounds for this decision.

Section 8. List of excluded companies

The Ministry shall publish a list of companies that have been excluded from the investment universe of the Fund or put under observation.

Section 9. Entry into force

These guidelines come into force on 1 March 2010. The Ethical Guidelines for the Government Pension Fund – Global, adopted by the Ministry of Finance on 19 November 2004, are repealed on the same date.

Appendix 2: Norwegian Government Pension Fund – Global: Ethical Guidelines 2004

Ethical Guidelines of the Norwegian Government Pension Fund – Global ('Ethical Guidelines'), issued 22 December 2005 pursuant to regulation on the Management of the Government Pension Fund – Global, former regulation on the Management of the Government Petroleum Fund issued 19 November 2004.

1.   Basis

The ethical guidelines for the Government Pension Fund – Global are based on two premises:

The Government Pension Fund – Global is an instrument for ensuring that a reasonable portion of the country's petroleum wealth benefits future generations. The financial wealth must be managed so as to generate a sound return in the long term, which is contingent on sustainable development in the economic, environmental and social sense. The financial interests of the Fund shall be consolidated by using the Fund's ownership interests to promote such sustainable development.

The Government Pension Fund – Global should not make investments which constitute an unacceptable risk that the Fund may contribute to unethical acts or omissions, such as violations of fundamental humanitarian principles, serious violations of human rights, gross corruption or severe environmental damages.

2.   Mechanisms

The ethical basis for the Government Pension Fund – Global shall be promoted through the following three measures:

Exercise of ownership rights in order to promote long-term financial returns based on the UN Global Compact and the OECD Guidelines for Corporate Governance and for Multinational Enterprises.

Negative screening of companies from the investment universe that either themselves, or through entities they control, produce weapons that through normal use may violate fundamental humanitarian principles.

Exclusion of companies from the investment universe where there is considered to be an unacceptable risk of contributing to:

- Serious or systematic human rights violations, such as murder, torture, deprivation of liberty, forced labour, the worst forms of child labour and other child exploitation
- Grave breaches of individual rights in situations of war or conflict
- Severe environmental damages
- Gross corruption
- Other particularly serious violations of fundamental ethical norms.

3. The exercise of ownership rights

3.1 The overall objective of Norges Bank's exercise of ownership rights for the Government Pension Fund – Global is to safeguard the Fund's financial interests. The exercise of ownership rights shall be based on a long-term horizon for the Fund's investments and broad investment diversification in the markets that are included in the investment universe. The exercise of ownership rights shall primarily be based on the UN's Global Compact and the OECD Guidelines for Corporate Governance and for Multinational Enterprises. Norges Bank's internal guidelines for the exercise of ownership rights shall stipulate how these principles are integrated in the ownership strategy.

3.2 Norges Bank shall report on its exercise of ownership rights in connection with its ordinary annual reporting. An account shall be provided of how the Bank has acted as owner representative – including a description of the work to promote special interests relating to the long-term horizon and diversification of investments in accordance with Section 3.1.

3.3 Norges Bank may delegate the exercise of ownership rights to external managers in accordance with these guidelines.

4. Negative screening and exclusion

4.1 The Ministry of Finance shall, based on recommendations of the Council on Ethics for the *Government Pension Fund – Global*, make decisions on negative screening and exclusion of companies from the investment universe.

The recommendations and decisions shall be made public. The Ministry may, in certain cases, postpone the time of public disclosure if this is deemed necessary in order to ensure a financially sound implementation of the exclusion of the company concerned.

4.2 The Council on Ethics for the *Government Pension Fund – Global* shall consist of five members. The Council shall have its own secretariat. The Council shall submit an annual report on its activities to the Ministry of Finance.

4.3 Upon request of the Ministry of Finance, the Council issues recommendations on whether an investment may constitute a violation of Norway's obligations under international law.

4.4 The Council shall issue recommendations on negative screening of one or several companies on the basis of production of weapons that through normal use may violate fundamental humanitarian principles. The Council shall issue recommendations on the exclusion of one or several companies from the investment universe because of acts or omissions that constitute an unacceptable risk that the Fund contributes to:

- Serious or systematic human rights violations, such as murder, torture, deprivation of liberty, forced labour, the worst forms of child labour and other child exploitation
- Grave breaches of individual rights in situations of war or conflict
- Severe environmental damages
- Gross corruption
- Other particularly serious violations of fundamental ethical norms

The Council shall raise issues under this provision on its own initiative or at the request of the Ministry of Finance.

4.5 The Council shall gather all necessary information at its own discretion and shall ensure that the matter is documented as fully as possible before making a recommendation regarding negative screening or exclusion from the investment universe. The Council may request Norges Bank to provide information as to how specific companies are dealt with in the exercise of ownership rights. Enquiries to such companies shall be channelled through Norges Bank. If the Council is considering recommending exclusion of a company, the company in question shall receive the draft recommendation and the reasons for it, for comment.

4.6 The Council shall review on a regular basis whether the reasons for exclusion still apply and may against the background of new information recommend that the Ministry of Finance reverse a decision to exclude a company.

4.7 Norges Bank shall receive immediate notification of the decisions made by the Ministry of Finance in connection with the Council's recommendations. The Ministry of Finance may request that Norges Bank inform the companies concerned of the decisions taken by the Ministry and the reasons for the decision.

Appendix 3: Guidelines for Norges Bank's Work on Responsible Management and Active Ownership of the Government Pension Fund – Global (GPFG)

Adopted by the Ministry of Finance on 1 March 2010 pursuant to Act no. 123 of 21 December 2005 relating to the Government Pension Fund, section 2, paragraph 2, and section 7.

Section 1. Norges Bank's work on responsible management

(1) The management of the assets in the Fund shall be based on the goal of achieving the highest possible return, cf. the Regulations of 22 December 2005 no. 1725 regarding the management of the Government Pension Fund – Global, section 2, paragraph 3. A good return in the long term is dependent on sustainable development in economic, environmental and social terms, as well as well-functioning, legitimate and effective markets.

(2) The Bank shall integrate considerations of good corporate governance and environmental and social issues in its investment activities, in line with internationally-recognised principles for responsible investment. Integration of these considerations shall occur in respect of the Fund's investment strategy and role as financial manager. In executing its management assignment, the Bank shall give priority to the Fund's long-term horizon for investments and that these are broadly placed within the markets included in the investment universe.

(3) The Bank shall develop internal guidelines that indicate how the considerations expressed in paragraph two are integrated into the investment activities of the various asset classes, for both the internally and the externally managed parts of the portfolio. In its management of the real estate portfolio, with regard to environmental protection the Bank shall give priority to considerations of energy efficiency, water consumption and waste management.

Section 2. Active ownership

(1) The Bank's primary goal in its active ownership is to safeguard the Fund's financial interests.

(2) Active ownership shall be based on the UN Global Compact, the OECD Guidelines on Corporate Governance and the OECD Guidelines for Multinational Enterprises. The Bank shall have internal guidelines for its exercise of ownership rights that indicate how these principles are integrated in its active ownership.

(3) Major amendments to the Bank's priorities in its active ownership shall be sent to the Ministry of Finance for comment before a final decision is made. The Bank's plans shall be subject to public consultation before being submitted to the Ministry.

Section 3. Contribution to the development of best practice in responsible investment

The Bank shall actively contribute to the development of good international standards in the area of responsible investment activities and active ownership.

Section 4. Reporting

(1) The annual report that is prepared pursuant to the guidelines for the management of the GPFG, section 4.3, paragraph 1 shall as a minimum contain the following account of the Bank's work on active ownership and integration of good corporate governance and environmental and social issues:

a) a report on the Bank's work integrating good corporate governance and environmental and social issues into its management, cf. section 1.

b) a report on the Bank's exercise of ownership rights and other aspects of its active ownership activities. The report should describe how the Bank has acted as the owner's representative in safeguarding the goals of sections 1 and 2. The Bank's voting record at annual general meetings and the Bank's guidelines for voting shall be made public.

c) an account of the Bank's contribution to the development of good international standards in activities concerning responsible investment and active ownership, cf. section 3.

(2) The quarterly report that is prepared pursuant to the guidelines for the management of the GPFG section 4.3, paragraph 2 shall as a minimum include an account of the main aspects of the Bank's active ownership during the last quarter.

Section 5. Entry into force

These guidelines come into force on 1 March 2010.

Bibliography

ABN AMRO, 'Sustainable Development' (2006); www.abnamro.com/com/about/sd/sd_policies.jsp.

AFP, 'Myanmar Refugees seek Belgium Trial for TotalFinaElf' (8 May 2002).

Allen, Mark and Jaime Caruana, 'Sovereign Wealth Funds – A Work Agenda', *International Monetary Fund* (29 February 2008); www.imf.org/external/np/pp/eng/2008/022908.pdf.

Allens, Arthur Robinson, 'Brief on Corporations and Human Rights in the Asia-Pacific Region', prepared for Prof. John Ruggie UN SRSG for Business and Human Rights, (2006); www.reports-and-materials.org/Legal-brief-on-Asia-Pacific-for-Ruggie-Aug-2006.pdf.

Allouche, José (ed.), *Corporate Social Responsibility* (New York: Palgrave, 2006).

Alston, Philip, 'The "Not-a-Cat" Syndrome: Can the International Human Rights Regime Accommodate Non-State Actors?', in Philip Alston (ed.), *Non-State Actors and Human Rights* (Oxford University Press, 2005), pp. 3–36.

Amnesty International, 'Sudan: The Human Price of Oil', AI Index: AFR 54/001/2000 (3 May 2000).

'Human Rights Principles for Companies', AI Index: ACT 70/01/98 (January 1998).

Aviva PLC, 'Corporate Social Responsibility Report 2007'; www.aviva.com/index.asp?

Backer, Larry Catá, 'Economic Globalization and the Rise of Efficient Systems of Global Private Law Making: Wal-Mart as Global Legislator', *Connecticut Law Review*, 39 (2006–7).

'The Norwegian Sovereign Wealth Fund: Between Private and Public', *Georgetown Journal of International Law*, 40 (2009).

Bakan, Joel, *The Corporation: The Pathological Pursuit of Profit and Power* (New York: Free Press, 2005).

Barnidge, Jr., Robert P., 'The Due Diligence Principle Under International Law', *International Community Law Review*, 81 (2006).

Basel Committee on Banking Supervision, Customer Due Diligence for Banks' (2002); www.bis.org/publ/bcbs85.pdf.

BASF, 'Corporate Report 2005: Our Values to Social Responsibility'; www.berichte.basf.de/en/2005/unternehmensbericht/02_unternehmen/10_werte/?id=V00-BJ.5GAzq2bir1dv.

Bazyler, Michael J., 'Litigating the Holocaust', *University of Richmond Law Review*, 33 (2000).

Beitz, Charles R., *Political Equality* (Princeton University Press, 1989).

Berman, Paul Schiff, 'From International Law to Law and Globalization', *Columbia Journal of Transnational Law*, 43 (2004–5).

BHP Billiton, 'Sustainability Report' (Full Report 2006); http://sustainability. bhpbilliton.com/2006/documents/BHPBillitonSustainabilityReport2006. pdf.

Birnbacher, D., 'Philosophical Foundations of Responsibility', in A. E. Auhagen and H. W. Bierhoff (eds.), *Responsibility: The Many Faces of a Social Phenomenon* (New York: Routledge, 2001), pp. 9–22.

Blomeyer-Bartenstein, Horst, 'Due Diligence', in *Encyclopaedia of Public International Law*, Vol. I (Amsterdam: Elsevier Science Publishers, 1987).

Boivin, Alexandra, 'Complicity and Beyond: International Law and the Transfer of Small Arms and Light Weapons', *International Review of the Red Cross*, 87 (September 2005).

Bomann-Larsen, L. and O. Wiggen (eds.), *Responsibility in World Business* (Tokyo: United Nations University Press, 2004).

British American Tobacco, 'Social Report' (2001/2002); www.corporateregister. com/a10723/bat02-soc-uk.pdf.

Brownlie, Ian, *Principles of Public International Law*, 5th edn (Oxford: Clarendon Press, 1998).

Business & Human Rights Resources Centre; www.business-humanrights.org.

Byers, Michael, *Custom, Power and the Power of Rules: International Relations and Customary International Law* (Cambridge University Press, 1999).

Carroll, Patricia M. C., 'Socially Responsible Investment of Public Pension Funds: The South Africa Issue and State Law', *New York University Review of Law & Social Change*, 10 (1980–1).

Cassel, Doug, 'Corporate Aiding and Abetting of Human Rights Violations: Confusion in the Courts', *Northwestern University Journal of International Human Rights*, 6 (2008).

Check, D. and R. Jones, 'S&B Seminar on Shareholder Rights and Responsibilities Attracts over 100 Delegates from Around the World', *Schiffrin & Barroway Bulletin* (Spring, 2006).

Chesterman, Simon, 'Oil and Water: Regulating the Behaviour of Multinational Corporations Through Law', *New York University Journal of International Law and Politics*, 36 (2004).

'The Turn to Ethics: Disinvestment from Multinational Corporations for Human Rights Violations – The Case of Norway's Sovereign Wealth Fund', *American University International Law Review*, 23 (2008).

Chirwa, Danwood Mzikenge, 'The Doctrine of State Responsibility as a Potential Means of Holding Private Actors Accountable for Human Rights', *Melbourne Journal of International Law*, 5 (2004).

Christenson, Gordon A., 'Attributing Acts of Omission to the State', *Michigan Journal of International Law*, 12 (1990–1).

Clapham, Andrew, 'Extending International Criminal Law beyond the Individual to Corporations and Armed Opposition Groups', *Journal of International Criminal Justice*, 6 (2008).

Human Rights Obligations of Non-State Actors (Oxford University Press, 2006).

'Remarks at the 2006 American Society of International Law, Annual Meeting', *American Society of International Law Proceedings*, 100 (2006).

Coleman, James, *Foundations of Social Theory* (Cambridge, MA: Harvard University Press, 1990).

Commission of the European Union, 'Communication from the Commission to the European Parliament, The Council, The European Economic and Social Committee and the Committee of the Regions' (27 February 2008); http://ec.europa.eu/internal_market/finances/docs/sovereign_en.pdf.

Committee on International Relations, US House of Representatives, 'The Internet in China: A Tool for Freedom or Suppression?: Joint Hearing before the Subcommittee Africa, Global Human Rights & International Operations and the Subcommittee on Asia and the Pacific', US House Committee on International Relations, Serial Nos. 109–57 (15 February 2006); www.foreignaffairs.house.gov/archives/109/26075.pdf.

Convention on the Prohibition of the Development, Production and Stockpiling of Bacteriological (Biological) and Toxin Weapons and on their Destruction (signed 10 April 1972, entered into force 26 March 1975).

Convention on the Prohibition of the Development, Production, Stockpiling and Use of Chemical Weapons and on their Destruction (adopted by the UN General Assembly on 30 November 1992 in A/RES/47/39).

Cooke, Jennifer, 'Finding the Right Balance for Sovereign Wealth Fund Regulation: Open Investment vs. National Security', *The Columbia Business Law Review*, 2 (2009).

Coomans, Fons and Menno T. Kamminga, *Extraterritorial Application of Human Rights Treaties* (Antwerp: Intersentia, 2004).

Corporate Europe Observatory (CEO), 'Shell Leads International Business Campaign Against UN Human Rights Norms', *CEO Info Brief* (March 2004); www.corporateeurope.org/norms.html.

Corten, Olivier, 'The Notion of "Reasonable" in International Law: Legal Discourse, Reason and Contradictions', *International and Comparative Law Quarterly*, 48 (1999).

L'Utilisation du 'Raisonnable' par le Juge International: Discours Juridique, Raison et Contradictions (Brussels: Bruylant, 1997).

Council on Ethics, 'Annual Report 2005' (Oslo: Government Pension Fund – Global, January 2006); www.regjeringen.no/pages/1957930/Årsmelding%20 2005%20eng.pdf.

'Annual Report 2006' (Oslo: Government Pension Fund – Global, January 2007); www.regjeringen.no/pages/1957930/engelsketikk_06.pdf.

'Annual Report 2007' (Oslo: Government Pension Fund – Global, January 2008); www.regjeringen.no/pages/1957930/Annual%20Report%202007.pdf.

'Annual Report 2008' (Oslo: Government Pension Fund – Global, January 2009); www.regjeringen.no/pages/1957930/etikkradet_engelsk08.pdf.

'Annual Report 2009' (Oslo: Government Pension Fund – Global, January 2010); www.regjeringen.no/pages/1957930/etikkradet_engelsk08.pdf.

'Letter dated 11 October 2007, on the Council's Assessment of Companies with Operations in Burma.' Unofficial English translation: www.regjeringen.no/pages/2018769/Burma%20letter%20english.pdf.

'Letter dated 18 April 2008, on the Council's Assessment of Investments in Israel Electric Corp.' Unofficial English translation: www.regjeringen.no/pages/2099873/IEC%20letter%20English.pdf.

'Letter dated 10 June 2008, Regarding Recommendation to Exclude the Company Monsanto Co. from the Investment Universe of the Government Pension Fund Global.' Unofficial English translation: www.regjeringen.no/pages/2105482/Brev_til_FIN_vedr_Monsanto%20ENG.pdf.

'Letter dated 19 March 2009, on the Council on Ethics Assessment of Investments in Companies with Activities in Israel.' Unofficial English translation: www.regjeringen.no/pages/2179095/Letter%20to%20Ministry%20March%202009.pdf.

'Other Documents' (March 2006–September 2009); www.regjeringen.no/en/sub/Styrer-rad-utvalg/ethics_council/Recommendations/Other-documents.html?id=458703.

'Recommendation of 11 April 2005 on Exclusion from the Government Petroleum Fund's Investment Universe of the Company Kerr-McGee Corporation.' Unofficial English translation: www.regjeringen.no/en/sub/Styrer-rad-utvalg/ethics_council/Recommendations/Recommendations/Recommendation-of-April-12–2005-on-exclu.html?id=425309.

'Recommendation of 16 June 2005 on the Exclusion of Companies that are Involved in the Production of Cluster Munitions.' Unofficial English translation: www.regjeringen.no/pages/1661742/Tilrådning%20klasevåpen%20eng%2015%20juni%202005.pdf.

'Recommendation of 19 September 2005, on the Exclusion of Companies that are Involved in Production of Nuclear Weapons.' Unofficial English translation: www.regjeringen.no/pages/1661428/Tilrådning%20kjernevåpen%20engelsk%2019%20sept%202005.pdf.

'Recommendation of 14 November 2005, Concerning Whether Investments in Total, Due to the Company's Operations in Burma, are Contrary to the Petroleum Fund's Ethical Guidelines (Total Recommendation).' Unofficial English translation: www.regjeringen.no/en/sub/Styrer-rad-utvalg/ethics_council/Recommendations/Recommendations/Recommendation-of-14-November-2005.html?id=425314.

'Recommendation of 15 November 2005 on the Exclusion of Wal-Mart Stores Inc. (Wal-Mart Stores Inc. Recommendation).' Unofficial English translation: www.regjeringen.no/en/sub/Styrer-rad-utvalg/ethics_council/Recommendations/Recommendations/Recommendation-of-November-15–2005 – on-e.html?id=423835.

'Recommendation of 15 February 2006 on Exclusion of Freeport McMoRan Copper & Gold Inc.: Published 6 June 2006.' Unofficial English translation: www.regjeringen.no/pages/1956975/F%20Recommendation%20Final.pdf.

'Recommendation of 6 September 2006, on Exclusion of Poongsan Corp.'

'Recommendation of 20 September 2006 Concerning Whether the Weapons Systems Spider and Intelligent Munition System (IMS) Might be Contrary to International law – Letter to Ministry of Finance from Advisory Council on Ethics.' Unofficial English translation: www.regjeringen.no/pages/1662930/Tilrådning%20Spider%20IMS%20%20English%2020.pdf.

'Recommendation of 20 November 2006 on the Exclusion of the Company Monsanto Co.' Unofficial English translation: www.regjeringen.no/pages/2105482/Recommendation%20Monsanto%20ENG.pdf.

'Recommendation of 15 May 2007 on Exclusion of Vedanta Resources Plc.' Unofficial English translation: www.regjeringen.no/Upload/FIN/Statens%20pensjonsfond/RecommendationVedanta.pdf.

'Recommendation of 15 May 2007 on Exclusion of the Companies Rheinmetall AG and Hanwha Corp.' Unofficial English translation: www.regjeringen.no/pages/2041987/Rheinmetall%20and%20Hanwha,%20Unofficial%20English%20transla.pdf.

'Recommendation of 5 September 2007 – New Assessment of the Company Rheinmetall AG.' Unofficial English translation: www.regjeringen.no/pages/2042008/Rheinmetall,%20Unofficial%20English%20translation%20Sept07.pdf.

'Recommendation of 15 November 2007 on Exclusion of the Company GenCorp Inc.' Unofficial English translation: www.regjeringen.no/en/sub/Styrer-rad-utvalg/ethics_council/Recommendations/Recommendations/Recommendation-of-November-15–2007-on-ex.html?id=496177.

'Recommendation of 15 November 2007 on Exclusion of the Company Serco Group Plc.' Unofficial English translation: www.regjeringen.no/pages/2042005/Serco%20Group,%20Unofficial%20English%20translation.pdf.

'Recommendation of 14 November 2008, on the Exclusion of the Company Dongfeng Motor Group Co. Ltd.' Unofficial English translation: www.regjeringen.no/pages/2162512/tilrådning%20Dongfeng%20English.pdf.

'Recommendation of 16 February 2009, on Exclusion of the Company Norilsk Nickel.' Unofficial English translation: www.regjeringen.no/pages/2267887/Recommendation%20-%20%20Final.pdf.

'Recommendation of 15 May 2009 on Exclusion of the Company Elbit Systems Ltd.' Unofficial English translation: www.regjeringen.no/pages/2236676/Tilrådning%20Elbit%20engelsk.pdf.

Crane, Andrew et al. (eds.), *The Oxford Handbook of Corporate Social Responsibility* (Oxford University Press, 2008).

Crawford, James, *The International Law Commission's Article on State Responsibility: Introduction, Texts and Commentary* (Cambridge University Press, 2005).

Crimm, Nina J., 'Post-September 11 Fortified Anti-Terrorism Measures Compel Heightened Due Diligence', *Pace Law Review*, 25 (2004–5).

Dankwa, Victor, Cees Flinterman and and Scott Leckie, 'Commentary to the Maastricht Guidelines on Violations of Economic, Social and Cultural Rights', *Human Rights Quarterly*, 20 (1998).

De Meester, Bart, 'International Legal Aspects of Sovereign Wealth Funds: Reconciling International Economic Law and the Law of State Immunities with a New Role of the State', *European Business Law Review* (2009).

De Schutter, Olivier, 'The Accountability of Multinationals for Human Rights Violations in European Law', in P. Alston (ed.), *Non-State Actors and Human Rights* (Oxford University Press, 2005), pp. 227–314.

De Schutter, Olivier (ed.), *Transnational Corporations and Human Rights* (Oxford: Hart Publishing, 2006).

Deva, Suriya, 'Acting Extraterritorially to Tame Multinational Corporations for Human Rights Violations: Who Should "Bell the Cat"?', *Melbourne Journal of International Law*, 5 (2004).

Dhooge, Lucien J., 'Condemning Khartoum: The Illinois Divestment Act and Foreign Relations', *American Business Law Journal*, 43 (2006).

'Darfur, State Divestment and The Commerce Clause', *North Carolina Journal of International Law and Commercial Regulation*, 32 (2007).

Dihr, Aaron A., 'Realigning the Corporate Building Blocks: Shareholder Proposals as a Vehicle for Achieving Corporate Social and Human Rights Accountability', *American Business Law Journal*, 43 (2006).

Dörmann, Knut, *Elements of War Crimes under the Rome Statute of the International Criminal Court* (Cambridge University Press, 2003).

Drake, Thomas E., *Quakers and Slavery in America* (Gloucester, MA: Peter Smith, 1965).

Economist, The, 'Sovereign-Wealth Funds: The World's Most Expensive Club' (26 May 2007).

Eide, A., 'Report on the Right to Food as a Human Right', United Nations Sub-Commission on the Promotion and Protection of Human Rights (1987); UN Doc. E/CN.4/Sub.2/1987/23.

Epstein, Richard A. and Amanda M. Rose, 'The Regulation of Sovereign Wealth Funds: The Virtues of Going Slow', *University of Chicago Law Review*, forthcoming.

Eriksen, Tore, 'The Norwegian Petroleum Sector and the Government Pension Fund – Global' (Oslo: Norwegian Ministry of Finance, June 2006); www.regjeringen.no/upload/FIN/Statens%20pensjonsfond/The_ Norwegian_Petroleum_Sector_te.pdf.

Eser, Albin, 'Individual Criminal Responsibility', in Antonio Cassese (ed.), *The Rome Statute of the International Criminal Court: A Commentary* (Oxford University Press, 2002), pp. 767–822.

Etzioni, Amitai, 'A Communitarian Note on Stakeholder Theory', *Business Ethics Quarterly*, 8 (1998).

European Coalition on Oil in Sudan, 'Unpaid Debt: The Legacy of Lundin, Petronas and OMV in Block 5A, Sudan 1997–2003' (Utrecht: ECOS, 2010).

FAFO, 'A Comparative Survey of Private Sector Liability for Grave Violations of International Law in National Jurisdictions' (2006).

'Project on Business and International Crimes: Assessing the Liability of Business Entities for Grave Violations of International Law, Nation Survey on Norway', 2004); www.fafo.no/liabilities/Norway%20version%20 standardized%20Nov%202004.pdf.

Federation Internationale des ligues des droits de l'Homme (FIDH), 'Position Paper 442/2', (15 March 2006); www.fidh.org/IMG/pdf/business442a.pdf.

Feinberg, J., 'Collective Responsibility', *The Journal of Philosophy*, 65 (1968).

Ferdinandusse, Ward, 'Out of the Black Box? The International Obligations of State Organs', *Brooklyn Journal of International Law*, 29 (2003–4).

Follesdal, Andreas, 'Political Consumerism As Chance and Challenge', in Michele Micheletti, Andreas Follesdal and Dietlind Stolle (eds.), *Politics, Products and Markets: Exploring Political Consumerism Past and Present* (New Brunswick, NJ: Transaction Press, 2004).

Forcese, Craig, 'Globalizing Decency: Responsible Engagement in an Era of Economic Integration', *Yale Human Rights & Development Law Journal*, 5 (2002).

Freeland, Charles, 'How Can Sound Customer Due Diligence Rules Help Prevent the Misuse of Financial Institutions in the Financing of Terrorism?', *European Journal of Law Reform*, 4 (2002).

G8 Summit 2007, 'Chair's Summary' (Heiligendamm, 8 June 2007); www.g-8. de/Webs/G8/EN/G8Summit/SummitDocuments/summit-documents.html.

Genocide Intervention Network, 'Sudan Peer Performance Analysis: An Analysis of the Historical and Forecasted Financial Performance of Companies Identified as "Highest Offenders" in Sudan'; www.sudandivestment.org/docs/sudan_peer_analysis.pdf.

Gibney, Mark et al., 'Transnational State Responsibility for Violations of Human Rights', *Harvard Human Rights Journal*, 12 (1999).

Gilson, Ronald J. and Curtis J. Milhaupt, 'Sovereign-Wealth Funds and Corporate Governance: A Minimalist Response to the New Mercantilism', *Stanford Law and Economics Online*, Working Paper No. 355 (18 February, 2008).

Gjessing, O. P. K. and H. Syse, 'Norwegian Petroleum Wealth and Universal Ownership', *Corporate Governance*, 15 (2007).

Goodin, R. E., *Protecting the Vulnerable: A Reanalysis of our Social Responsibilities* (University of Chicago Press, 1985).

Green, Jersey M., 'The Imposition of Vicarious Liability Through Joint Venture', *Trial Talk*, 38:168 (1990); reprinted at: www.preeosilverman. com/CM/Articles/Articles29.asp#_ednref1.

Greene, Edward F. and Brian A. Yeager, 'Sovereign Wealth Funds – A Measured Assessment', *Capital Markets Law Journal*, 3 (2008).

Haight, Matthew and James Hazelton, 'Financial Markets: A Tool for Social Responsibility?', *Journal of Business Ethics*, 52 (2004).

Halvorsen, Kristin, Norwegian Minister of Finance, 'Sovereign Wealth Funds as Serious Financial Investors', *Financial Times* (15 February 2008).

Hampton, Jean, 'Contract and Consent', in Robert E. Goodin and Philip Pettit (eds.), *A Companion to Contemporary Political Philosophy* (Oxford: Blackwell, 1993), pp. 379–93.

Hardimon, M. O., 'Role Obligations', *The Journal of Philosophy*, 91:7 (1994).

Held, David, *Democracy and the Global Order* (Cambridge: Polity Press, 1995).

Held, David and Anthony McGrew, *The Global Transformations Reader: An Introduction to the Globalization Debate* (Oxford: Polity Press, 2000).

Hessbruegge, Jan Arno, 'The Historical Development of the Doctrines of Attribution and Due Diligence in International Law', *New York University Journal of International Law and Politics*, 36 (2003–4).

Hessbrügge, Jan Arno, 'Human Rights Violations Arising from Conduct of Non-State Actors', *Buffalo Human Rights Law Review*, 11 (2005).

Hirschman, Albert O., *Exit, Voice, and Loyalty* (Cambridge, MA: Harvard University Press, 1970).

Hoffman, William C., 'The Separate Entity Rule In International Perspective: Should State Ownership of Corporate Shares Confer Sovereign Status For Immunity Purposes?', *Tulane Law Review*, 65 (1990–1).

Human Rights Watch, 'Oil Companies Complicit in Nigerian Abuses: Nigeria – Human Rights Watch World Report' (New York: Human Rights Watch, 1999).

'*The Enron Corporation: Corporate Complicity in Human Rights Violations*' (New York: Human Rights Watch, 1999).

'*Sudan, Oil, and Human Rights*' (New York: Human Rights Watch, 2003).

Ignatieff, Michael, 'Human Rights, Power, and the State', in Simon Chesterman, Michael Ignatieff and Ramesh Thakur (eds.), *Making States Work: State Failure and the Crisis of Governance* (Tokyo: United Nations University Press, 2005).

International Commission of Jurists, Expert Legal Panel Report 'Corporate Complicity & Legal Accountability' (Geneva: ICJ, 2008); www.icj.org/IMG/Volume_3.pdf.

Presbyterian Church of Sudan v. *Talisman Energy, Inc.*, On Petition for Writ of Certiorari to the United States Court of Appeals for the Second Circuit: 'Brief of the International Commission of Jurists and the American Association for the International Commission of Jurists, *Amici Curiae*, Supporting Petitioners'.

International Council on Human Rights Policy, *Beyond Voluntarism: Human Rights and the Developing International Legal Obligations of Companies* (Versoix: International Council on Human Rights Policy, 2002).

International Court of Justice, 'Reparation for Injuries Suffered in the Service of the United Nations, Advisory Opinion': ICJ Reports (11 April 1949); www.icj-cij.org/docket/files/4/1835.pdf.

International Law Commission, 'Draft Articles on Responsibility of States for Internationally Wrongful Acts ("DASR")' (New York: UN International Law Commission, 2001).

'Report of the International Law Commission on the Work of its Fifty-Third session', UN GAOR, 56th Session., Supp. No. 10, UN Doc. A/56/10 (New York: UN International Law Commission, 2001), pp. 43–59.

Jochnick, Chris, 'Confronting the Impunity of Non-State Actors: New Fields for the Promotion of Human Rights', *Human Rights Quarterly*, 21 (1999).

Jonas, H., *The Imperative of Responsibility: In Search of an Ethics for the Technological Age* (University of Chicago Press, 1984).

Joseph, S., *Corporations and Transnational Human Rights Litigation* (Oxford: Hart Publishing, 2004).

Jungk, Margaret, 'Defining the Scope of Business Responsibility Abroad', *Human Rights & Business Project* (Copenhagen: Danish Centre for Human Rights, 2005), pp. 1–12; www.humanrightsbusiness.org/files/320569722/file/defining_the_scope_of_business_responsibility_.pdf.

Kamchibekova, Damira, 'State Responsibility for Extraterritorial Human Rights Violations', *Buffalo Human Rights Law Review*, 87 (2007).

Kamijyo, Miki, 'The "Equator Principles": Improved Social Responsibility in the Private Finance Sector', *Sustainable Development Law & Policy*, 4 (2004).

Kamminga, M. and S. Zia-Zarifi (eds.), *Liability of Multinational Corporations Under International Law* (The Hague: Kluwer, 2000).

Karliner, Joshua and Bruno Kenny, 'Responsibility vs. Accountability', *International Herald Tribune* (1 July 2002).

Keenan, Patrick and Christiana Ochoa, 'The Human Rights Potential of Sovereign Wealth Funds', *Georgetown Journal of International Law*, 40 (2009).

Keller, Amy D., 'Sovereign Wealth Funds: Trustworthy Investors or Vehicles of Strategic Ambition – An Assessment of the Benefits, Risks and Possible Regulation of Sovereign Wealth Funds', *Georgetown Journal of Law & Public Policy*, 7 (2008).

Kelly, E., 'The Burdens of Collective Liability', in D. K. Chatterjee and D. E. Scheid (eds.), *Ethics and Foreign Intervention* (Cambridge University Press, 2003), pp. 118–39.

Kendall, Joe et al., 'The Diligence Due in the Era of Globalized Terrorism', *International Lawyer* 36 (2002).

Kimmitt, Robert M., 'Public Footprints in Private Markets: Sovereign Wealth Funds and the World Economy', *Foreign Affairs*, 87 (2008).

Knoll, Michael S., 'Ethical Screening in Modern Financial Markets: The Conflicting Claims Underlying Socially Responsible Investment', *The Business Lawyer*, 57 (2001–2).

Kobrin, Stephen J., 'Oil and Politics: Talisman Energy and Sudan', *New York University Journal of International Law and Politics*, 36 (2004).

Koh, Harold Hongju, 'Transnational Legal Process', *Nevada Law Review*, 75 (1996).

'Why Transnational Law Matters', *Penn State International Law Review*, 24 (2005–6).

Korsgaard, C. M., *Creating the Kingdom of Ends* (Cambridge University Press, 1996).

Kraakman, Reinier H. et al., *The Anatomy of Corporate Law: A Comparative and Functional Approach* (Oxford University Press, 2004).

Krasner, Stephen D., 'Structural Causes and Regime Consequences: Regimes As Intervening Variables', *International Organization*, 36, 2 (1982).

Kronke, Herbert, 'Capital Markets and Conflict of Laws', *Recueil des Cours*, 286 (2000).

Kronman, Anthony, 'Contract Law and Distributive Justice', *Yale Law Journal*, 89 (1980).

Kumar, Rahul, 'Defending the Moral Moderate: Contractualism and Common Sense', *Philosophy and Public Affairs*, 28 (1999).

'Reasonable Reasons in Contractualist Moral Argument', *Ethics*, 114 (2003).

Kurtz, Lloyd, 'Socially Responsible Investment and Shareholder Activism', in Andrew Crane et al. (eds.), *The Oxford Handbook of Corporate Social Responsibility* (Oxford University Press, 2008), pp. 259–61.

Kutz, Christopher, 'Acting Together', *Philosophy and Phenomenological Research*, 61:1 (2000).

Complicity: Ethics and Law for a Collective Age (New York: Cambridge University Press, 2000).

Landler, Mark, 'Norway Keeps Nest Egg From Some U.S. Companies', *New York Times* (4 May 2007).

Langland, Eric, 'Misplaced Fears Put to Rest: Financial Crisis Reveals the True Motives of Sovereign Wealth Funds', *Financial Times* (7 January 2009).

Lawrence, Robert F. and William L. Thomas, 'The Equator Principles and Project Finance: Sustainability in Practice?', *Natural Resources & Environment*, 19 (2004–5).

Leader, Sheldon, 'Human Rights, Risks, and New Strategies for Global Investment', *Journal of International Economic Law*, 9 (2006).

Lobe, Jim, 'U.S.-Burma: Sanctions Campaign Keeps Rolling', *IPS-Inter Press Service* (15 May 1997).

Luxton, Peter, 'Ethical Investment in Hard Times', *The Modern Law Review*, 55 (1992).

MacDonald, Jeffrey, 'Congress's Dilemma: When Yahoo in China's not Yahoo', *Christian Science Monitor* (14 February 2006); www.csmonitor.com/2006/0214/p01s04-usfp.html.

Mansley, Mark, 'Private Financial Actors and Corporate Responsibility in Conflict Zones', in Karen Ballentine and Heiko Nitzschke (eds.), *Profiting from Peace: Managing the Resource Dimensions of Civil War* (Boulder, CO: Lynne Rienner, 2005).

Marcks, Eric, 'Avoiding Liability for Human Rights Violations in Project Finance', *Energy Law Journal*, 22 (2001).

Marriott International, Inc., 'Human Rights Policy Statement' (2006); http://ir.shareholder.com/mar/downloads/HumanRightsStatement.pdf.

May, L., *Sharing Responsibility* (University of Chicago Press, 1992).

McCorquodale, Robert, 'Spreading Weeds Beyond Their Garden: Extra-territorial Responsibility of States for Violations of Human Rights by Corporate Nationals', *The American Society of International Law Proceedings*, 100 (2006).

McCorquodale, Robert and Penelope C. Simons, 'Responsibility Beyond Borders: Extraterritorial Violations by Corporations of Human Rights Law', *Modern Law Review*, 70 (2007).

Mill, John Stuart, *On Liberty [1859]*, ed. Mary Warnock (Glasgow: Collins, 1962).

Mitchell, N. J., *Agents of Atrocity: Leaders, Followers, and the Violation of Human Rights in Civil War* (New York: Palgrave, 2004).

Monshipouri, M., C. E. Welsh and E. T. Kennedy, 'Multinational Corporations and the Ethics of Global Responsibility: Problems and Possibilities', *Human Rights Quarterly*, 25 (2003).

Monsma, David and John Buckley, 'Non-Financial Corporate Performance: The Material Edges of Social and Environmental Disclosure', *University of Baltimore Journal of Environmental Law*, 11 (2003–4).

Moran, G., *A Grammar of Responsibility* (New York: The Crossroad Publishing Company, 1996).

Myers, Joseph M., 'The Silent Struggle against Terrorist Financing', *Georgetown Journal of International Law*, 6 (2005).

Nagel, Thomas, 'The Problem of Global Justice', *Philosophy & Public Affairs*, 33 (2005).

Nassauer, Friedemann, *Sphärentheorien' zu Regelungen der Gefahrtragungshaftung in verträglichen Schuldverhältnissen* (Marburg: Elwert, 1978).

Nexen Inc, 'Nexen Human Rights Policy' (2003); www.nexeninc.com/files/Policies/Human_Rights_Policy.pdf.

Norman, R., *Ethics, Killing and War* (Cambridge University Press, 1995).

Norwegian Central Bank (Norges Bank), *NBIM Investor Expectations on Children's Rights* (Norges Bank Investment Management, 2010); www. e-pages.dk/nbim/7/.

Norwegian Government Pension Fund – Global, 'Ethical Guidelines of the Norwegian Government Pension Fund – Global ("Ethical Guidelines"), Issued 22 December 2005 pursuant to regulation on the Management of the Government Pension Fund – Global, former regulation on the management of the Government Petroleum Fund issued 19 November 2004.

'Ethical Guidelines of the Norwegian Government Pension Fund – Global ("Ethical Guidelines"), Guidelines for Observation and Exclusion from the Government Pension Fund – Global's Investment Universe' (as amended 1 March 2010). English translation: www.regjeringen.no/en/sub/styrer-rad- nes.html?id=425277.

'Guidelines for Norges Bank's Work on Responsible Management and Active Ownership of the Government Pension Fund – Global (GPFG), Adopted by the Ministry of Finance on 1 March 2010 pursuant to Act no. 123 of 21 December 2005 relating to the Government Pension Fund, section 2, paragraph 2, and section 7': www.regjeringen.no/mobil/en/dep/fin/ Selected-topics/the-government-pension-fund/responsible-investments/ Guidelines-for-Norges-Banks-work-on-responsible-management-and-active-ownership-of-the-Government-Pension-Fund-Global-GPFG. html?id=594253.

'Regulations on the Management of the Government Pension Fund – Global dated 22 December 2005, No. 1725 (as amended 1 March 2010); www. regjeringen.no/en/dep/fin/Selected-topics/the-government-pension-fund/ the-guidelines-for-the-management-of-the.html?id=434605.

Norwegian Government White Paper, NOU 2003:22, on the Ethical Guidelines of the Government Pension Fund (Report from the Graver Committee) (Oslo, 11 July 2003). English version: www.regjeringen.no/ nb/dep/fin/tema/andre/Etiske-retningslinjer/Graverutvalget/Report-on-ethical-guidelines.html?id=420232.

Norwegian Petroleum Fund Advisory Commission on International Law, 'Memorandum to the Ministry of Finance: Question of Whether Investments in Singapore Technologies Engineering can Imply a Violation of Norway's International Obligations, Ministry of Finance' (Oslo, 22 March 2002); http:// www.regjeringen.no/en/dep/fin/Selected-topics/andre/Ethical-Guidelines-for-the-Government-Pension-Fund   –   Global-/Advisory-Commission-Documents/Advisory-Commission.html?id=413581&epslanguage=EN-GB.

'Memorandum to the Ministry of Finance: Question of Whether an Investment through the Petroleum Fund Can Constitute a Human Rights Violation', (2002); www.regjeringen.no/mobil/se/dep/fin/tema/statens_pensjonsfond/ ansvarlige-investeringer/Advisory-Commission-Documents/advisory-commission-220302.html?id=105699.

Novartis, 'Policy on Corporate Citizenship' (2001); www.corporatecitizenship. novartis.com/downloads/managing-cc/02_2003_policy_on_corporate_ citizenship.pdf.

Nowrot, Karsten, 'The 2006 Interim Report of the UN Special Representative on Human Rights and Transnational Corporations: Breakthrough or

Further Polarization?', *TELC Policy Papers on Transnational Economic Law*, 20 (2006).

Nussbaum, Martha C., *Sex and Social Justice* (New York: Oxford University Press, 1999).

Nyberg, Maurice, 'At Risk from Complicity with Crime', *Financial Times* (27 July 1998).

Nystuen, Gro, 'Response to Criticism Concerning the Exclusion of Companies from the Norwegian Government Pension Fund', *Dagens Næringsliv* (11 September 2006).

Occidental Petroleum, 'Occidental Petroleum Corporation Code of Business Conduct', (amended 2004, 2007); www.oxy.com/PUBLICATIONS/PDF/code.pdf.

Olson, Martha J., 'University Investments with a South African Connection: Is Prudent Divestiture Possible?', *New York University Journal of International Law and Politics*, 11 (1979).

Organisation for Economic Co-Operation and Development, *Corporate Governance of State-Owned Enterprises: A Survey of OECD Countries* (Paris: OECD Publishing, 2005).

'Sovereign Wealth Funds and Recipient Country Policies' (OECD Investment Committee, 4 April 2008); www.oecd.org/dataoecd/34/9/40408735.pdf.

Pierson, Paul, *The New Politics of the Welfare State* (Oxford University Press, 2001).

Pieth, Mark, 'Customer Due Diligence for Banks', in Mark Pieth (ed.), *Financing Terrorism* (Dordrecht, Boston, London: Kluwer Academic Publishers, 2002).

Pisillo-Mazzeschi, Ricardo, 'The Due Diligence Rule and the Nature of the International Responsibility of States', *German Yearbook of International Law*, 35 (1992).

Pogge, Thomas, *World Poverty and Human Rights* (Cambridge: Polity Press, 2002).

Prakash, Sethi S., 'Investing in Socially Responsible Companies is a Must for Public Pension Funds – Because there is No Better Alternative', *Journal of Business Ethics*, 56 (2005).

Prosser, William, *Prosser and Keeton on Torts*, 5th edn (St. Paul, MN: West Publishing, 1984).

Punch, Maurice, 'Why Corporations Kill and Get Away with It: The Failure of Law to Cope with Crime in Organizations', in André Nollkaemper and Harmen van der Wilt (eds.), *System Criminality in International Law* (Cambridge University Press, 2009), pp. 42–68.

Ramasastry, Anita, 'Corporate Complicity: From Nuremberg to Rangoon. An Examination of Forced Labor Cases and Their Impact on the Liability of Multinational Corporations', *Berkeley Journal of International Law*, 20 (2002).

'Secrets and Lies? Swiss Banks and International Human Rights', *Vanderbilt Journal of Transnational Law* 31 (1998).

Ramsey, Michael D., 'International Law Limits on Investor Liability in Human Rights Litigation', *Harvard International Law Journal*, 50 (2009).

Ravikoff, Ronald B. and Myron P. Curzan, 'Social Responsibility in Investment Policy and the Prudent Man Rule', *California Law Review*, 68 (1980).

Rawls, John, *A Theory of Justice* (Cambridge, MA: Harvard University Press, 1971).

Renan, Ernest, *Discours et Conferences* (Paris: Calman-Levy, 1887), pp. 277–31.

Richardson, Benjamin J., 'Enlisting Institutional Investors in Environmental Regulation: Some Comparative and Theoretical Perspectives', *North Carolina Journal of International Law and Commercial Regulation*, 28 (2002–3).

Roche, 'Human Rights' (2006); www.roche.com/corporate_responsibility/employees/human_rights.htm=.

Roht-Arriaza, Naomi, 'From Country-Based to Corporate Campaigns', *Berkeley Journal of International Law*, 21 (2003).

Rose, Paul, 'Sovereigns as Shareholders', *North Carolina Law Review*, 87 (2008).

Ruggie, John G., 'Business and Human Rights: Mapping International Standards of Responsibility and Accountability for Corporate Acts. Report of the Special Representative of the Secretary-General (SRSG) on the Issue of Human Rights and Transnational Corporations and Other Business Enterprises', UN Doc. A/HRC/4/035 (United Nations Human Rights Council, 9 February 2007).

'Promotion and Protection of Human Rights: Interim Report of the Special Representative of the Secretary-General on the Issue of Human Rights and Transnational Corporations and Other Business Enterprises', UN Doc. E/CN.4/2006/97 (United Nations Human Rights Council, 22 February 2006).

'Promotion and Protection of all Human Rights, Civil, Political, Economic, Social and Cultural Rights including the Right to Development. Protect, Respect and Remedy: A Framework for Business and Human Rights – Report of the Special Representative of the Secretary-General on the Issue of Human Rights and Transnational Corporations and Other Business Enterprises', UN Doc. A/HRC/8/5 (7 April 2008).

'Promotion of all Human Rights, Civil, Political, Economic, Social and Cultural Rights, including the Right to Development. Business and Human Rights: Towards Operationalizing the "Protect, Respect and Remedy" Framework'. Report of the Special Representative of the Secretary-General on the Issue of Human Rights and Transnational Corporations and Other Business Enterprises', UN Doc. A/HRC/11/13 (22 April 2009); www2.ohchr.org/english/bodies/hrcouncil/docs/11session/A.HRC.11.13.pdf.

'Putting the "Protect, Respect and Remedy Framework" Into Practice' (29 April 2010); www.institutehrb.org/blogs/guest/putting_the_protect_respect_remedy_framework_into_practice.html.

'Report of the Special Representative of the Secretary-General on the Issue of Human Rights and Transnational Corporations and Other Business Enterprises: Further Steps toward the Operationalization of the "Protect, Respect and Remedy"-Framework' UN Doc. A/HRC/14/27 (9 April 2010); www.reports-and-materials.org/Ruggie-report-2010.pdf.

'State Responsibilities to Regulate and Adjudicate Corporate Activities under the United Nations' Core Human Rights Treaties' (Harvard University, 12 February 2007); www.humanrights.ch/home/upload/pdf/070410_ruggie_2.pdf.

'State Responsibilities to Regulate and Adjudicate Corporate Activities under the United Nations' Core Human Rights Treaties – Individual Report on the International Covenant on Civil and Political Rights: Report No. 3' (Office of the United Nations High Commissioner for Human Rights, June 2007); www.reports-and-materials.org/Ruggie-ICCPR-Jun-2007.pdf.

'State Responsibilities to Regulate and Adjudicate Corporate Activities under the United Nations' Core Human Rights Treaties – Individual Report on the United Nations Convention on the Elimination of All Forms of Discrimination against Women: Report No. 4' (Office of the United Nations High Commissioner for Human Rights, September 2007).

'Taking Embedded Liberalism Global: The Corporate Connection', in David Held and Mathias Koenig-Archibugi, *Taming Globalization* (Cambridge University Press, 2003).

'The Theory and Practice of Learning Networks', *Journal of Corporate Citizenship*, 5 (2002).

Saland, Per, 'International Criminal Law Principles', in Roy S. K. Lee, *The International Criminal Court: The Making of the Rome Statute* (The Hague: Kluwer, 1999).

Sasson, Saskia, 'The State and Economic Globalization: Any Implications for International Law?', *Chicago Journal of International Law*, 109 (2000).

Satz, Debra M., 'Liberalism, Economic Freedom, and the Limits of Markets', *Social Philosophy and Policy*, 24:1 (2007).

Savarese, Eduardo, 'Issues of Attribution to States of Private Acts: Between the Concept of De Facto Organs and Complicity', in *Italian Yearbook of International Law*, vol. XV (University of Siena, 2005), pp. 111–36.

Saxon, Matthew, 'It's Just Business, Or Is It? How Business and Politics Collide With Sovereign Wealth Funds', *Hastings International and Comparative Law Review*, 32 (2009).

Scanlon, Thomas M., 'The Aims and Authority of Moral Theory', *Oxford Journal of Legal Studies*, 12 (1992).

What We Owe to Each Other (Cambridge, MA: Harvard University Press, 1998).

Scharpf, Fritz W., 'The Viability of Advanced Welfare States in the International Economy: Vulnerabilities and Options', *Journal of European Public Policy*, 7 (2000).

Scheffer, David J., *Presbyterian Church of Sudan* v. *Talisman Energy, Inc.*, On Petition for Writ of Certiorari to the United States Court of Appeals for the Second Circuit: 'Brief of David J. Scheffer, Director of the Center for International Human Rights, as Amicus Curiae in Support of the the Issuance of a Writ of Certiorari' (19 May 2010).

Scheffler, S., 'Relationships and Responsibilities', *Philosophy and Public Affairs*, 36 (1997).

Scott, Craig, 'Multinational Enterprises and Emergent Jurisprudence on Violations of Economic, Social and Cultural Rights', in Asbjørn Eide,

Catarina Krause and Allan Rosas, *Economic, Social and Cultural Rights: A Textbook* (The Hague: Nijhoff, 2001), pp. 563–96.

Shamir R., 'Between Self-Regulation and the Alien Tort Claims Act: On the Contested Concept of Corporate Social Responsibility', *Law & Society Review*, 38 (2004).

Shell, 'Business and Human Rights: A Management Primer', (1998); www.shell.com/static/envirosoc-en/downloads/management_primers/business_and_human_rights_primer.pdf.

Shinn, Matt (ed.), 'The 2005 Business & Human Rights Seminar Report: Exploring Responsibilities and Complicity' (London, 8 December 2005).

Shue, H., *Basic rights: subsistence, affluence and US foreign policy* (Princeton University Press, 1996).

Simmons, A. J., *Moral Principles and Political Obligations* (Princeton University Press, 1979).

Skogley, Sigrun and Mark Gibney, 'Transnational Human Rights Obligations', *Human Rights Quarterly*, 24 (2002).

Smith, Adam, 'How the Commerce of the Towns Contributed to the Improvement of the Country', Book 3, ch. 4 in *An Inquiry into the Nature and Cause of the Wealth of Nations* [1776] (New York: The Modern Library, Random House, Inc, 1937).

Solomon, Jill, *Corporate Governance and Accountability*, 3rd edn (Chichester (UK): Wiley, 2010).

Sornarajah, M., 'Linking State Responsibility for Certain Harms Caused by Corporate Nationals Abroad to Civil Recourse in the Legal System of Home States', in Scott Craig (ed.), *Torture As Tort* (Oxford University Press, 2001).

Spar, Debora L., 'The Spotlight and the Bottom Line: How Multinationals Export Human Rights', *Foreign Affairs*, 77 (1998).

Sparkes, Russell and Christopher J. Cowton, 'The Maturing of Socially Responsible Investment: A Review of the Developing Link with Corporate Social Responsibility', *Journal of Business Ethics*, 52 (2004).

Spiro, Peter J., 'New Players on the International Stage', *Hofstra Law & Policy Symposium*, 2 (1997).

Steinhardt, Ralph G. and Anthony D'Amato (eds.), *The Alien Tort Claims Act: An Analytical Anthology* (New York: Hotei Publishing, 1999).

Stumberg, Robert, 'Preemption & Human Rights: Local Options after Crosby v. NFTC', *Law and Policy in International Business*, 32 (2000–1).

Sullivan, Danny, 'Google License To Operate In China Questioned; Will Disclosure Have To Go?' (21 February 2006); http://blog.searchenginewatch.com/060221-091709.

Summers, Lawrence, 'Funds that Shake Capitalist Logic', *Financial Times* (29 July 2007).

Sverdlik, Stephen, 'Collective Responsibility', *Philosophical Studies*, 51 (1987).

Syse, H. and H. Ingierd, 'What Constitutes a Legitimate Authority?', *Journal of Social Alternatives*, 24 (2005).

Temple, David, 'China's Search Engine Landscape', Multilingual Search (6 January 2006); www.multilingual-search.com/china-search-engine-landscape-article/06/01/2006.

Thomas, Daniel C., *The Helsinki Effect: International Norms, Human Rights, and the Demise of Communism* (Princeton University Press, 2001).

Truman, Edwin M., 'Sovereign Wealth Funds: The Need for Greater Transparency and Accountability', Peterson Institute for International Economics, Policy Brief, No. PB07–6 (August 2007); www.petersoninstitute.org/publications/pb/pb07–6.pdf.

Sovereign Wealth Funds: Threat or Salvation? (Washington, DC: Peterson Institute for International Economics, 2010).

UN Commission on Human Rights, 'Resolution 2005/69 of Economic and Social Council' UN Doc. E/CN.4/2005/L.87 (15 April 2005).

'Situation of Human Rights in Myanmar: Report of the Special Rapporteur, Paulo Sérgio Pinheiro', UN Doc. E/CN.4/2005/36 (2 December 2004).

UNEP Finance Initiative and UN Global Compact, *'Principles for Responsible Investment'* (New York: United Nations Environmental Program, 2006).

UN Global Compact Office, 'The Ten Principles of the Global Compact' (New York: United Nations Global Compact Office, 2004); www.unglobalcompact.org.

'Transparency and Anti-Corruption: Results of the Consultation Process on the Introduction of a Principle against Corruption' (New York: United Nations Global Compact Office, 10 May 2004); www.unglobalcompact.org/docs/issues_doc/7.7/result_consultation.doc.

'Report of the Informal Consultation with the Institutional Investor and Business Communities: Responsible Investment in Weak or Conflict-Prone States' (New York: United Nations Global Compact Office, 17 January 2007); www.unglobalcompact.org/docs/news_events/meeting_reports/Meeting_Report_Final.pdf.

UN Global Compact Office and OHCHR, *'Embedding Human Rights in Business Practice'* (New York: United Nations Global Compact Office, 2004); www.unglobalcompact.org/docs/issues_doc/human_rights/embedding.pdf.

UN Human Rights Council, 'Report of the United Nations High Commissioner on Human Rights on the sectoral consultation entitled "Human Rights and the Financial Sector"', UN Doc. A/HRC/4/99 (7 March 2007).

UN Office of the High Commissioner for Human Rights (OHCHR), 'Report of the United Nations High Commissioner on Human Rights on the Responsibilities of Transnational Corporations and Related Business Enterprises with Regard to Human Rights', UN Doc. E/CN.4/2005/91 (15 February 2005).

UN Press Release, 'Secretary-General Proposes Global Compact on Human Rights, Labour, Environment, in Address to World Economic Forum in Davos', UN Doc. SG/SM/6881 (1 February 1999).

UN Principles for Responsible Investment Initiative, 'Principles for Responsible Investment', www.unpri.org/principles/.

UN Security Council, 'Resolution 1747 (2007) on Iran', UN Doc. S/RES/1747 (2007).

UN Sub-Commission on the Promotion and Protection of Human Rights, 'Sub-Commission Decision 1999/101', UN Doc. E/CN.4/SUB.2/DEC/1999/101 (3 August 1999).

'Resolution 2003/16', UN Doc. E/CN.4/Sub.2/2003/L.11 (13 August 2003).

Van Liedekerke, Luc, Jef Van Gerwen and Danny Cassimon, *Exploration in Financial Ethics*, Ethical Perspectives Monograph Series (Leuven: Peeters Publishers, 2000).

Vandekerckhove, Wim Jos Leys and Dirk Van Braeckel, 'That's Not What Happened and It's Not my Fault Anyway! An Exploration of Management Attitudes Towards SRI-Shareholder Engagement', *Business Ethics: A European Review* 16 (2007).

Vedanta Resources Plc., 'Corporate Governance Report' (2008); http://ar2008. vedantaresources.com/corpgovreport.aspx.

Vetlesen, A. J., *Evil and Human Agency: Understanding Collective Evildoing* (New York: Cambridge University Press, 2005).

Menneskeverd og ondskap: Essays og artikler 1991–2002 (Oslo: Gyldendal Norsk Forlag, 2003).

Wallace, Wendy L., 'Are States Denied A Voice? Citizen-Driven Foreign Policy After Crosby v. National Foreign Trade Council', *Case Western Reserve Journal of International Law*, 52 (2002).

Watchman, Paul Q., 'Banking on Responsibility', *Freshfields Bruckhaus Deringer* (July 2005); www.freshfields.com/publications/pdfs/practices/12057.pdf.

Watson, Alan, *Legal Transplants: An Approach to Comparative Law* (Edinburgh: Scottish Academic Press, 1974).

Weisman, Steven R., 'Sovereign Funds Stir Growing Unease: As Foreign State-Controlled Investors Gain Leverage, Washington Starts to Fret', *International Herald Tribune* (21 August 2007).

Weissbrodt, David, 'Business and Human Rights', *University of Cincinnati Law Review*, 74 (2005).

'Draft Human Rights Codes for Companies', UN Doc. E/CN.4/Sub.2/2000/ WG.2/WP.1/Add.1 (25 May 2000).

Weissbrodt, David and Muria Kruger, 'Norms on the Responsibilities of Transnational Corporations and Other Business Enterprises with Regard to Human Rights', *American Journal of International Law*, 91 (2003).

Wells, C., *Corporations and Criminal Responsibility*, 2nd edn (Oxford University Press, 2001).

Werle G., 'Individual Criminal Responsibility in Article 25 ICC Statute', *Journal of International Criminal Justice*, 5 (2007).

Wesley, John, 'The Use of Money: Sermon 50' (1872); http://wesley.nnu.edu/ john-wesley/the-sermons-of-john-wesley-1872-edition/sermon-50-the-use-of-money/.

Whitney, Ambassador Benson K., 'Pension Fund Divestment: Meeting Norwegian Fairness Standards?' (Oslo: Norwegian Institute of International Affairs (NUPI), 1 September 2006).

Williams, Bernard, *Ethics and the Limits of Philosophy* (Cambridge, MA: Harvard University Press, 1986).

Williams, Grayling M., 'In Support of Azania: Divestiture of Public Pension Funds As One Answer to United States Private Investment in South Africa', *Black Law Journal*, 9 (1984).

Wong, Anthony, 'Sovereign Wealth Funds and the Problem of Asymmetric Information: The Santiago Principles and International Regulations', *Brooklyn Journal of International Law*, 34 (2009).

Wood, Stepan, 'In Defense of the Sphere of Influence: Why the WGSR should not follow Professor Ruggie's Advice on Defining the Scope of Corporate Social Responsibility', submitted to the Working Group on Social Responsibility (WGSR) of the International Organization for Standardization (ISO) (Copenhagen, 17–21 May 2010).

Wright, Christopher and Alexis Rwabizambuga, 'Institutional Pressures, Corporate Reputation, and Voluntary Codes of Conduct: An Examination of the Equator Principles', *Business and Society Review*, 111 (2006).

Young, Iris Marion, 'Responsibility and Global Labor Justice', *Journal of Political Philosophy*, 12 (2004).

Index